Andrew R. Gottlieb, PhD

Out of the Twilight
Fathers of Gay Men Speak

*Pre-publication
REVIEWS,
COMMENTARIES,
EVALUATIONS . . .*

"**G**ottlieb is trying to tackle the problem of a father and his gay son directly, by speaking to the father. The obvious seems to have taken many decades to begin . . . and Gottlieb is brave enough to sail into uncharted waters."

Charles Silverstein, PhD
Founding Editor,
Journal of Homosexuality

"**D**r. Gottlieb's elegant study brings the fathers of gay men into sharp focus and makes an important contribution to the literature on homosexuality. The chapter of stories is extremely compelling and, I believe, will become essential reading for anyone who is struggling to come out as the parent of a gay son. Dr. Gottlieb's scholarship is evident throughout, particularly in the Discussion chapter, where the research is well placed in a theoretical context and implications for clinical practice are presented."

Debra Bader, CSW
Private practice,
Westchester County, NY

Out of the Twilight
Fathers of Gay Men Speak

HAWORTH Gay & Lesbian Studies
John P. De Cecco, PhD
Editor in Chief

Out of the Twilight
Fathers of Gay Men Speak

Andrew R. Gottlieb, PhD

Harrington Park Press®
An Imprint of The Haworth Press, Inc.
New York • London • Oxford

Published by

Harrington Park Press®, an imprint of The Haworth Press, Inc., 10 Alice Street, Binghamton, NY 13904-1580

Quoted lines in Chapter 1 are from *Death of a Salesman* by Arthur Miller. Copyright 1949, renewed © 1977 by Arthur Miller. Used by permission of Viking Penguin, a division of Penguin Putnam Inc.

Chapter 2 includes brief quotations from *Funny Boy* by Shyam Selvadurai. Text: Copyright 1994 by Shyam Selvadurai. By permission of William Morrow and Company, Inc.

Cover design by Monica L. Seifert.

The Library of Congress has cataloged the hardcover edition of this book as:

Gottlieb, Andrew R.
    Out of the twilight : fathers of gay men speak / Andrew R. Gottlieb.
      p.   cm.
    Includes bibliographical references and index.
    ISBN 0-7890-0614-6 (hard)
    1. Gay men—Family relationships—Psychological aspects. 2. Fathers and sons—Psychological aspects. 3. Parents of gays—Psychology. 4. Homosexuality, Male—Psychological aspects. 5. Psychoanalysis and homosexuality. I. Title.

HQ76 .G67 2000
306.874'2—dc21
                                                        99-055438

ISBN: 1-56023-951-4 (pbk.)

To my father and to the memory of my mother

ABOUT THE AUTHOR

Andrew R. Gottlieb, PhD, is the Clinical Supervisor at Hudson Guild Mental Health Services in New York City and a private practitioner specializing in the treatment of children, adolescents, and gay men. Dr. Gottlieb's work on the mourning processes in children has been published in the *Clinical Social Work Journal.*

The darkness declares the glory of light

T. S. Eliot
Murder in the Cathedral

CONTENTS

Foreword

A child's disclosure to the family that he or she is homosexual can be a shattering experience, often precipitating a crisis that can be overwhelming for all. Published stories by parents of gay children have almost all attested to the initial trauma involved in learning that their children were different in a way they had never expected and never wished for. Most of these stories have been told from the viewpoint of a mother and have related how, from this initial crisis and through a series of stages, their relationship with their gay child evolved from initial shock and denial into one of acceptance and appreciation. Seldom have these stories been told from the viewpoint of fathers.

In this insightful and important book, Andrew Gottlieb uses historical and literary perspectives in a well-researched and psychologically sound manner to provide the background for his study, one that uses narrative or storytelling as a way to understand personal experience. Here, twelve fathers of gay sons were interviewed in depth, reporting how they proceeded through various stages of adapting to their sons' disclosure of their homosexual orientation.

As readily acknowledged by Dr. Gottlieb, the major weakness of his study is that the subjects had to be willing to be interviewed. Thus, they comprised a biased sample of fathers who had not rejected their gay sons nor became alienated from them, fathers who made the valiant attempt to understand their sons and to stay involved in their lives. Many fathers *and* mothers of gay children do not choose to do this. But, despite this limitation, this study has much to offer in furthering our general understanding of the processes parents experience in resolving significant crises in their adult lives and particularly crises involving their adult children. As the author notes, when the crisis involves a child's stigmatized identity, the parent who chooses to openly support and stand by the child, in effect, now shares that stigmatized identity and must overcome the many obstacles that identity imposes.

But happily, for the majority of fathers in this study, the author found that the crisis of homosexuality, first perceived as a danger, eventually became an opportunity, a second chance, even a "rebirth" for both father and son. For most of these fathers, the resolution of the disclosure of their sons' homosexuality was a positive experience, which resulted in a closer and more intimate father-son relationship.

A very significant finding was that a father's ability to identify with his son was a major factor in eventually being able to accept and appreciate his son's sexual orientation. Further, many of these fathers idealized their sons' high intelligence, creativity, or artistic gifts. It appears that this idealization, even overidealization, facilitated the father's identification. Dr. Gottlieb hypothesizes that perhaps the fathers' focus on their sons as ideal lessens the importance of their sexuality. This finding merits further study. Therapists working with parents of gays who are having difficulty accepting their children might find it helpful to encourage parents to focus more on their child's positive qualities and less on his or her sexual orientation.

This book is well-written and carefully researched. It is a hopeful book in that most of these fathers were able, through their love for their sons, to overcome the socially sanctioned prejudices toward homosexuality and to achieve a relationship with them that many heterosexual pairs of fathers and sons do not enjoy. Books of this nature will help us to gradually dissipate the irrational antigay prejudice that still pervades our society.

Jean M. Baker, PhD
Author of *Family Secrets:
Gay Sons—A Mother's Story* (1998)

Preface and Acknowledgments

You have in your hand a study written partly in storybook form. The first of these stories—the Introduction—follows the father through the more traditional psychoanalytic writings, describing him one-dimensionally, solely as a facilitator of his child's growth, ending with the notion of father as twilight figure. Chapter 1 quickly reverses course and looks at the crisis of fatherhood and what obstacles *he* must overcome as he navigates through his son's life cycle. The first section of Chapter 2 gives a historical overview of shifting portraits of the father in writings about homosexuality relative to his place in its origins; the second section describes the many ways he has responded in the face of the crisis of homosexuality. Chapter 3, "Methodology," is a story about the research itself. In fashioning the narratives that comprise Chapter 4, I attempt to paint a portrait of each individual father as I saw him and as he saw himself. Chapter 5, "Findings," describes the father and son individually and in relationship over time as seen through a categorical lens. The final chapter, "Discussion," links with and amplifies existing theory with a focus on those tasks of adult development which have impacted on the father separately as well as on the father-son relationship.

The themes of these stories partially revolve around presence and absence, losing and being found. Throughout, I attempt to put together different facets of the person we call *father*, hoping that, piece by piece, he begins to take shape, moving from the background more into the foreground, progressively emerging as more real, as a person in his own right—"out of the twilight."

Even though a book may have a single author, many others contribute, each in their own special way. In that spirit, I would like to thank my dissertation advisory committee, Drs. Mary Ann Jones, Maryellen Noonen, and George Frank, particularly Dr. Jones for her clear-headedness, for helping me to stay on track, and for giving me the freedom to "pull out all the stops" and set this theme to music; to my former teacher, pianist Lambert Orkis, for serving as an inspiration to me over the years through his uncompromising pursuit of beauty and excellence; to my professional colleagues, Michele Dubowy and Janine Reimen, for providing a daily dose of love and support, as well as a special thanks to Ann Takahashi for doing the interview with Pei and for her unswerving interest in me and in this project; to Edwin Musselman, for twenty years of friendship; to my Aunt Elayne and Aunt Phyllis, for their interest and caring; to my partner, Michael McCormick, for his love and understanding; to my auditor, Lisa Catanzaro, for being another pair of eyes; to my patients and supervisees, for teaching me much about myself, sometimes more than I want to know; to the Fahs-Beck Fund for Research and Experimentation, for providing me with a generous grant; to the administrative and editorial team at The Haworth Press beginning with Dr. John P. De Cecco, editor in chief, and Bill Palmer, for accepting my proposal and for taking a chance with a relative newcomer, to Melissa Devendorf, Andrew Roy, Karen Fisher, Peg Marr, Jessica Hinton, and Dawn Krisko, for their collective attention to detail, their responsiveness, and their accessibility to me which helped to move the various parts of production along with remarkable ease; and, most of all, to the fathers in this study, for inviting me into their lives for this brief moment in time, without whom this book could not have been written.

To all of you I say, thank you.

Introduction

"What About Father?"

In his article, "Analytic Play and Its Relationship to the Object," Green (1993) expands Winnicott's (1965b) view that there is no such thing as an infant apart from maternal care with his own assertion that "[n]o mother-child couple exists without a father somewhere" (Green, 1993, p. 220). The title of Winnicott's (1964) essay, "What About Father?" succinctly characterizes the tenuous relationship the psychoanalytic movement has had with him over the last hundred years, recognizing his presence but not completely understanding his place. As Green (1993) implies, a father always exists somewhere—but where? He has been an enigma.

Much of what has been written in the traditional psychoanalytic literature has been from the standpoint of the father's impact on the developing child. It is only more recently that we have begun to explore the child's impact on the developing father—the subject of the present study. Let me briefly survey the more classical writings beginning with Burlingham (1973), who categorically delineates Freud's references to the father-son relationship. Of these, the case of Little Hans (Freud, 1909/1977) holds a particularly important place, coming at that moment in time when Hans stands at the threshold of his move out of the maternal orbit, cautiously entering the oedipal universe. Not only does Hans's father help him to resolve the more immediate symptom—his phobia—but also by way of that process, helps his son to resolve preoedipal issues, i.e., separation-individuation and identity conflicts, thereby facilitating identification with him. As Fineberg (1986) suggests, perhaps "the Oedipal complex was the cure rather than the cause of Hans's phobia" (p. 442).

The ego psychological perspective further developed this theme of the father helping the child to evolve out of the symbiotic union with the mother. Although Mahler, Pine, and Bergman (1975) are clear that father "belongs to an entirely different category of love objects from mother" (p. 91), they are less clear about what those exact differences are. Working within a Mahlerian framework, Abelin (1971, 1975) begins to crystallize the specific dimensions of the father's role. Although he says the child's relationship with the father originates later in the *symbiotic subphase* than does the one with the mother, the former takes on increased importance during the *practicing subphase*, representing " 'nonmother' space" (1971, p. 246), providing the child opportunities "for the elated exploration of reality" (p. 246), while simultaneously allowing for a return to " 'home base' [i.e., mother] for periodic refueling" (p. 246). During the *rapprochement* crisis, the father continues to provide a safe haven, a refuge, while the child's relationship with the mother is more ambivalently charged: "During the course of the separation-individuation process, the father becomes aligned with reality, not yet as a source of constraint and frustration, but rather as a buttress for playful and adaptive mastery" (p. 249).

Ross (1994) stresses that "a father now offers to a child an image of another integral object in relation to but not fused with the mother . . . [likening] himself to this distinct object, whose presence thereby lends its support and constancy to a child's nascent, tenuous, and labile representation of self" (p. 90). During this period, the father is "pre-competitive, pre-ambivalent, non-retaliatory, [and] idealized" (Demby, 1990, p. 149). In plainer language, Viorst (1987) observes that the "father presents an optional set of rhythms . . . a second home base, . . . [making] it safer to roam . . . someone to turn to when we need to resist the lure of re-merger with mother—and when we need to mourn that paradise lost" (p. 73). Greenspan (1982) identifies the father as *the second other*, one who offers "his hand to the youngster who is trying to swim to shore, while fighting off the malevolent phallic dragons that wish once again to submerge the child in the dangerous undifferentiated waters" (p. 135).

Moving beyond Anna Freud's (1966) notion of *identification with the aggressor* (pp. 109-121) as the defensive mechanism by which the Oedipus complex gets resolved, Loewald (1980) treats the boy's positive identification with the father, which serves to buffer "the danger of the womb" (p. 15), as equal in importance to the more usual configuration of a "positive libidinal relation to the mother" (p. 15) against the backdrop of "paternal castration threat" (p. 15). It is during the oedipal period that a father's presence should complement the mother's, serving to crystallize a son's ideas about gender and sex differences, ideally being receptive to and admiring of the ways in which his child expresses sexual identity through a celebration of his own body and his sense of self (Ross, 1994). However, fathers may attempt to "thwart or abet their sons' increasingly phallic aggressions. They may also invite or else disparage an object love and identificatory longing that take on quasi-homosexual overtones" (p. 91).

Although ego psychology shifted its concerns to include preoedipal development, moving away from the Freudian focus of the father's role as it related almost exclusively to oedipal conflicts and their resolution, nevertheless, the father's task of assisting the child with separation from the mother remained common to both psychologies.

Although object relations theorists moved psychoanalysis even farther away from its phallocentric center through an emphasis on maternal care and its vicissitudes, we find the importance of the father's role echoed in Klein (1975) as well. She writes:

> If the boy can turn some of his love and libidinal desires from his mother's breast towards his father's penis, while retaining the breast as a good object, then his father's penis will figure in his mind as a good and creative organ . . . a precondition for the boy's capacity to develop his positive Oedipal desires. (p. 411)

Of course, this is no easy matter, given the wish to destroy and the fear of being destroyed that Klein attributes to the infant's unconscious. Winnicott's work (1964, 1965a, 1965b) emphasizes the importance of the father in creating a safe environment for the mother, freeing her to be able to fully attune herself to her infant. Fairbairn (1952), however, reduces the child's relationship with the father to a recapitulation of the one he had with the mother, delineating no clear differences between the two except for the obvious biological ones, describing him as "a parent without breasts" (p. 122).

In his psychology of the self, Kohut (1977) restores the father. He theorizes that consolidation of self takes place by way of two relational lines: the first through "the establishment of the child's cohesive grandiose-exhibitionistic self" (p. 185) by way of the *mirroring selfobject* (usually the mother); the second through "the establishment of the child's cohesive idealized parent-imago" (p. 185) by way of the *idealizing selfobject* (usually the father). These developmental moves are sequential—from mother to father—in ways similar to the ones described by the other schools of thought. Further, Kohut emphasizes that the resolution of oedipal conflicts is solely dependent on the response of the selfobjects:

> If the little boy . . . feels that his father looks upon him proudly as a chip off the old block and allows him to merge with him and with his adult greatness, then his Oedipal phase will be a decisive step in self-consolidation . . . despite the unavoidable frustrations of his sexual and competitive aspirations. (p. 234)

These examples from the four psychologies—Drive, Ego, Object Relations, Self—provide a sense that the predominant thrust of psychoanalytic writings regarding the father, heretofore, has been around how he helpfully facilitates his child's development in the first years of life, moving the boy or girl away from the mother-child matrix and into a larger, more exciting world. Only with the advent of the women's movement, increased divorce rates, greater numbers of fathers having custody, and shared caretaking responsibilities (Neubauer, 1986; Parke and Tinsley, 1984) have we begun to discover who the father really is apart from this narrowly defined role; how what he has experienced in relation to his child helps him to further develop as a person in his own right, in turn moving him away from the parental matrix and into a more expansive interpersonal universe.

Greenacre (1966) writes that the father "is probably most frequently sensed as a twilight figure, taking shape one way or another, actually associated with morning and evening; only appearing periodically in the full light of day" (p. 197). Although she is talking here about how the infant/child experiences the father—as "a murky figure 'off there'" (p. 198)—it seems that he has remained "a murky figure" (p. 198) within psychoanalytic writings as well. Over the past twenty years, however, we have attempted to acknowledge him, to call attention to his presence in a way that has not been done before. This is long overdue.

One place where the father continues to hide is in the lives of gay men, this despite or perhaps because of his critical importance as the primary erotic object (Isay, 1990). In my own clinical work, I am continually struck by the fact that there is frequently more of an obvious emotional connection between a gay man and his mother while the relationship with his father is more tenuous, sometimes fraught with tremendous conflict. He appears less real, a shadowy, "twilight figure," if he appears at all.

Much of what has been written on the father-gay son dyad has been from the perspective of the gay son. Almost nothing has given us a full account of the father's experience—how *he* perceived that moment of recognition of his son's difference and the effect that that moment had on him as a parent and as a person. My purpose here is to try to bring the father out of the "twilight . . . in[to] the full light of day" (Greenacre, 1966, p. 197), attempting to make him more human, to transform him into a real, less transferential object, full of flesh and blood, full of frailties and vulnerabilities. In so doing, we may come to better understand him and his struggles and, ultimately, come to better understand gay men and their struggles.

Green (1993) was right. A father always exists somewhere. This is an attempt to find him.

Chapter 1

Child to Father

O rising stars!
Perhaps the one I want so much will rise, will rise with some
of you.

Walt Whitman
"Out of the Cradle Endlessly Rocking"

As Colarusso and Nemiroff (1979) correctly observe, psycho-analysis has long been dominated by its concentration of efforts in formulating a comprehensive theory of child and adolescent development in contrast to its comparative lack of attention to the period of adulthood. Certainly physical and emotional changes during earlier phases of the life cycle are much more obvious and observable compared with changes in the later phases, which tend to be much more subtle and minute. In their view, however, "adulthood is an ongoing, dynamic process" (p. 61), a "continuing 'evolution' of existing psychic structure" (p. 62), contrasting with the more traditional view of the adult as "a finished product" (Freud, Nagera, and Freud, 1965, p. 10), solely measured by whether or not one has completed all prior developmental stages. While Erikson's (1963) *eight ages of man* (pp. 247-274) are predicated on the notion that each successive age is built on the prior one, nevertheless, he gives equal importance to all of them. His work was a major breakthrough in how we conceptualize adult development. Of particular relevance for my study are the later ages—*generativity* and *ego integrity*. Additionally, the existence of separate polarities within the adult male and the push toward integration (Levinson et al., 1978) all offer a framework for hypothesizing about a father's acceptance of his gay son—the mechanisms by which this might come about and the meanings it might have.

In a series of landmark papers, Theresa Benedek (1959, 1970a, 1970b) opens the door to an examination of parenthood, moving it away from the more traditional biological/sociological perspectives toward a more psychobiological one. Implicit in her work is the theme of mutually reinforcing processes between parent and child that she terms *emotional symbiosis,* defined as "a reciprocal interaction . . . which, through . . . 'introjection-identification,' creates structural change" (1959, p. 392). In other words, there is an interpersonal spiraling which includes taking in the object and the affect of that object's attitude toward the self, impacting on the esteem of both the parent and the child. This is complicated by the child's reviving unresolved developmental dilemmas in the parent, that is, conflicts the parent had with his or her own parent, now providing either the opportunity for resolution and further integration or exacerbating the pathologic manifestation. "Parenthood . . . inevitably revives one's own infantile life with all its problems of affection and aggression, nurturance and dependence" (Blum, 1990, p. 29). Jacobson's (1964) reference to parents' identification with their children, important in both early childhood and in parent-adult child relationships, appears to be a key ingredient in parents' acceptance of their gay or lesbian children.

Schwartz (1984) expands these ideas by stating that

> ongoing developmental processes in the child which entail dynamic interactions between representations of self and object . . . are actualized in interpersonal exchanges between child and parent, while in the parent the regressively elicited imagos of his past are in psychodynamic exchange with mental representations of the child in the present. (p. 366)

More simply, there is an interplay of forces colliding which includes the self and object representations of both parent and child occurring in their respective past and present. Specifically, the parents' response to the child is shaped by a combination of identifications with both their child and their own parents as well as by their positive and negative transferential reactions. In self psychological terms, Elson (1984) uses the symbol of the *double helix* to describe "a twin process" (p. 299) in which "the forming and firming narcissism within the child and the further transformation of narcissism in the parents" (p. 299) work in tandem, all processes which continue for both child and parent throughout life.

Although these dynamics are present despite the gender of the dyad, they carry a special kind of tension, a special poignancy perhaps, for the parent and child of the same gender—mother/ daughter, father/son. It is here that the potential for narcissistic gratification and/or narcissistic injury is probably greatest. It may be easier, more natural to consider that particular child an extension of the parent's self. Manninen (1993) notes that "the son grants the father the imperishability of the father's masculinity . . . and hence . . . what the gods have promised through the ages: eternity" (p. 40). Given this high degree of investment, conflict is inevitable.

Although evidence of the son's fear of infanticide is more commonly found, the theme of the father's need to destroy his son, sometimes out of a fear of being destroyed *by* him, is recorded in virtually every conceivable form as well. The Bible tells us of Abraham's consent to sacrifice his son, Isaac, per God's request. Greek myths tell the story of Uranus, the primordial father of the gods, who persecuted his own children and in turn was castrated by his son, Cronus, who himself was then overthrown by his son, Zeus (Graves, 1955). Certainly fairy tales speak to this theme in their own symbolic ways. The oedipal tale *Jack and the Beanstalk* is a fight to the finish between the boy and the father/Ogre—who will "eat" whom first, who has the greatest phallic strength. By virtue of his quickness and cunning, Jack is hailed as the conquering hero, as the oedipal victor—no small achievement for a little boy. But it was a close call.

While psychoanalysis has given much attention to the Oedipus complex, the *Laius complex* (Devereux, 1953; Ross, 1982a, 1982b, 1983; Silverstein, 1981), by comparison, has been largely ignored. As Ross (1982b) reports, Laius, Oedipus' father, was subjected to much trauma stemming from the early loss of his own father and expulsion by his uncle, forcing him to wander Greece prior to his return years later to reclaim the throne. What was it that lay behind Laius' demand for his wife, Jocasta, to give up their baby and leave Oedipus abandoned on the mountaintop? Of all the traits that Ross attributes to Laius—"narcissism," "jealousy," "possessiveness," "imperious violence," "coward[ice]" (pp. 180-184)—"the last straw" (p. 183) was his perception of the exclusivity of the mother-child relationship, fueling his intense envy and his wish to murder. In line with Freud's (1915/1959) idea that the instincts are subject to reversals, Devereaux (1953) suggests that there was a "self-castrative" (p. 134) element present in Laius' attempted murder of Oedipus, implying an underlying wish to be a woman and, as Ross (1982b) adds, "perhaps . . . a mother" (p. 183). This final idea seems like a common thread running through some of the literature as we will see in the review that follows.

FATHERHOOD: A STATE OF CRISIS

A crisis may be developmental, situational, or both. It may act as a progressive force, a regressive force, or both. The Chinese word for *crisis* is formed by two characters—one signifying *danger*, the other signifying *opportunity*. In any language, a crisis represents a turning point, a fork in the road. Whether developmental or situational, progressive or regressive, all crises have certain common features. Rapoport (1965) observes that crises are temporal in nature; they are phasic, having "a beginning, middle and end" (p. 26); they may be marked by specific cognitive states—confusion, diminished reality-testing and problem-solving abilities—and affective states—a sense of helplessness. Resolution of the crisis results in corrected perceptions furthered by new knowledge, improved capacity to manage affects, and expanded problem-solving potential.

Fatherhood presents a crisis. From a sociological perspective, this crisis might be triggered by the incongruity existing between the cultural pressures to assume an irrevocable parental role and the *paucity of preparation, abruptness of transition,* and *lack of guidelines* (Rossi, 1968, p. 35) that characterize our society's approach to parenthood. From a psychological perspective, this crisis may be connected to the father's uncertainty about his identity and role, his changing relationship with his family, a revival of oedipal competition and fear of retaliation, his need for symbiotic union, a possible crisis in sexual identity, or a sense of his own limitations versus the possibility of self-expansion and immortalization (Ross, 1994). In examining fatherhood as a crisis, we can look at both what happens to a father as he traverses with his son through the normal stages of development—the subject of this chapter—and what happens when he is confronted by specific situations unique to him and to his family, the crisis of homosexuality, for example—the subject of the next chapter.

First, what is it that provides the motivation for fatherhood? Diamond (1986) gives us a framework for understanding the complex interplay of multiple forces that drive this need. Some of these originate in the preoedipal period—a wish to bear a child—or in the oedipal period—a wish to impregnate one's mother and an envy of female childbearing capacity—all of which Jacobson (1950) discusses in her paper, "Development of the Wish for a Child in Boys." Some of these derive from more present concerns—a generative wish to expand both the self and the marital relationship as well as a reparative wish to revitalize one's own parents (Diamond, 1986).

Shor and Sanville (1978) address the notion that marriage may be a *primary illusion,* that is, an attempt to repair all the imperfections of earlier relationships: "the chosen spouse was to be all that the former caretakers and mentors had failed to be, and such perfection would of course cure all our deficits and perfect us" (p. 9). Diamond (1986) suggests that this longing for primary illusion may be at the root of a father's wish to parent as well: "The prospects of parenthood promise the possibility of recapturing fusional love without sacrificing autonomy. . . . Wishes to be unambivalently loved and admired . . . offer unlimited possibilities for repair among adult males so needy of gratifying their healthy symbiotic wishes" (p. 455). As husbands and fathers, men are continually striving to fill the gap between the ego ideal and the real self in all its limitations. Fatherhood offers fulfillment to his partner both as a mother and as a sexual being in a way that he could not do for his own mother as a child. He can now claim a sense of completeness: "I and only I suffice to my partner" (Manninen, 1993, p. 36). It is only the relationship with his son, however, that promises "narcissistic continuity," thereby achieving "the masculine ideal," creating "a blessed imperishability" (p. 40).

> My boy, Bill!
> I will see that he's named after me,
> I will!
> My boy, Bill!

He'll be tall and as tough as a tree,
Will Bill!

Billy Bigelow
"Soliloquy" from *Carousel*
(Ephron and King, 1956)

Ross (1984) emphatically states that "fatherhood cannot be treated as a discrete, static psychological event" (p. 382). Rather, "an ongoing *paternal* 'dialogue'" (p. 382) takes shape by way of the reciprocity between father and son. This is so right from the period of expectant fatherhood. Much has been written concerning emotional and psychosomatic symptomatology triggered by events in the lives of prospective fathers (Gerzi and Berman, 1981; Gurwitt, 1982; Hartman and Nicolay, 1966; Herzog, 1982b; Jarvis, 1962; Jessner, Weigert, and Foy, 1970; Lacoursiere, 1972; Osofsky, 1982; Wainwright, 1966; Zilboorg, 1931). Themes centering on "merging, borrowing, donating, feeding, relinquishing, hurting, feeling depleted, losing; recognizing what is self and what is other, how things are connected, and mechanisms of disconnection; tolerating bisexuality, yet retaining confidence in one's own core-gender identity" (Herzog, 1982b, p. 314) all emerge.

In his richly evocative, one-of-a-kind analysis, Gurwitt (1982) takes us through the final phase of a four-year treatment focusing on the stages of a young father-to-be, who "[s]omehow . . . must bridge the male-female within, the real and the fantasized, the past and the present, starting life and the fear of injury and death, being a child-son-daughter and a parent-father-mother" (p. 284). Throughout the four periods of prospective fatherhood—*getting ready, impregnation-conception/bridging, midpregnancy*, and *coming-to-terms* (pp. 279-294)—the author traces the regressive and progressive shifts that occur in the patient as he reexamines and reexperiences the relationships that were, the relationships that are, and the relationships-to-be, reworking these into a more unified, more consolidated form, crescendoing into a rebirth of self.

Not all cases have such a happy ending. Lacoursiere (1972) reports a situation in which the pregnancy and subsequent birth of a child triggered symptoms of withdrawal, then suicidal and homicidal thoughts, escalating into a psychotic break. Two years later, a second child had a more extreme effect, with the patient actually losing the sense of his own identity, wondering if he himself was the baby, all of which was symptomatic of an acute, undifferentiated schizophrenic/paranoid reaction.

While the timing and quality of symptoms are "related to major unresolved conflicts and developmental difficulties" (Osofsky, 1982, p. 227), these may be less overt, more transient in nature, and more amenable to intervention. Psychosocial factors such as the degree of financial stability, family/community supports, and the stability of the marital relationship all contribute to the ways in which this new fact of life is or is not integrated. Whatever the degree of severity, core issues such as the intensifying of dependency needs, the rivalry of the (sibling) child, and the reawakening of oedipal conflicts (Zayas, 1987) probably occur in some form in most men consciously or otherwise.

A word about the *couvade syndrome* or "sympathy pains." In summarizing this literature, Zayas (1987) links their existence to envy of a woman's childbearing capacities, anxiety about the pregnancy, and guilt around impregnating and causing physical discomfort, suggesting that his induced pain may be an unconscious attempt to relieve her suffering by taking it on himself. It may also "represent a defensive identification with the woman that shrouds the man's latent hostility and sexual aggression" (p. 17). The prevalence of this as a cross-cultural phenomenon has also been observed (Reid, 1975). Jessner and her colleagues (1970) remind us that because the father does not have the benefit of those psychophysiological events that govern the life of the mother-to-be, pregnancy must be experienced "second hand . . . [through] experiential components such as hope, appropriation, and responsibility. The meaning of fatherhood is grafted upon the procreative act. There is a sense in which fatherliness crystallizes in a decision and a responsibility recognized and accepted" (p. 239), if all goes well, that is.

> But for the newborn . . . he had a peculiar sentiment, not of pity alone but even of tenderness. . . . Several times a day he went to the nursery, and remained there. . . . At such moments especially Karenin felt quite calm and at peace with himself.

> Levin, gazing at this tiny piteous being, vainly searched his soul for some indications of paternal feeling. He felt nothing

for it but repulsion. . . . There was nothing merry or joyful in it; on the contrary, there was a new and distressing sense of fear.

Tolstoy, *Anna Karenina*

Greenberg and Morris (1982) employ the term *engrossment* in an attempt to describe the particular qualities of the father's relationship with his newborn. By this they mean "a sense of absorption, preoccupation, and interest" (p. 88) covering everything from an increased sense of visual and tactile awareness to a perception of the perfection of the infant, intense elation, and a burgeoning sense of self-esteem.

Pruett (1983) argues that engrossment is inadequate in describing the far-reaching, psychic restructuring that the infant and toddler can potentially cause in the father, which can be analogous to the mother's relationship with her growing fetus. His study focuses on fathers who were the primary caretakers of children ranging in age from two to twenty-four months. He periodically assessed both the children in terms of developmental tasks and the fathers themselves in terms of their patterns of caretaking and their relationships with their wives. He finds confirmation of the father's capacity to form "intense reciprocal nurturing attachments" (p. 273) and uses the term *biorhythmic synchrony* (p. 266) to capture the special attunement between father and child. Pruett feels that this caregiving capacity may be rooted in maternal identification as well as in identification with the child, furthering "resolution of the father's disappointment and grief over *his* own father's nonnurturance" (p. 269).

Blos (1985) describes his work with a forty-year-old man who experienced intense ambivalence toward his son, which began during his wife's pregnancy and continued all through the birth process, infancy, and toddlerhood. Themes related to "overpowering jealousy" (p. 29) beginning with the physical changes in his wife's body, "the baby's theft of the breasts . . . envy and resentment . . . guilt and self-blame" (p.29), rejection and abandonment, all culminated in "murderous intentions" (p. 29). This climaxed with an upsurge in jealousy and hostility when his son began to walk as the man exclaimed, "Now there are two erect men ambulating in my house" (p. 29).

Blos posits the source of these feelings as "residual affects related to the birth of his [the patient's] brother" (p. 29), now reignited by the birth of his own son. This merging of feelings toward the sibling combined "with oedipal residues" (p. 29) point up the complex interplay that commonly exists between the fatherhood and the sonship experience. In treatment, this patient was eventually able to mourn the loss of love he never received from his own father and, by way of the transference, move toward a higher level of development and, one would hope, become a better parent in the process.

Similarly, Bolen (1990) views the estrangement between father and son as being rooted in the notion of son as rival. From pregnancy, a husband may have a sense that he is being abandoned by his wife as she becomes more inwardly focused and less available to him, perhaps a recapitulation of the experience of being abandoned by his own mother as she became more preoccupied with the impending birth of a younger sibling. The prospect of fatherhood may bring about fears of being trapped accompanied by feelings of dread and resentment at his new responsibilities. The newborn further converts his wife as now first and foremost a mother, eating away at the exclusivity of their relationship as a couple. All of this could set the stage for a father who is abusive and/or neglectful.

> Fee-fi-fo-fum,
> I smell the blood of an Englishman,
> Be he alive, or be he dead
> I'll have his bones to grind my bread.
>
> Ogre to Jack
> "Jack and the Beanstalk" (Jacobs, 1967)

> O dearest, dearest boy! my heart
> For better lore would seldom yearn,
> Could I but teach the hundredth part
> Of what from thee I learn.
>
> William Wordsworth
> "Anecdote for Father"

Anthony (1970b) captures the difficulties that parents confront when trying to deal with the seductiveness of the oedipal child, often treating him "with an inconsistent mixture of teasing acceptance and angry repudiation, at times admired and at times laughed at" (p. 276). In most instances, "a silent revolution" (p. 277) takes place without the parents becoming too aware of the proceedings; in other instances, "oedipal discontent ensues" (p. 276), during which time the frustrations of the child become paramount and threaten family equilibrium. The oedipal behavior of the child reactivates the oedipal behavior of the parent, sometimes arousing a tremendous amount of guilt for parent and child alike.

Anthony's (1970b) case of Mark, age five, the second oldest of four boys, provides an unusual example. A change in the mother's work schedule necessitated that the father run his architectural business from home, making him now the primary caretaker. Increased contact with the father led to Mark's revealing "clues" (p. 282) to him—intense interest in girls' "wee-wees" (p. 282), aggressive ideas about the mother, dreams of violence against the younger brother—all of which induced much guilt in Mark, who insisted that the only way to rid himself of these thoughts was to "cut [his] brain out" (p. 283). This in turn induced a range of responses in the father—awe, wonder, gratitude. He felt honored to gain entry into his son's private world, cementing the growing bond between them. Marital tensions developed, however. To the degree that the mother became increasingly infuriated with Mark, the father became increasingly intrigued. With the latter assuming a more "therapeutic" (p. 284) stance, that is, listening to and reassuring his son, Mark grew less preoccupied over time. A clear identification with his father developed concurrent with his turning toward peers as a source of gratification. The marital relationship eventually improved as well.

In this case, little overt aggression was directed toward the father. The closest Mark got was reported in dream material when he expressed his desire for "another daddy who when you g[e]t a shot in the arm would give you something that would stop it from hurting" (p. 282). Although Mark seemed to be more in contact with his negative feelings toward his mother and brother, the fact that he was able to tell his father about the dream at all is significant. To be aware of and express aggression to him directly would have been too threatening. Clearly, Mark felt that he needed his father for survival. More importantly, though, what seems special about this case is the sense of longing between father and son and their desire to be close to each other. Portrayed is a real intimacy and exclusivity that is rarely written about, usually too threatening to acknowledge, frequently walled off by a fortress of defenses. But Anthony has given us a rare and a poignant glimpse into the meaning that this relationship can have.

> I wish that my little Pinocchio might be a real boy. Wouldn't that be nice? Just think! A real boy, a real boy.
>
> Geppetto to Figaro, the cat
> *Pinocchio* (Disney, 1940)

Kestenberg (1970) reflects the parents' predicament in watching their child transform from one stage to the next. The perpetual cycle of reacquainting themselves with this stranger necessitates that the parents transform themselves in the process as well. This requires a continuous relinquishing of the child that was and the parent that was and a willingness to reconstruct those images in light of new developmental realities. The period of latency poses this challenge. Like Pinocchio, the latency child is released into the world without strings, leaving the parents "partially childless" (p. 295), requiring them to newly reorganize their lives in some ways, giving up their narcissistic investment in the child as their possession, acknowledging his newly emerging sense of autonomy. Geppetto's longing for a "real boy" helped him to transform his sense of himself as just a wood-carver to incorporate a sense of himself as a father. Although delighted at first, he was probably unprepared for the problems ahead. When Pinocchio did not return from school that first day, he was panic-stricken and set out in search of him, only to endanger himself in the process. But Pinocchio proved himself "father of the [m]an" (Wordsworth, 1913, p. 461), rescuing Geppetto from inside the whale. Pinocchio finally became "real." Geppetto finally became a father.

> I can see him when he's seventeen or so—
> And start-in' in to go with a girl!
> I can give him lots of pointers, very sound,
> On the way to get 'round any girl.
>
> Billy Bigelow
> "Soliloquy" from *Carousel*
> (Ephron and King, 1956)

This pervasive happily-ever-after feeling so characteristic of latency is shattered by adolescence. As Anna Freud (1958) observes, "[t]he inner balance achieved" in the prior developmental period "is preliminary . . . and precarious" and does not allow for both quantitative and qualitative changes "which are both inseparable from puberty" (p. 264). With these tremendous internal and external shifts come changes relative to primary object ties. Withdrawal of cathexis can take the form of either sudden or more gradual "flight" (p. 269), transferring the freed libido to parent substitutes and/or to contemporaries, whose views are diametrically opposed to those of the parents, now "the adolescent's main oppressors and persecutors" (p. 271).

Anthony (1970a) states that parental response to the adolescent is dictated by three factors: a collective reaction based on a stereotyping of the adolescent; an idiosyncratic reaction based on the specific personalities involved; and a transference reaction based on unconscious influences of earlier relationships. He asserts that polarized and stereotypical thinking may shape parental views and, I think, bears striking similarity to the ways in which society perceives its gay and lesbian children:

> as victimizer and victim; as dangerous and endangered; as sexually rampant, requiring restraint, and as sexually inadequate, needing encouragement; as emotionally maladjusted, crying out for treatment, and as emotionally free, emitting a breath of fresh therapeutic air onto stale adult conflicts; as an enviable object to be cut down and as a repository of the adult's unfulfilled ambitions to be built up; as a redundant family member to be extruded with as much haste as decency will permit and as a lost object to be mourned in passing. (p. 310)

In his discussion of early adolescence, Blos (1970) notes that the child's decathecting of the primary objects is seriously impaired "if the parents persevere at the level of a relationship that earlier befitted the sexually immature child" (p. 248). Manifestation of this occurs along a wide continuum: "It extends from ignoring the sexual maturation of the pubertal child to eagerly soliciting his genital activity; from tenaciously eliciting . . . affection and compliance to withdrawing from him as an intolerable source of disappointment and frustration" (p. 238).

The father of thirteen-year-old Ben sought to elevate himself through his son's accomplishments and simultaneously to repair the relationship with his own emotionally unavailable father by forging a closeness with Ben, thus placing his son in a "paternal position" (p. 245). A need for his son to submit to his domination was tied to the father's need to be loved. His attempt to relive his own childhood "by proxy" (p. 248) solidified the interdependence of father and child, creating confusion in Ben and "the calamity of drive arrest" (p. 248).

Cohen and Balikov (1974) observe the parents' difficulties in maintaining a secure sense of themselves in the face of narcissistic injury generated by the adolescent revolt. One solution—a retreat into parental abdication—may be manifested in several ways: denial of conflict; overidealization of the adolescent; imitation of them for the sake of preserving archaic bonds; and filicidal impulses and fantasies. The treatment of Mr. A., a forty-two-year-old writer, is illustrative of some of these.

Despite the hospitalization of his sixteen-year-old son, Jim, for a depressive reaction, Mr. A. continued to deny that his son was depressed. His need to idealize Jim as "perfect and happy" (p. 230) was linked to a need to idealize himself as a good parent. The father could not see Jim as separate. Mr. A.'s own father, while college-trained and athletic, was mostly described as passive-dependent. A longing for a father with whom he could more fully identify was reawakened by his need to idealize his son, thus preserving the tie with his own father. *Isolation of affect* was the primary defense within a rigid character armor, impairing empathic relatedness to Jim who, like Blos' (1970) thirteen-year-old Ben, was unable to use his father to further his development. With treatment, Mr. A. was able to achieve some measure of separation from his own parents and was more able to comfortably move into a position of authority within his present family, thereby being more available to help Jim further the "second individuation process of adolescence" (Blos, 1967).

As Rangell (1970) notes, the Oedipus complex does not end with the phallic stage and the formation of the child's superego. Rather, it is an ever-evolving force that becomes reactivated all through the life cycle: a "continual moving stream . . . propelling itself from within and susceptible to attraction from without" (p. 332). Nowhere would this be truer than for the father in the throes of dealing with his adolescent and adult son. As the latter matures and assumes mastery and control over his own life, the father must relinquish his own authority in the process, potentially igniting a sense "of impotence, loss, dissolution, and resignation" (Colarusso and Nemiroff, 1982, p. 321). This could take the form of trying to reestablish control or, as noted above, partial or complete abdication. Filicidal fantasies sometimes surface.

> So Abram rose, and clave the wood, and went,
> And took the fire with him, and a knife.
> And as they sojourned both of them together,
> Isaac the first-born spake and said, My Father,
> Behold the preparations, fire and iron,
> But where the lamb for this burnt-offering?
> Then Abram bound the youth with belts and straps,
> And builded parapets and trenches there,
> And stretchèd forth the knife to slay his son.
> When lo! an angel called him out of heaven,
> Saying, Lay not thy hand upon the lad,
> Neither do anything to him. Behold,
> A ram, caught in a thicket by its horns;
> Offer the Ram of Pride instead of him.
> But the old man would not so, but slew his son,
> And half the seed of Europe, one by one.
>
> Wilfred Owen
> "The Parable of the Old Man and the Young"
> (Reprinted by permission
> of New Direction Publications Corporation)

Although this parable is a reflection of Owen's outrage against "[w]ar, and the pity of [w]ar" (1964, p. 31), he uses the paradigm of father and son to invoke the larger catastrophe, making it less anonymous, more immediate and real.

A pivotal scene in the film *Shine* (Scott and Hicks, 1996) finds teenage pianist and prodigy David Helfgott learning that he has been offered a full scholarship to the Royal Academy of Music in

London. His father, Peter, a tense, controlling, embittered, frightened man, suspicious of everyone and everything outside the parameters of his own ever-shrinking world, tries to stop him from leaving. He contemptuously scoffs at the mere suggestion that David "can just do as [he] please[s]." His sadistic need to dominate his son is fueled on one hand by the fact that most of his own family had been wiped out in the Holocaust. He wants to make David suffer the way *he* has suffered. He wants to destroy him the way his own family and he himself has been destroyed, thereby solidifying the family bond. His is an *identification with the aggressor* (Freud, 1966). On the other hand, he is terrified at the very thought of losing David, his only son. David is his whole world. David feels the weight of this awesome responsibility and must get out. Peter is desperate, knowing that without David, he will not survive. Out of his desperation comes his final, aching plea:

> You go, you will never come back into this house again. You will never be anybody's son. The girls will lose a brother. Is that what you want? You want, you want to destroy your family? . . . David, David, if you love me, you will stop this nonsense. You will not step out the door. David, you go, you will be punished for the rest of your life. My David, don't go.

Colarusso and Nemiroff (1982) suggest "that the representation of the concept, father, within the adult self undergoes evolution as the experience of fatherhood changes" (p. 323). This is determined by the father's experience as a son past and present; as a father past and present; and through other related experiences as a spouse, a mentor, and a protégé past and present. Perhaps no one illustrates this better than the character of Willy Loman (Miller, 1949), who was plagued by the fact that he never really knew his own father:

> Willy [to brother, Ben]: All I remember is a man with a big beard (p. 48). . . . Dad left when I was such a baby and I never had a chance to talk to him and I still feel—kind of temporary about myself. (p. 51)

Willy's *father hunger* (Herzog, 1980, 1982a) necessitated the creation of father surrogates throughout his life: his brother, Ben;

the elderly salesman, Dave Singleman, who at eighty-four could just "pick up a phone, and be remembered and loved and helped by so many different people" (Miller, 1949, p. 81), convincing Willy "that selling was the greatest career a man could want" (p. 81); and friend and neighbor, Charley, who gives him money, a job offer, and bits of unsolicited advice: "The only thing you got in this world is what you can sell. And the funny thing is that you're a salesman, and you don't know that" (p. 97).

Having never really had a father seriously impairs Willy's capacity to *be* a father. He projects onto his sons, Happy and especially Biff, his inflated, well-liked, successful false self, masking his deflated, disliked, unsuccessful true self. Although these projections incapacitate Biff, he is able to ultimately come to terms with them. In his fury, Biff says:

> I am not a leader of men, Willy, and neither are you. You were never anything but a hard-working drummer who landed in the ash can like all the rest of them! I'm one dollar an hour, Willy! I tried seven states and couldn't raise it. A buck an hour! Do you gather my meaning? I'm not bringing home any prizes any more, and you're going to stop waiting for me to bring them home! . . . Pop, I'm nothing! I'm nothing, Pop. Can't you understand that? There's no spite in it any more. I'm just what I am, that's all. . . .Will you let me go, for Christ's sake? Will you take that phony dream and burn it before something happens? (pp. 132-133)

"Biff Loman is lost" (p. 16), proclaims Willy. What he really means is that that part of him as represented by Biff—his hopes and dreams—is lost. Biff is a mirror of Willy's wandering, impoverished, fatherless self. Biff survives because he can see this. Willy kills himself rather than face inevitable truths. This theme of child as lost object (Freud, 1967) is a common one found in fairy tales, folklore, and myths and to which we now turn our attention. It is a dynamic that captures the father's struggle as he tries to locate the presence of his gay son, one mirrored in the son's struggle as he tries to locate the presence of his father.

Chapter 2

In Search of the Father

O you singer solitary, singing by yourself, projecting me,
O solitary me listening, never more shall I cease perpetuating
  you.

Walt Whitman
"Out of the Cradle Endlessly Rocking"

In a letter to an American mother, who had written to Freud over her concern about her son's homosexuality, he wrote back consolingly by saying that this condition

> is assuredly no advantage but it is nothing to be ashamed of, no vice, no degradation, it cannot be classified as an illness; we consider it to be a variation of the sexual function produced by a certain arrest of sexual development. Many highly respectable individuals of ancient and modern times have been homosexuals, several of the greatest men among them (Plato, Michaelangelo, Leonardo da Vinci, etc.). It is a great injustice to persecute homosexuality as a crime and cruelty too. (Freud, 1951, p. 787)

Regarding the possibility of an actual change in sexual orientation, he continued:

> [W]e cannot promise to achieve this. In a certain number of cases we succeed in developing the blighted germs of heterosexual tendencies which are present in every homosexual, in the majority of cases it is no more possible. It is a question of the quality and the age of the individual. The result of treat-

ment cannot be predicted. What analysis can do for your son runs in a different line. If he is unhappy, neurotic, torn by conflicts, inhibited in his social life, analysis may bring him harmony, peace of mind, full efficiency, whether he remains a homosexual or gets changed. (p. 787)

Many things can be gleaned from Freud's response to this "grateful mother." First, it points out the rather ambiguous, equivocal position Freud held in relation to the origins of homosexuality. His public stance—that homosexuality should not be considered an illness—contrasts with his clinical stance—that it is an arrest or fixation point on the road to heterosexuality. Freud's struggle to remain clinically neutral was certainly affected by the times and culture in which he lived. For our purposes, what remains pertinent is the fact that this letter was written by a *mother*. Although it is not clear if a copy of her letter to Freud exists, it *is* clear from his response that she expressed great anguish over her son's situation. But, what about the father? What did he feel? Was he in the picture at all?

Most psychoanalytic writings on male homosexuality concern the nature of its origins. Does the father have a role there? Freud (1905a/1965, 1905b/1977, 1910/1964, 1920b/1968) repeatedly affirms that homosexuality derives from a combination of innate and environmental factors. The weight of these differed both qualitatively and quantitatively, depending on if one was: an *absolute invert*, one whose object choice was exclusively tied to members of one's own gender; an *amphigenic invert*, one whose object choice vacillated between males and females; or a *contingent invert*, one whose object choice was circumstantially bound (1905a/1965, p. 23). Of the contributing environmental or familial factors, Freud observes that "[t]he absence of a strong father in childhood not infrequently favours the occurrence of inversion" (p. 34). Freud concurs with Sadger (in Freud, 1910/1964), who observes the presence of "masculine women . . . who . . . push the father out of his proper place" (p. 49). Freud notes being "more strongly impressed by cases in which the father was absent from the beginning or left the scene at an early date" (p. 49), predisposing the son to identify with the mother. These interlocking dynamics have traditionally been considered critical in the formation of male homosexual identity.

In the *Three Essays* (1905a/1965), later recapitulated in the *da Vinci* monograph (1910/1964) and in *Group Psychology and the Analysis of the Ego* (1921/1971), Freud theorizes that the son's intense fixation on the mother results in his ultimate identification with her. This occurs by way of a regression to a position between autoeroticism and narcissism, leaving him with a need to seek out sexual objects like himself, loving them in the same way in which his mother loved him, thereby preserving the archaic, infantile bond. Object choice, therefore, is not based on erotic feelings per se, but rather is a choice based on castration anxieties, all of which results in a "ceaseless flight from women" (1905a/1965, p. 33). Freud's contention is that homosexual identity becomes consolidated partially out of the son's fear of his father and/or the physical/emotional absence of his father.

Many of these ideas are echoed in the work of Fenichel (1945), who summarizes the etiology of male homosexual identity as follows:

> The probability of homosexual orientation is increased the more a boy tends to identify with the mother. Children in general tend to identify themselves more with the parent from whom they have experienced the more impressive frustrations. This explains Freud's findings that those men are more inclined to become homosexual who have had a "weak" father or no father at all. (p. 337)

In the decades that followed Freud's death, the psychoanalytic perspective on homosexuality became further rigidified, moving away from the tolerance evident in Freud's work (Lewes, 1989). In some ways, this was understandable. Those analysts fleeing Nazi persecution before World War II were preoccupied with acceptance in this country. Unsure about their professional futures, they did not want to compromise themselves by challenging prevailing attitudes. With McCarthyism on the rise and purges of homosexuals from government routine, more conservative trends ensued, sowing the seeds for the emergence of a more pathological model (Isay, 1990).

Among the chief architects of the environmental perspective was Irving Bieber. Although a major study authored by him and colleagues Dain, Dince, Drellich, Grand, Gundlach, Kremer, Rifkin, Wilbur, and Bieber (1965) was widely acclaimed at the time, it has since been widely challenged (Churchill, 1971; Friedman, 1988; Lewes, 1989). At the core is their claim to have uncovered the one and only cause of male homosexuality: a combination of a *close-binding intimate mother* and *detached father* (Bieber et al., 1965). They write that "[t]he [homosexual] son emerged as the interactional focal point upon whom the most profound parental psychopathology was concentrated" (p. 310). Their work shaped analytic thinking for decades despite the fact that this research was: (1) based on questionnaires completed by the patients' analysts, opening up possibilities for distortion in reporting their patients' histories; (2) drawn from a small sample of 106 patients, two-thirds of whom were either schizophrenic or character disordered; (3) focused on the periods of latency and adolescence rather than on the psychosexual events around the oedipal period; and (4) carried out by analysts who were already convinced of the psychopathology of homosexuality and of its roots in familial dysfunction. So the theme of the detached/absent father as causal for male homosexuality persisted.

A flurry of research activity occurred right before and after the Bieber study that supported his findings. West (1959) examined abstracts of case records of adult psychiatric inpatients matched for age and diagnosis that included no identifying information relative to their sexual orientation. He concludes that there is evidence to suggest "a typical parental constellation" (p. 94) in the backgrounds of the homosexual patients—an "over-intense mother and unsatisfactory father relationship" (p. 94), which are not as significant separately as they are in combination. In contrast, there are a number of other studies (Apperson and McAdoo, 1968; Chang and Block, 1960; Snortum et al., 1969; Thompson et al., 1973) in which subjects are drawn from nonclinical settings. Despite this, these studies all support the traditional psychoanalytic perspective of a father who is experienced as rejecting and detached, leading the authors to see this as a contributing factor in the etiology of male homosexuality.

Particular mention should be made of Evans' (1969) conclusions. Despite the fact that his results are similar to those of Bieber, he does not say conclusively that exposure to the combination of a close-binding intimate mother and a detached, hostile father is necessarily etiologically significant in the formation of male homosexuality. He emphasizes that the son himself plays a crucial role in determining the ways in which his parents relate to him. He writes "that the father of a homosexual son becomes detached and/or hostile because he does not understand or is disappointed in the son is just as tenable as that the son becomes homosexual because of the father's rejection" (p. 134). His perspective sheds a different light on this matter and foreshadows later psychoanalytic ideas. Although Siegelman (1974) finds his sample of 307 homosexual subjects to be less close to their fathers than are his heterosexual subjects, a subsample scoring low on neuroticism reveals no significant differences in familial relations, leading him to "seriously question the existence of *any* association between family relations and homosexuality *vs.* heterosexuality" (p. 16). Milic and Crowne (1986) observe that homosexual sons believe their fathers to be less loving and more rejecting than their heterosexual counterparts, but the authors did not go on to draw any conclusions about etiology.

In summarizing some of these studies, Friedman (1988) points out that even though "[t]he weight of the evidence . . . seems . . . to implicate a pattern of family interactions in the development of homosexual men . . . a big leap is necessary in order to conclude that homosexuality is likely to be *caused* by exposure to this type of family situation" (p. 71). Bell, Weinberg, and Hammersmith (1981) find that homosexual sons have a more conflictual relationship with their fathers than do heterosexual sons, but they also point out that this fact in itself "is not a very good predictor of a boy's eventual sexual preference. Too many other experiences must follow for it to have any effect at all" (p. 56). Hooker (1969) broadly considers whether sexual predisposition, learning, and environmental factors separately or in combination play a part in the formation of a homosexual identity and whether certain phases of development are more critical than others.

Along more traditional lines, Socarides (1982) gives particular weight to the *abdicating father,* who is emotionally unavailable to help his son *disidentify* (Greenson, 1978) from his mother. He writes:

> Although most homosexual men portray their fathers as weak, passive, or unable to stand up against the mother, it should not be assumed that all abdicating fathers give the appearance of submission and defeat. Some adopt an affective stance of arrogance, hostility, and superiority, compensatory defensive reactions to what they unconsciously and/or consciously perceive as the insurmountable challenge of fatherhood. . . . In effect, the fathers sacrificed their sons in order to escape their wives. (Socarides, 1982, p. 512)

In a similar vein, Nicolosi (1991) assesses homosexuality as "almost always the result of problems in family relations, particularly between father and son" (p. 25). A failure in *father-salience* (p. 50), that combination of dominance and nurturance which would invariably propel the son out of the maternal orbit, leads to alienation from all males: "By eroticizing what he feels disenfranchised from, the homosexual man is still seeking this initiation into manhood" (p. 42).

Discussing the development of masculine identity in a somewhat different, less pathological way, Jungian analyst Guy Corneau (1991) argues that there is a split between the ways in which men perceive the realm of the body—the internal world (senses, feelings)—and the ways in which they perceive the realm of the mind—the external world (the workplace). The former is associated with all that is mother; the latter is associated with all that is father. Mother is an insider; father is an outsider. Over time, men learn to amputate the female parts of themselves—the *anima.* Corneau claims that the homosexual son, who may be more in touch with his anima, fails to see himself reflected in the eyes of his father, fails to identify with him, and so turns to other men to reinforce his sense of masculinity: "Homosexuality may thus be said to express an unconscious search for the father and for a male identity" (p. 27). Coming from a more traditional English object relations perspective, Layland (1981) also views homosexual activity as related to being "in search of a loving father." I wonder if the reverse might also be true, that the more rejecting father fails to see himself reflected in the eyes of his homosexual son, fails to identify with *him* because the son may represent that which is emotional and erotic in the father's own nature, and this must be repressed at all costs.

In his work on transsexuality, transvestism, and homosexuality, Stoller (1976) does not see any clear patterns emerging in the fathers of effeminate homosexuals: "Some of them are as distant and uninvolved as are the fathers of transsexuals and some fetishistic cross-dressers, while others are angry, punitive, frightening men to their sons" (p. 150). In their tripartite study, Freund and Blanchard (1983) isolate cross-gender behavior in childhood as the most contributory factor in the emotionally distant relationship between homosexual males and their fathers as opposed to just the sons' erotic preference for male partners per se. In a cross-cultural survey, Whitam and Zent (1984) find that early cross-gender behaviors are common in all the homosexual groups in the four societies they examine—the United States, Guatemala, Brazil, and the Philippines. However, parental reactions to these behaviors appear to be more extreme in the Anglo-Saxon world, particularly in the United States. The authors claim that the father's hostility and detachment so frequently noted in the literature are not causative of homosexuality, but rather "culturally variable reactions to culturally invariable behavior" (p. 432) related to his awareness of and his disappointment over his homosexual-to-be son.

In studying a group of "sissy boys" and their families over a fifteen-year period, Green (1987) looks specifically at whether or not their early cross-gender behaviors—dressing in female clothing, playing with dolls, voicing a preference to be a girl—were correlated with later adult sexuality. He finds that 75 percent of them developed either homosexually or bisexually. Although he weighs in multiple factors that might contribute to this including biological factors, the psychology of the parents, and sociological patterns in the environment, part of the picture he paints is one of "feminine boy"-father alienation. He feels that this is fueled by the boy's identification with the mother as "it is she who is successful in obtaining love and affection from the father . . . [which] [r]egrettably, for the son . . . drives the father further away" (p. 377). This, combined with a sense of alienation from male peers, culminates in *male-affect starvation,* perhaps motivating "the later search for love and affection from males" (p. 377).

All of this culminates in Isay's (1987, 1990, 1997) formulation, which builds on Green's. He concludes that the gay male child brings a constitutionally driven sexual orientation to the oedipal situation, identifying with the mother, sometimes taking on opposite-sex characteristics in order to secure the father's interest and love. Thus oedipal rivalry is between the mother and son *for* the father, a dynamic observed earlier by Legman (in Bell, Weinberg, and Hammersmith, 1981, p. 54). Sensing this, perhaps preconsciously or unconsciously, the father may withdraw from his son in fear and confusion, leaving the sense of his being detached and aloof, more as a *result* of the recognition of his son's difference rather than as a causative factor in its formation. The estrangement between father and son that eventually develops may be a defensive posturing based on the anxiety about erotic feelings and their meaning to each of them. This construction is based on a reinstating of Freud's idea that sexuality is (partially) inborn. The difference here is that Isay would consider (homo)sexuality completely innate, an idea that Freud (1905a/1965) would have considered "crude" (p. 28). However, Isay's remains a compelling argument.

It should be emphasized that Isay is talking less about the origins of homosexuality than about the quality of object relationships and how these develop in gay men. This theme is found in the work of Silverstein (1981) as well, who writes about the father as a "phantom . . . who lives within the son and is sometimes projected onto the son's lover. He is an idealized father . . . who was desired then and is demanded now" (p. 26). Silverstein states that unresolved father/son conflict can contribute to the development of certain character types in the son, the latter becoming either a *rejector* or a *suitor* (pp. 27-30), complicating the son's capacity to engage in satisfying love relationships. Further, he suggests that the previously mentioned Laius complex is a metaphor that typifies "the relationship between a father and his homosexual-to-be son" (p. 314), representing the "unconsummated love" between the two. This is built around the son's experience of being rejected by the father for another (usually the mother or sibling), the father's avoidance of physical contact with his son, and his rejection of his son as "sexual suitor" (p. 314), all of which may be connected to a homosexual threat experienced by the father.

What is important to bear in mind here is that the images of the father that are scattered throughout psychoanalytic writing—Freud's castrating, all-powerful father, Bieber's detached father, Isay's fearful, anxious, confused father, Silverstein's phantom father—are, in the end, all projections, all reconstructions, all seen through the eyes of the adult son and his therapist. As valid and as real as those are, they do not tell the whole story. We need to hear from the father himself in order to complete the picture.

HOMOSEXUALITY: A STATE OF CRISIS

It *is* the end of the world.

Owen to Rose
The Lost Language of Cranes
(Leavitt, 1987)

In Leavitt's (1987) novel, *The Lost Language of Cranes,* Philip anxiously reveals his homosexuality to his parents, Owen and Rose. His mother responds with sadness and reserve, fearful of what will become of her son, wondering if some secrets are best kept *as* secrets. His father is in a state of shock, barely responding to Philip at all. It is only after his son leaves the apartment that he gives full vent to his feelings, expressing the kind of wailing that only comes from deep within the soul. Why is Owen so distraught? For whom does he mourn? He mourns not only for his son but for himself, for those lost years of his own life, the years he spent in hiding, too ashamed of who *he* was. Now he feels he must come to terms. Through Philip, he sees what he could have been and what he now wants to be. In some ways, "[i]t *is* the end of the world" (p. 176), the world that was safe and familiar. Despite his protests, despite the fact that Rose is everything to him, we sense that he will leave that world now, will leave Rose for something, for someone, for himself perhaps. It is the eleventh hour. There is no turning back. He must finally acknowledge his own homosexuality.

Although most fathers are not faced with Owen's crisis, it may feel like "the end of the world" for some when trying to come to grips with their son's homosexuality, as it could have life-altering implications for themselves as well. Anderson (1987) has conceptualized parental reactions as "a multistage process" (p. 166) similar to the stages of grief, a theme that Borhek (1993, pp. 27-36) takes up as well. At the core, initial awareness of their child's homosexuality is experienced as a loss on many levels. The first stage, *shock and denial,* is characterized by externalizing the issue, attempting to protect themselves from the painful reality and its implications. This may be followed by the second stage, *anger and guilt,* in which attempts to pin blame and correct parenting practices (depending on the age of the child) become the focus. The final stage, *acknowledgment,* is characterized by some degree of acceptance of the child's same-sex attractions and of its likelihood for continuation.

DeVine's (1984) series of phases has more specificity. The first, *subliminal awareness,* is marked by suspicion of a family member's homosexuality, but maintenance of the "status quo . . . [through] covert denial" (p. 11) is the rule; the second, *impact,* begins when the truth is made known and a crisis ensues, threatening homeostasis; the third, *adjustment,* may involve attempts to maintain the family's equilibrium, "bargaining" with the homosexual member first to "change" (p. 13) or at least to hide; the fourth, *resolution,* involves the family's acknowledgment of their loss and an opportunity to begin the mourning process; the fifth and final phase, *integration,* involves a full acceptance of the homosexual member. Obviously, all of these phases/stages describe general trends. They are not separate and distinct, but fluid and overlapping (Borhek, 1993). The possibility of getting stuck in denial—*the ostrich effect* (Griffin, Wirth, and Wirth, 1986, pp. 14-16)—or at any other point remains possible (Muller, 1987; Vargo, 1998). However, just as the child has his or her own process of coming out, these suggest that parents have *their* own process of coming out as well (Aarons, 1995; Baker, 1998; Borhek, 1979, 1988, 1993; Dew, 1995; Fairchild and Hayward, 1989; Griffin, Wirth, and Wirth, 1986; Shyer and Shyer, 1997), representing what Borhek (1993) calls a kind of "two-way mirror" (pp. 1-7).

The beginning of this process is tragically illustrated by the Friedmans (Silverstein, 1977), an Orthodox Jewish family whose lives revolved around religious practices. The father, the firstborn in his family of origin, owned a small business. He did not fulfill his own family's expectation that he would become a rabbi, something which left him feeling extremely guilty and emasculated. This dissipated somewhat after the birth of Marvin, his firstborn. Father and son were quite close during those early years. When his father was away on business trips, Marvin would sleep with his father's picture underneath his pillow, soothing away the loneliness during those difficult periods. Tragedy struck, however, when he was eight years old. His father's business failed, forcing the family into bankruptcy, necessitating that they sell their home and move into a small apartment, sometimes needing to borrow money from relatives to make ends meet. This narcissistic injury set in motion the father's memories of a host of other past failures, leaving him embittered and enraged: "When he looked at Marvin . . . he saw only a reflection of his own shame . . . his feelings of failure. In his own eyes he had failed his firstborn son. For this reason he had to reject the boy" (p. 84).

Marvin's sexual fantasies and experiences seemed at some level to recreate the lost relationship with his father, always seeking affection from older men. Foremost was his need for security and a need to feel wanted. Through the father's awareness of Marvin's many late-night phone calls and his association with a friend, a dancer, who was obviously gay, the father gradually came to realize the truth: "You're a fag. I think you're crazy. . . . I'm going to call up the doctor and tell him you're a fag. I want you committed to an institution. You're no good anyway" (p. 87).

Marvin plotted revenge, taking aim at his father, hitting him where it hurt—his masculinity. On the day of his sister's wedding, Marvin, dressed like Bette Davis, strutted his stuff onto the floor, extended his hand, adorned with a long cigarette holder, and said, "Anybody have a light?" (p. 90) That was the beginning of the end. Leaving the wedding early, Marvin went home to bed, only to be awakened by loud noise, bright lights, two policemen, men in white coats, and his father, who had told the authorities that his son had threatened his life. Right before Marvin was taken through the doors of the mental hospital strapped to a stretcher, he turned to his father and said, "Well, I hope you're satisfied, Mr. Friedman. You'll never see your son again" (p. 91). Not too long after his release, the father died—a broken man.

In analyzing this case, Silverstein indicates that Marvin was relieving the father in the sense that, momentarily, he took the focus off his father's sense of failed masculinity and placed it squarely on himself, together creating the role of Marvin as "chosen one" (p. 96), allowing his father to function, albeit marginally. The father's guilt and shame regarding his own failings became projected onto his son. In different ways, both were in conflict about what it meant to be a man. This modern-day Willy/Biff Loman (Miller, 1949) were mirror images of one another, both caught up in their feeling that they had disappointed themselves and each other. It was an all-out war. Both sides lost. They were never able to come to any mutual understanding about what had happened. Perhaps Marvin himself was able to work all of this through in his own treatment and come to some resolution. We will never know.

Bernstein (1990) identifies some recurring themes in relation to attitudes and issues relevant to parents' grappling with their child's homosexuality. She delineates these as follows: social stigma; causality; spousal and self-blame; fears of social isolation and discrimination against the child; the possibility of a change to a heterosexual orientation; disclosure to family and friends; and fears of losing their child if they remained unaccepting. Certainly the theme of (potential) loss permeates these issues—a loss of their own and the child's social status in the family and in the community, a loss of an image of themselves as good parents, a loss of a sense of who their child really is, a loss of the child to a new family of gay people, the potential or actual physical loss of their sons to AIDS, and a loss of their hopes and dreams of expanding the dimensions of their relationships with their children through the experience of being grandparents.

Regarding the last issue, Myers (1982) notes that parents sometimes experience a sense of "disillusionment" (p. 139), particularly if this is their only child, and especially if that child is a son. With no other chance to carry on the family name, parents may be inclined to become guilt inducing out of their own desperation and disappointment. Parents might also experience their child's homosexuality as a rejection of their values and, with it, a rejection of themselves as people with little control or influence in their child's life (Borhek, 1993). The specificity of these reactions may be determined by a number of interlocking factors: the preexisting quality of the parent-child relationship; parents' age; concern about and dependency on status and conventional social customs; flexibility/ rigidity of defenses; and interpretation of religious doctrine (Vargo, 1998). Negative reactions are normal. What varies is only "form, intensity, and duration" (p. 49).

Funny Boy (Selvadurai, 1997) is the story of growing up gay in Sri Lanka. Arjie, our boy hero, prefers to spend his time and is more at home in the company of girls. This gives him ample opportunities to engage in fantasy play, a chance to take "voyages of imagination" (p. 4). For him, boys' games are "incomprehensible" (p. 4). One of his raisons d'être is the game "bride-bride." By virtue of being the most imaginative, he always assumes the role of the heroine:

> by the sari being wrapped around my body, the veil being pinned to my head, the rouge put on my cheeks, lipstick on my lips, kohl around my eyes—I was able to leave the constraints of my self and ascend into another, more brilliant, more beautiful self, a self to whom this day was dedicated . . . a self magnified . . . an icon, a graceful, benevolent, perfect being upon whom the adoring eyes of the world rested. (p. 5)

All of his girl cousins are in awe of him and are glad to play along, all except Tanuja, nicknamed "Her Fatness," that is. She thinks this is unfair since Arjie is "not even a girl" (p. 11). Obviously, *she* wants to play the bride. Fed up, she stoops to saying, "You're a pansy . . . [a] faggot" (p. 11). "Go away, you fatty-boom-boom!" (p. 11) the others shout, a show of support for Arjie's right to be bride. "Her Fatness" runs to get her mother, Kanthi Aunty.

When Kanthi Aunty finds out who is calling her daughter "fatty," Arjie is unmasked. She drags him—sari, hairpins, and all—to where all the adults, including his mother and father, are convening, making him the object of ridicule the way her daughter was treated. All the aunts and uncles howl with laughter. "[L]ooks like you have a funny one here" (p. 14), says Cyril Uncle to the father. Neither mother nor father thinks this very funny, however. Both are shocked and humiliated. Later that evening, father tears into his wife. "How long has this been going on?" he demands to know. When she says that all this "was as new to [her] as it was to [him]," he makes her accountable: "You should have known. You should have kept an eye on him. . . . If he turns out funny like that Rankotwera boy, if he turns out to be the laughingstock of Colombo, it'll be your fault" (pp. 14-15).

> I want to be your friend, Tom. I know there's something between fathers and sons that makes it hard for them to be friends. But, I'd like to try.
>
> Herb, *Tea and Sympathy*
> (Berman and Minnelli, 1956)

"Sister Boy" is what the young men call eighteen-year-old Tom Lee, the central character in the film *Tea and Sympathy*. Although his sexuality is ambiguous, what is clear is that others perceive him as homosexual. The word itself is never mentioned, however, only implied. Set on a college campus, it tells the story of a sensitive, tortured youth at odds with others and at odds with himself. He just does not fit in, no matter how hard he tries. When his father, Herb, comes for a visit, he is shocked at the ways in which his son is openly taunted and ridiculed. Although it is apparent that Tom longs for a deeper connection with his father, Herb has no idea how to relate to his son except by way of trying to make a man out of him, ultimately realizing how difficult that will be. In conversation with the housemaster, Bill Reynolds, Herb exposes his humiliation and his exasperation:

> Why isn't he a regular fellow, Bill? He's had every chance to be since he was knee-high to a grasshopper—boys' camps, boarding schools. I've always seen to it that he was associated with regular guys. Why doesn't some of it rub off? . . . He's going to have to learn to run with the other horses. I want to be proud of him. That's why I had him in the first place. But he makes it so difficult for me. My associates ask me what he wants to be and I have to tell them that he hasn't made up his mind because I just won't tell them that he wants to be a folksinger.

In the film *The Wedding Banquet* (Hope, Schamus, and Lee, 1993), Wei-Tung is trapped. Although he has been in a stable, five-year relationship with his lover, Simon, in New York, he feels that out of a sense of obligation he must respond to his parents' long-distance requests to marry and give them a grandchild. His mother has signed him on with Taipei's "best singles club" and alerts him (by cassette) that he will be receiving an application that asks about his "ideal woman." She implores him not to "be so choosy."

To meet their demands, Simon talks Wei-Tung into marrying Wei-Wei, a painter, also from mainland China. She is Wei-Tung's tenant, a squatter who gives him paintings in lieu of rent money. In theory, this scheme should allow her to stay in the country and should effectively get Wei-Tung's parents off his back, at least for a while. However, after his parents learn that their son and Wei-Wei are planning to settle down, they take it upon themselves to come to New York to arrange the wedding. Panic ensues.

After the rather unceremonious marriage ritual at City Hall and an elaborate wedding banquet arranged by a former army comrade, the plan unravels when two crises collide—the father is hospitalized for a mild stroke and Wei-Wei learns that she is pregnant. In the hospital corridor, Wei-Tung confesses to his mother that he is gay and that "Simon is [his] real friend." She becomes confused and hysterical, vowing that her husband "must not know" the truth about "his only precious son." Both mother and son aim at shielding the father. It is too late. He already knows.

In a concluding scene, the father sits with Simon on the dock by the water and presents him with a birthday gift—an envelope filled with money—saying to Simon, "Wei-Tung is my son so you are my son, also." Simon is shocked. The father insists on a vow to keep this *their* "secret, for [the good of] the family," a secret that everyone is trying to hide, a secret now shattered. At the airport before boarding the plane for the long trip home, the father gratefully says to Simon, "Thank you for taking care of our son," heartfelt words that reflect his confirmation of the sanctity of their union.

Our children are only the sum of *us,* what *we* add up to.

Harry, *The Sum of Us*
(McElroy, Dowling, and Burton, 1994)

In the Australian film *The Sum of Us,* we look in on the relation-ship between Harry Mitchell, a middle-aged widower, and his twenty-four-year-old gay son, Jeff, a plumber, living together in Sydney. Although straight ("life without women would be like bar-becue without beer") and liberal-minded ("I made up my mind, that no matter what, he'd be his own man"), Harry encourages Jeff to "find some nice young fella [and] get set up in life." However, when Jeff succeeds in bringing a "bloke," Greg, back to the house, no sooner are they warming up for "a bit of action" than Harry prances through the living room under the pretense of getting a beer. Harry and Greg quickly begin to engage in some intimate discussion about Greg's family, work, and sex life. (They also engage in some inti-mate acts as well—urinating together on Harry's tomato patch, *sans* Jeff.) Greg cannot "hack" their domesticity and abruptly leaves the scene. His own problems notwithstanding, Greg is reading the un-conscious message to stay away from Harry and Jeff who, in their own way, desperately cling to each other.

In contrast, Greg's relationship with his father is troublesome in a different way. He is not out of the closet to his parents and is always going to the pub, leaving his father suspicious about his activities. "So, where are you going—dancing?" he says contemptuously. Lat-er that night, Greg explains to Jeff that his father is "like a stranger . . . someone I live with but don't know very well and don't like very much." His father's suspicions are confirmed when he sees his son, dressed as a cowboy, dancing in the local gay pride parade, being broadcast "all over the late news." Early the next morning when he tries to sneak into the house, hoping his parents will not hear him, Greg is angrily confronted by his father: "Get out! Get out of here now! You can come back once for your things when I'm not here. Then, that's it. I never want to see you again."

Clearly, both fathers act out their discomfort in different ways. We learn early on that after Harry's own father died, his mother established a relationship with another woman for the next forty years. The two were eventually separated when it became apparent that they could not physically care for themselves any longer. Feel-ing partly responsible for that and for his mother's death shortly thereafter, Harry compensates for his guilt by trying to push Jeff into a relationship, unconsciously sabotaging it in the process. His attempts at being open and liberal-minded seem a bit forced. His lack of boundaries is forgiven when we realize that he does not want to lose his son, now the most important person to him. Life alone would be unbearable.

We know nothing about Greg's father. But as we watch him discover his son's secret, his horror and mortification grab us. His hopes and dreams shatter forever. Obviously, Greg wanted his father to know the truth, but could not find another way to tell him. The narcissistic wound is deep. Out of his own pain, he needs to get rid of Greg. Whatever Greg represents is too horrifying for him to contemplate. Perhaps he is not willing to see his son partly as the sum of himself.

The Twilight of the Golds (Colichman et al., Marks, 1996) takes us into a future where we can find out everything about an infant before birth—gender, the presence of birth defects, even sexual orientation. Rob has been one of the doctors responsible for engineering some of these medical breakthroughs. He is married to Suzanne. On the verge of becoming parents, they find out that their son-to-be will probably be gay. Suzanne's brother, David, is also gay. Should she have the baby? Old wounds reopen as David wonders what *his* parents might have done with the information had they had it at the time of his birth. When David pushes his father, Walter, to tell him how he really feels about his being gay, Walter admits:

> Maybe Suzanne would be an only child. Maybe we wouldn't have to think about the things that you make us think about. And how do I really feel? I'll tell you. I think you're sick and diseased and if there were a cure, I'd want you cured. That's how I really feel.

While Walter dialogues with Suzanne about the moral dilemma that this presents to her future, he reflects on the time when David was "dumped" by his boyfriend in college. His son had called him and his wife, asking them if he could come home so that they could soothe him, so that they could help him grieve. Walter denied his request, telling David "that he'd have to get through it on his own," a decision he might have made differently if presented with the situation now. With regret he reflects, "When my son needed me the most, I wasn't, . . . I wasn't there for him. I wasn't there."

After Suzanne implores Rob to tell her of his own feelings about the possibility of their having a gay son and what that might mean for him individually and for them as a couple, Rob admits that out of his own shame, he might have to leave the marriage. The last we hear of him, he has separated from Suzanne, but is visiting her and their son on weekends. Will he return for good?

In the Gloaming (Nugiel and Reeve, 1997) follows Danny, a young gay man with AIDS, through his return home to make peace with his family and to die. After standing outside his parents' house, looking around at the place in which he grew up, one filled with so many memories, he anxiously knocks on the front door. His father, Martin, answers. The two smile at each other uncomfortably before the older man takes his son's hand, quickly calling his wife, Janet, to the scene to tell her that their son has arrived. She comes immediately, rescuing them from their mutual discomfort. The distance between father and son is painful and obvious.

Much of this quiet, exquisite film revolves around the central characters of mother and son as they further solidify what has been an exclusive and special relationship. Many of their most intimate discussions concerning favorite holidays, favorite movies, marriage, relationships, love, even sexuality, take place "in the gloaming," during the twilight hour, "that time of longing between day and night, that mystery." The intimacy between them grows to the same extent that the distance between Danny and his father widens. "He doesn't have a clue as to who I am," he confides to his mother.

In the final scene after Danny dies and his body is taken from the home, Janet momentarily goes into her son's bedroom to sit and think. Her husband, who inquires about the funeral arrangements, breaks the silence. "I suppose he told you what he wanted," he says to his wife. She replies that he had, except for his not being quite sure what kind of music would be suitable. Father recollects that their son seemed to like the bagpipes he heard at his grandfather's funeral. Janet concurs. Regretfully, tearfully, Martin looks at his wife and inquires, "Would you please tell me what else my boy liked?"

The empirical literature tells a similar story in its own way. In those studies that address disclosure of homosexuality to parents, a large percentage of the subjects who participated were mothers (Ben-Ari, 1995a, 1995b; Holtzen and Agresti, 1990; Robinson, Walters, and Skeen, 1989). Fathers were also less likely to have been informed of their child's sexual orientation than mothers (Bell and Weinberg, 1978; Ben-Ari, 1995b; Boxer, Cook, and Herdt, 1991; Cramer and Roach, 1988; D'Augelli, 1991; D'Augelli, Hershberger, and Pilkington, 1998; Savin-Williams, 1989) or siblings (Bell and Weinberg, 1978) out of fear of possible retribution (D'Augelli, Hershberger, and Pilkington, 1998; Savin-Williams, 1994). However, while parents may go through a period of mourning subsequent to disclosure (Robinson, Walters, and Skeen, 1989), relationships with their gay children, including the father/son dyad, have been shown to not only improve over time (Holtzen and Agresti, 1990), but in some cases get even better than the period prior to disclosure (Cramer and Roach, 1988; Muller, 1987).

While fathers' accounts of their responses to their sons' homosexuality are difficult to uncover, mothers' stories abound. Borhek's (1979) *My Son Eric* is one of these, documenting a mother's struggle to come to terms with her own religious convictions and how these might be understood and reconciled alongside her son's homosexuality. As we witness Mary's exploration of the deeper layers of her self, homosexuality becomes transformed into a metaphor for the darker, barely known regions of the psyche—"a dangerous inner wolf, prowling on the outskirts of our safe, tidy, outer life" (p. 130). Although her ex-husband and Eric's father, Tom, is mentioned, he stays as much on the periphery of her narrative as he does in their lives. This takes nothing away, however, from the heroic and often moving account of her journey through "[t]he long dark night . . . into a morning of joy" (p. 143).

Aarons (1995) tells the story of another Mary—Mary Griffith—who changes from a Christian fundamentalist, one who "used the Bible and its verses—one for every occasion—as sentinels against the fearsome agents of Satan, who she knew must be contriving to infiltrate her comfortable suburban bubble" (p. 43), to an activist for the gay cause. That bubble eventually "ruptured" (p. 78) after her son Bobby's disclosure, then again four years later when, at age twenty, he threw himself into the path of an oncoming trailer, his body thrown under the overpass, instantly demolished. Aarons constructs a portrait of Bobby mostly through his diaries, "a map of [his] inner landscape" (p. 170), a place where he could cry out "like an angry Job" (p. 171), reaching for a life that might have been, but which, ultimately, remained unreachable.

Although he had a close relationship with his mother, Bobby's connection with his father, Bob, was much more tenuous. As a young boy, he recalls being at the breakfast table and building "a barrier between [his] dad and [him]self with the cereal box and milk carton . . . pretend[ing] he wasn't there" (p. 96). For Bob, "*gay* was alien, irrelevant, incomprehensible" (p. 62). For Mary, her son's suicide proved transformative. Through her guilt and anger, she reshaped herself into a national spokesperson for Parents and Friends of Lesbians and Gays (P-FLAG). Reticent and self-conscious, it was a role she could never have imagined for herself just a few years before. With no pretense and nothing to hide, her story had a directness of appeal—"the imprint of truth" (p. 178)—and, through it all, she was "born again" (p. 229).

Dew's (1995) book, *The Family Heart*, a sensitive, poetic, and thoughtful memoir, forever interweaves the past with the present, the internal with the external landscapes. Although husband, Charles, is much more of a presence here, he still does not fully emerge. At first, Dew is confounded by her sense of grief after her oldest son, Stephen, comes out, at odds with the fact that he "was right there . . . alive and healthy" (p. 37). Too, she is confused by her sense of shame, as surely "there was nothing . . . shameful about Stephen" (p. 21). Contradictions abound between the images of the child she knows and the gay son that stands before her. Along the way, she collides head-on with one of her demons—bigotry:

> a stale-breathed, slothful beast, ancient and exuding a mild stench of sour ease and satisfaction. I was too tired and sad to hold out against its acquaintance any longer, so at last I looked it full in the face and was heartbroken by its awful familiarity. It is the monster of silence and inaction abroad in the world, a permutation of evil. (p. 140)

On one level, this tender, loving book is about the disruption of family—"a clumsy, bumbling sort of creature, lurching along through the decades" (pp. 76-77). On another level, it is about a mother's remorse about holding her children responsible for her happiness and her need for immortality—destructive forces that unknowingly shape and sometimes destroy lives. The writing of her book represents an attempt to undo some of the damage she feels she may have done in the process, that realization resulting in a redefinition and a reclaiming of her family.

Borhek's (1993) "two-way mirror" (pp. 1-7) is literally given form in *Not Like Other Boys* (Shyer and Shyer, 1997). Sad and humorous, harrowing and uplifting, it presents alternating accounts of a mother and son who, separately and together, slowly and inevitably come to the realization, the confirmation, and finally the acceptance of Chris's homosexuality. Aware of the possibility since her son was four years old, Marlene diligently read and consulted with the experts, reaching for the truth of what she knew in her heart all along. Chris's disclosure, "something like touching the burner on an unlit stove that turns out to be red hot anyway" (p. 227), while no surprise, was a reality she was still unprepared for. Her husband, Bob, was not much help. His denial proved to be "industrial-strength" (p. 126). In the process of learning to look at this reality, Marlene was able to see the other realities in her life a little bit more clearly, too. In her final words, she seems to make a plea to herself and possibly to all parents not to judge themselves too harshly:

> We were simply human, amateur parents, very much victims of our culture and our time. Now we have to give our son his dignity, make up for all the marauding affronts and disparagements that went before, and . . . watch over him penitently for the rest of our lives. (p. 256)

Baker (1998) brings her talents as a clinician, as a writer, and as a mother together to. tell the story of her relationships with her *two* gay sons, with a special focus on Gary, the younger one. Unique here are the brutally honest ways in which she self-examines, underlining that her training as a psychologist, rather than helping, interfered in the process of acceptance, at least at first, so inundated was she with the idea of homosexuality as "deviance" (p. 76).

Combing through the details of her children's lives, it is as if she is still looking for ways she could have been a better parent—ways she could have prepared her sons for the eventuality of their gayness, ways she could have reacted once Gary disclosed to her, ways that she allowed her own feelings to consume her. Perhaps her professional training ultimately helped, though, giving her access to regions of herself that other parents might not have in such abundance. Little did she know at the time that Gary's revelation was only a preparation for his AIDS diagnosis and the horrors that would bring. The courage that her son summoned in dealing with his illness was certainly matched by the courage of his mother. The harrowing last two years of Gary's life and Baker's continuing efforts to advocate on behalf of gay and lesbian youth movingly stand as a testament to the resiliency of the human spirit.

Now That You Know (Fairchild and Hayward, 1989), a guide for parents of gays and lesbians written *by* parents (two mothers, that is) which includes accounts of parents' stories, mostly recounts mothers' experiences. Only one father of a gay man, Jim, speaks openly. He acknowledges having difficulties "hitting it off" (p. 57) with his son Rick when he was younger, grappling with ways to relate to him. After Rick came out, Jim's initial impulse to support him was supplanted by greater awareness of his own pain. Although admittedly feeling proud of Rick's professional accomplishments, he continually struggles with his own prejudices. One is left feeling that this struggle will ultimately pay off in the form of a more open, honest, authentic relationship between the two.

Jack's story (Griffin, Wirth, and Wirth, 1986) strikes a similar chord. A well-educated professor working in a prestigious university, he, too, was not initially in touch with the full range of feelings when confronted with his son Chris's homosexuality. Like Jim, Jack had difficulties making contact with Chris throughout childhood. Whatever he tried seemed doomed to fail. Over time, however, Jack has been able to use this crisis to forge a closer connection with his son, not only understanding his views about homosexuality better, but realizing just "how crippling" (p. 153) his conservative background has been for him, leaving him "freer . . . to take other risks" (p. 154) as he faces life's challenges.

While these two vignettes and the texts from which they come were mostly designed to be helpful to other parents, guiding them through the long, arduous, roller coaster of emotions that accompanies a journey that would tax even the most experienced of explorers, they remain just that—vignettes. McDougall's (1998) compilation of letters written by parents of gay children for other parents covers the same ground. Of the fifty parents represented, only five are fathers. Bernstein's (1995) *Straight Parents, Gay Children*, written by the father of a lesbian, while it contains much in the way of anecdotal material, is really a sociohistorical account of the P-FLAG movement. Other material, whether for parents (Borhek, 1993; Caplan, 1996; Fairchild, 1979), professionals (Wells-Lurie, 1996), or both (Owens, 1998; Vargo, 1998; Weinberg, 1973), while empathic, tends to sound instructional. Clearly, fathers' experiences are underrepresented in the literature.

With *Sudden Strangers* (Fricke and Fricke, 1991) we begin to get a fuller glimpse into the father/gay son relationship. Written jointly by Aaron Fricke and his father, Walter Fricke, it essentially tells the story of the writing of their book and how it came to symbolize the story of their relationship. As Aaron writes in the introduction:

> The book changed as our father/son relationship changed, and each transformation of the book reflected the transformations in our relationship. It is neither the same book nor the same relationship that we started with six years ago. This was a book that had to be lived, not simply written. (pp. ix-xi)

Among his initial associations to his son's homosexuality, Walter recounts an incident in which Aaron, then four years old, inadvertently opened what he thought was the front door to the pharmacy he and his father were going to, but which turned out to be a cellar door, and he tumbled headfirst down the flight of stairs. By the time Walter got to him, "Aaron was standing firmly upright, unscathed" (p. 59). The fear of losing his son "to a darkened unknown" (p. 60) juxtaposed against his confidence in his son's capacity to stand "firmly upright, unscathed" (p. 59) were two central, competing metaphors in Walter's attempts to come to grips with his son's homosexuality. He writes about his experience of feeling utter helplessness in watching Aaron's withdrawal in adolescence, unable to fathom what it could be that was so troubling to his son—"a darkened unknown" (p. 60). At seventeen, however, Aaron was gaining nationwide attention, filing a lawsuit against his school to win the right to attend the senior prom with his boyfriend. Although not proud of his son's homosexuality, he *was* proud of his son's willingness to stand "firmly upright, unscathed" (p. 59). Walter's story is a plainly written, direct, unique account of a father in the throes of internal and external forces he does not fully comprehend. But his willingness to struggle with them ultimately gave way to an open, honest reconciliation with his son.

In a touching epilogue, Aaron recounts the sudden death of his father from pancreatic cancer shortly after the book's completion. Perhaps it was only through their mutual experiences of losing each other—physically, psychically—that, paradoxically, they were finally able to find each other.

Few fathers have taken the risk of allowing us into their private worlds, of allowing us to see their pain, their suffering, their pride, their joy, their humanity. When this has happened, it has been revelatory. But it has not happened often enough. This closet door has remained shut, perhaps bolted. Why have fathers left themselves out? Have *we* left them out? The fathers in this study *have* taken this risk. They speak in their own words. They emerge "out of the twilight."

Chapter 3

Methodology

In this chapter, I tell the story of the study. I cover: *sampling—* size, type, and recruitment; *the sample itself; data collection; trustworthiness; the interview; reactions;* and *data analysis.* Interspersed with the theoretical is a personal account, my own individual responses to each of the steps in the research process. I will begin with some general remarks about qualitative research, grounded theory and narrative, and the reasons for my choices for this particular study.

OVERVIEW

The German word *verstehen* refers to the capacity to empathically understand the experience of the other. The ability to reproduce in one's mind the ways in which that other thinks, feels, integrates, and interprets experience is the essence of qualitative research (Bogdan and Taylor, 1975). The researcher's mission is to be able to penetrate and translate those experiences in a way that captures both a sense of what is common and a sense of what is unique. The self becomes "bracketed" (Mirvis and Louis, 1985, p. 231), meaning that one keeps in abeyance one's presuppositions and enters into the situation with a sense of newness, hearing it all as if for the first time.

Ely and colleagues (1991) state that qualitative research might be described better in terms of the characteristics of its method rather than by a definition. They observe that events are understood in their natural contexts, that subjects "speak for themselves" (p. 4), and that experience is seen as a unified whole. From this perspective, a subject is a storyteller, helping the researcher to fathom his or her experience. Simultaneously, the researcher maintains a "bird's eye view," alert to commonalities and differences among subjects.

The experience of fathers of gay men has been a topic very much in the closet. The particular sensitivity of this area of inquiry, I felt, could only be captured through a research modality that was equally sensitive. Quantitative methods would not have been able to adequately reflect the infinite nuance and color of this human drama. Only an approach that was as free of bias as one could get; only an approach which tries to disengage the researcher from any preconceived ideas could have done justice to the richness of feeling and detail that I found here; only a qualitative method could help these stories and these storytellers come alive. Polkinghorne (1988) writes that learning about human beings by way of the more traditionally scientific research approaches have not sufficiently helped to eradicate the problems that we face individually and as a society. He argues that other avenues, other complementary methods need to be explored, ones more uniquely suited for the study of the human experience.

Strauss and Glaser developed their *grounded theory* approach in the late 1960s. Less a method than a style, it is concept-driven, placing *constant comparison* and *coding paradigms* squarely at its center, making way for "conceptual development and density" (Strauss, 1987, p. 5). The primary goal is theory construction, tapping into the researcher's capacity to look at phenomena in new ways. As practitioners and researchers, it is our obligation not to simply try to verify what we think we already know. We must also develop capacities to look at things creatively. The problems we are asked to tackle daily require it. Grounded theory affords this opportunity and this challenge.

In addition to this way of analyzing the material, I wrote narratives of each father's life. The *narrative* as a form, widely used in literature, is now increasingly used in the social sciences as a natural way to study lives (Connelly and Clandinin, 1990; Polkinghorne, 1988; Riessman, 1994; Sarbin, 1986). Although a definition of the term remains inexact, it "generally refers to a particular kind of text organized around consequential events in the teller's life" (Riessman, 1994, p. 67). Polkinghorne (1988) defines it as an "organizational scheme expressed in story form" (p. 13). As Riessman (1994) and White (1981) observe, there may also be a moral tone underneath the telling. I use the combination of grounded theory and narrative in complementary ways. The former reflects, in minute detail, the many sides of the fathers seen comparatively; the latter reflects each father as a separate, whole person.

ABOUT SAMPLING

Sample size invariably involves judgments. Obviously the sample must be sufficiently large that there is enough material upon which to build concepts and theories that have meaning and weight. The larger the sample, the more one's observations can be substantiated and considered "reliable" (Judd, Smith, and Kidder, 1991, p. 307). My original thought was that six subjects would be enough to begin to see consistent patterns in the material. As I progressed, however, I began to add other dimensions to the interview and felt I needed a larger number to ensure that my findings were consistent. So in the end, my sample included twelve fathers. By then there had been sufficient replication of the material. Themes and hypotheses had fully emerged. There did not seem to be any "genuinely new insights" (Taylor and Bogdan, 1984, p. 83) by the final interview. The point of *saturation* (Strauss, 1987) had been reached.

Of course, exactly when to leave the field is another judgment one must make on one's own. Ely and her colleagues (1991) suggest that one criterion might be the degree to which the researcher "can talk for the participants" (p. 91). Has the researcher been sufficiently immersed in the experiences of the subjects to be able to empathize with and express their views as if those views were his or her own? I would say that by the end of the interviewing, I felt secure that I could represent my subjects accurately enough to help others see them as they were representing themselves to me.

My sample type was a *nonprobability-purposive* one. I made an attempt to handpick subjects who reflected a range of characteristics in terms of race, nationality, religion, and age at the time of the study as well as at the time at which they learned about their sons' sexuality. A range of responses to homosexuality was also key. Looking for commonalties within this broad cross section, I thought, might give the study wider application. Hearing the same or at least a similar story from subject to subject would lend greater weight to the findings. Obviously my subjects would have to have enough time to devote to this process and would have to have given their experiences some prior thought, combining these with a willingness and a capacity to share those ideas in a way that would be accessible to myself and to others (Taylor and Bogdan, 1984). In a sample of this type, care must be taken not to generalize the findings, as the degree to which the subjects are truly representative of the population under consideration is never clear (Reid and Smith, 1989).

My subjects were recruited in different ways. I began my search by distributing hundreds of flyers on the streets around central meeting places for gay people—the Lesbian and Gay Community Services Center, A Different Light Bookstore, the corner of Seventh Avenue and Christopher Street—and at some gay-related events— the AIDS Walk, a street fair sponsored by SAGE (Senior Action in a Gay Environment), and two Gay Pride Marches, one in Queens and one in Manhattan. I think the word *dismal* would accurately reflect the response I received. Many people ignored me, making a concerted effort to ensure that I was totally out of their reach as they passed me by. Some looked at the flyer, read it, and gave it back to me, saying matter-of-factly or antagonistically, "I'm not the father of a gay man." One person said with annoyance and with obvious pain, "My father won't speak to *me*. He certainly isn't going to speak to *you!*" Many took flyers and read them as they continued walking. Some said that they would ask their fathers or someone else's father. Some were curious about the project, wondering whether it was for a book. One person said that he would fax it to other organizations.

Despite the many hours of effort, I never got any leads from flyers I personally gave out. I felt angry and discouraged. Early on, I began to feel acutely aware that I had chosen the wrong topic. Since it seemed too late to pick another area of study, I thought that I had better make the best of it and try to understand why I was doing this in the first place.

Concurrently, I was posting notices at both of my places of employment and at gay establishments, either by going there myself or by sending the flyer to the organization. I contacted key people of various gay-related institutions—the Hetrick-Martin Institute, the AIDS Center of Queens County, Gay Men's Health Crisis, the *Philadelphia Gay News*—as well as various gay groups—Gay-Bi Fathers Forum, GAPIMNY (Gay Asian-Pacific Islander Men of New York), Asians and Friends, APICHA (Asian and Pacific Islander Coalition on HIV/AIDS), the Queer Coop of Columbia University, the Gay Academic Union, Gay Men of African Descent, and the Neutral Zone. I put an advertisement in the GAPIMNY newsletter and notices in newsletters of Gay Men of African Descent, Asians and Friends, Gay-Bi Fathers Forum, and CLAGS (Center for Lesbian and Gay Studies of City University). I also spoke with other clinicians in the gay community—Ralph Blair, Charles Silverstein—people visible and known. I made contact with gay academicians at Columbia University, Brooklyn College, and City University. In terms of more mainstream efforts, I went to a couple of the local churches and spoke with religious leaders, I advertised in the *Amsterdam News,* and left flyers in more visible locales—a laundromat, a bookstore, and a couple of office buildings. I spoke with friends, family, colleagues, other students, and neighbors. A few tried to actively recruit while others put up flyers. Some did both. A colleague posted information on the Internet.

Simultaneously, I was making contact with P-FLAG, a national organization supporting those struggling with the fact that someone close to them is either gay or lesbian. Through that organization, I met my first subject, Marty. He in turn found Mitchell, who in turn found Peter and Luis, all of whom were members as well. This *snowball* (Reid and Smith, 1989, p. 179) approach proved useful. While in Puerto Rico, I called the P-FLAG chapter there and found Juan Miguel Jr. Through the P-FLAG/API (Asian-Pacific Islander) chapter in California, I was able to find Pei.

I came to understand that a few of these men, activists for the gay cause, were like missionaries, who needed to "spread the word," although it was not clear to me exactly why they felt that they wanted or needed to do this. Did they feel guilty about causing their sons' homosexuality? Did they want their sons to live in a world that was less prejudiced? Did they want better relationships with their sons? All three perhaps?

For the sake of balance, it was clear that I could not get all of my subjects through P-FLAG. This might skew my findings. Eventually, I found Harry by way of his son and Neal by way of his daughter-in-law, both through flyers I left at the institute where I was employed. I found Ronald through his son, who is Harry's son's boyfriend—another snowball! Walter saw the notice I published in CLAGS. Glenn is the father of a colleague I have known informally for several years. Daniel, the gay father, was a referral through the editor of a gay newspaper. Although I did get two leads from one particular friend, these never materialized into subjects.

In the process of recruitment, many people I spoke with reflexively assumed that I was looking for *gay* fathers—not fathers of gay men. This is how I got Daniel, for example. Someone thought I was looking for gay fathers of gay sons. Surely my flyer or what I told people about who I was looking to interview was clear—or so I thought. Because this misperception happened with such regularity, I feel that it is worth noting. How to explain it?

The fact that I am gay and was usually recruiting my subjects within a gay-related context certainly fueled this. However, perhaps the idea of trying to understand the experience of fathers of gay men was a foreign one in some ways. After all, who except other parents might be interested in *that*? On a deeper level maybe this investigation represented a threat. Under threat, distortion takes place. It could be that gay men might be just as fearful of knowing about and understanding the experiences of their fathers as their fathers are of knowing about and understanding the experiences of their sons. Perhaps their disinterest was related to the disinterest they felt their fathers had in them. All this remains speculative.

THE SAMPLE ITSELF

The fathers who volunteered did, in fact, reflect a range of backgrounds. Racially, two are Hispanic, one is Asian, and nine are Caucasian. In terms of nationality, six are of Eastern European descent, one is Chinese, one is Argentinean, one is Canadian, one is English-Scottish-Welsh, one is Irish-English, one is Puerto Rican. Religiously, six are Jewish, one is a practicing Catholic, two were born Catholic but are nonpracticing, one is Baptist, one is Methodist, one is agnostic. Eleven are heterosexual; one is homosexual. Eight were born in this country and four were not—one is originally from Argentina, one from Russia, and one from China. One was born and lives in Puerto Rico. They range in age from fifty to eighty-five. (Their gay sons are from seventeen to fifty.) Six are retired; five are working; one is working part-time. Five are married to their first wives; two are married to their second wives; one married, divorced, then remarried his first wife; two are divorced and unmarried; the gay father is divorced and currently lives alone; one is widowed. All were or had been functioning in some type of professional capacity: a doctor; a lawyer; a guidance counselor; two businessmen; a chef; a director of a publishing company; a vice president of a theater advertising agency; an electrical engineer turned social worker; a college teacher; a supervisor of a maintenance department; and a manager at a computer company. They live in four different states and, as I noted, one lives in Puerto Rico— seven in major cities, five outside of them. At the time of the interviews, they had known conclusively of their sons' homosexuality anywhere from one to seventeen years. In Neal's situation, his son, who lives with a lover and their adopted child, never formally disclosed. However, Neal "suspected" about thirty years ago.

Clearly, my subjects reflect a range of backgrounds and experiences in certain ways. However, since all of these particular fathers were willing to be interviewed, they could *not* reflect a range of experiences in other ways. What about the fathers who felt that they could not talk to anyone about this, now or ever? Or fathers who thought that their gay sons were either mentally ill, going against religious doctrine, or were just plain evil? What about their experiences? As I could not find anyone who strongly held any of these beliefs, realistically I could not factor them into my work. This study is only reflective of a certain kind of father, a certain kind of experience. As I noted previously, the findings cannot be generalized to the population as a whole.

Prior to meeting them, I spoke with eleven of my subjects over the phone, broadly outlining the study and my expectations for their participation. I mailed the Consent Form and Statement to Subjects (see Appendixes A and B) to them before the interview. Prior to interviewing Juan Miguel Jr. in Puerto Rico, I spoke and had lunch with José, a gay man and the founder of the P-FLAG chapter in that country, briefing him on the nature of my research. He in turn spoke with Juan Miguel Jr.'s son, who in turn spoke with his father and brought him to the interview. All of the subjects signed the Consent Form and kept copies of this and the Statement to Subjects.

Upon meeting them, I spent some time reviewing with the fathers those areas of their experience I was particularly interested in hearing about, and addressing any concerns they may have had. All of them followed through with all phases of the process. In three cases—Marty, Mitchell, and Peter—I did a second in-person interview. (One of those was necessary because of some technical problems I encountered. The other two were done to amplify the material.) Ten of the interviews were done in the subjects' homes, one was done in a professional office, and one was done in the hotel at which I was staying in Puerto Rico. In all cases, I had telephone contact with the subjects at some point after the interviews, either to fill in some of the gaps in the data and/or to get approval of the narratives that I constructed. The interview with Pei was a special situation. Since he lives on another coast, a colleague of mine, who was visiting her family there, interviewed him. She followed the Interview Guide (see Appendix C) exactly as I had constructed it and exactly as I had trained her to do. I myself had telephone contact with Pei both before and after the interview. All of the subjects were promised a summary of my findings in their final form, published or otherwise. Guarantees of confidentiality, the right to review transcripts, and the right to withdraw at any time were emphasized.

DATA COLLECTION

The primary data collection strategy was in-depth interviewing, "face-to-face encounters between the researcher and informants" (Taylor and Bogdan, 1984, p. 77), ones that may take on the quality of "a conversation," with a focus on understanding the experiences of the other "in their own words." Paget (1983, p. 86) defines this process as one in which interviewer and interviewee are "doing something not just saying something," that is, there is "a mutual search" for meaning.

As Marshall and Rossman (1995) observe, this method has its strengths and limitations. Certainly a strength of the interview process is that it allows large amounts of data to be gathered quickly along with immediate follow-up and clarification. Also, observing nonverbal behavior may amplify the verbal material, adding to the understanding of meaning. Regarding limitations, data analysis is time consuming. Beyond this, the notion of truth is an important one to highlight. Taylor and Bogdan (1984) point out that while there is an effort to create relationships with subjects that promote honesty and integrity, we must also be aware of the fact that people may try to present themselves in the best possible light. I remained unsure, for example, if the fathers were always giving me a true picture of their sons—so idealized were they, on one hand, so vulnerable on the other. Would other fathers talk about their sons, straight or gay, in these ways, too? I was left wondering.

Spence (1986) calls attention to the concept of *narrative smoothing*. What he means by this is that therapists select the material they respond to with patients, "pressing certain interpretations more than others, supporting . . . certain kinds of explanations, or 'hearing' one meaning . . . as opposed to others" (p. 213), for example. It also means that what they report in the published cases will only illustrate and further *their* way of conceptualizing or understanding the material. It may not necessarily reflect the original meaning.

Let me propose here that another kind of smoothing can also take place by way of the subject. Quite literally, participants select what they choose to tell and/or what they choose not to tell, shaping the ways they are viewed by others and by themselves. As Polkinghorne (1988) observes, "the story selected to be told can function to present a particular image of the teller" (p. 164). Mishler (1986) concurs, observing that the stories one tells can serve "a self-protective and status-maintaining function vis-à-vis the interviewer" (p. 247). I became more aware of this dynamic as the interviews progressed and especially later in the analysis of the data. It also came up while I worked with a few of the fathers on their individual narratives. As Mishler points out, this aspect of the subject's reporting does not necessarily point to the interviewing process as "a flawed and faulted method" (p. 248). Rather, it speaks to the importance of including "analysis of the interview situation and process in order to arrive at a fuller and more adequate interpretation of respondents' answers to our questions" (p. 248). In the end, I could only work with and reflect upon the material in the ways in which it was presented to me. That then becomes part of the research.

Along the participant-observer continuum, my role here was that of a *limited observer* (Ely et al., 1991, p. 45). Unlike the more *active participant*, who not only observes but becomes "immersed in the lives of others" (Peshkin, 1985, p. 270), becoming part of the community studied, my role was much more circumscribed and did not extend outside the parameters of the research itself. As a limited observer, my mission was always clear. Unlike some active participants, I was not masquerading as someone else. My research task— to understand as completely as possible about the experiences of these fathers—was known by my subjects as just that. Whatever the nature of one's role within a qualitative study, the notion of *self as instrument* (Mirvis and Louis, 1985, pp. 230-232) applies across the board. This is the idea that we, as researchers, are uniquely capable of responding to a range of cues, viewing phenomena holistically, processing ideas as they occur, and using our knowledge as a basis for testing out new ideas (Reid and Smith, 1989). This requires a belief in the capacity to trust one's feelings, thoughts, and intuition, i.e., "to follow [one's] nose" (Connelly and Clandinin, 1990, p. 7), and the courage to put those ideas forth without an incapacitating fear of criticism that inevitably follows any study (Becker, 1967). In short, "the interviewer . . . is the research tool" (Taylor and Bogdan, 1984, p. 77).

TRUSTWORTHINESS

Given that the researcher and the research tool are one and the same, the establishment of trust in one's findings becomes more fundamental than ever. Although the procedures for ensuring trustworthiness are better established and more replicable in quantitative research, the concepts of *validity*—"the extent to which a measure corresponds to the 'true' position of a person or object on the characteristic being measured" (Reid and Smith, 1989, p. 199)— and *reliability*—the extent to which a measure is consistent in its results over time and in its use by independent researchers (Reid and Smith, 1989)—need to be considered in qualitative research as well. How are we as the primary research instrument held accountable? This is accomplished through a number of different avenues: (1) prolonged engagement; (2) triangulation; (3) negative case analysis; (4) peer review; and (5) member-checking (Ely et al., 1991, pp. 96-102, 158-167).

Prolonged engagement means spending the requisite amount of time necessary for the subjects to develop sufficient trust for the researcher to get the real stories. This combined with *persistent observation* allows for a sifting out of the relevant from the irrelevant and a construction of an in-depth understanding of the material (Ely, 1991). But, "how long is prolonged" (p. 96)?

In certain situations, my contact with the fathers extended many months past the first interview. With Mitchell, I did an in-person follow-up four months after the initial contact. The first discussions of the narratives of Marty, Glenn, Mitchell, Juan Miguel Jr., and Harry took place several months after our meetings. With Marty, my last telephone contact was twenty months after our two interviews in order to fill in some missing data. I had telephone contact with Walter seventeen months after our interview. For a study of this nature, I would say that this constitutes prolonged engagement.

Triangulation is the process of obtaining data from multiple sources to amplify the interview material and thereby gain a fuller understanding of the subject and his world (Taylor and Bogdan, 1984). A few fathers showed me pictures of their sons. (I got to meet Harry's son in the process of setting up the interview, Juan Miguel Jr.'s son right before the interview, and Luis's son during the interview. I spoke with Ronald's son over the phone. I had already known Glenn's son professionally for several years.) In terms of anything in writing, though, I was never privy to anything more than a letter and a Father's Day card from Marty's son, Gary. Although Mitchell shared something that he himself had written for a religious service developed for gay people and their families, parts of which I incorporated into his narrative, most of the fathers said that they had nothing from their sons in writing and nothing they themselves had written. I suppose triangulation could also include talking with other family members about the father's experience.

But my thought was that I wanted to make this a pure, entirely subjective perspective without "muddying the waters."

Negative case analysis is the process by which one tirelessly explores for situations that disprove developing hypotheses. When found, one is obligated to incorporate them in some way. This continual revision and rethinking also reshapes the data collection procedures as well, all of which goes into making the research credible (Judd, Smith, and Kidder, 1991). As Reid and Smith (1989) observe, data collection and data analysis are ongoing and intertwined. In this inductive process, the categories and hypotheses flow from and emerge out of the data, not the other way around. Most of the stories I listened to, while different in context, were not drastically different in tone and thematic content. All of the fathers, with the possible exception of Harry, fell along a continuum of acceptance of their sons' gayness. Some have obviously struggled deeply with this fact of their lives; some seem not to have struggled much at all; others were more in the middle. I had the sense that I was listening to a theme and variations. Although there were no cases that really disproved emerging hypotheses, Harry's mere acknowledgement of his son's homosexuality stood in contrast to the position of the other fathers, perhaps helping me to more clearly define the construct *acceptance*.

Ely and her co-writers (1991) argue for the necessity of *peer review*. This could take place in a group or individually. Because I was under some time constraints—working as a supervisor and administrator at an agency, as a therapist at a training institute and at my own practice—I thought that employing an individual auditor would better meet my particular needs. The person I chose for this role is a clinical social worker with several years of experience as a practitioner and supervisor. She had no prior connection to this study, no emotional involvement with me or with any of my subjects, and no experience with the area under investigation. Being home with a newborn child, she had time to devote to the task and was eager for intellectual stimulation and challenge. Because of these factors, I thought she was equipped to be as objective as anyone. Her job was to read the transcripts of the interviews as well as the narratives that I had prepared on the fathers in order to root out any obvious bias.

Some of her criticism was aimed at the sense that I was too freely interpreting what the subject was saying. She indicated that what I reflected did not always flow from what was said, that I reshaped it into something I wanted to hear at certain points. Also, she thought that sometimes I adopted too familiar a stance, either with the intention of educating the subjects or possibly trying to engage them more fully. (However, Spradley [1979] observes that "easygoing talk interspersed here and there throughout the interview will pay enormous dividends in rapport" [p. 59].) The auditor thought that these elements could have had the temporary effect of compromising objectivity at those moments in the interview. These did not occur in equal measure during each interview, but only in certain spots and with certain fathers more than with others. These were all things I tried to be aware of while conducting the interviews that followed those she reviewed.

Since the job of a qualitative researcher is to capture the essence of the other's experience, one obvious way to test this is through *member-checking*, that is, conferring with the very individuals one is writing about (Ely et al., 1991, pp. 165-167). As I have noted previously, the narratives that I constructed were sent to the fathers for their editing and approval. Connelly and Clandinin (1990) observe "that it is common in collaborative ventures to either work with participants throughout the writing . . . or to bring written documents back to participants for final discussions" with writing and living being "coincident activities . . . always [working] in tandem" (pp. 11-12). Mishler (1986) also suggests that there be a full collaboration between subject and researcher, in effect, "sharing control" (p. 249), so that the meaning of the story remains authentically represented. Spradley (1979) is insistent that we "safeguard" (p. 36) not only the rights and the interests of our subjects but their sensitivities as well. In an unusual move, he reports that in the process of writing about the life of James Sewid, a Kwakiutl Indian in British Columbia, he made the subject a full partner in the book by having him cosign the publication contract entitling him to a share of the royalties. Their final manuscript includes changes the subject and his wife suggested, "changes which reflected their sensitivities, not mine" (p. 36), Spradley observes.

It was in this spirit of collaboration that I chose to involve the fathers in a similar way. I wanted to ensure that what I was writing had the ring of authenticity and that the narratives would not be contaminated with my own interpretation, which might result in a distortion of the portrayals. Five of the fathers—Juan Miguel Jr., Walter, Ronald, Daniel, and Neal—were completely satisfied with my representation of them and asked for no changes. Juan Miguel Jr. even said that I made him sound "better" than he thought he had during our interview. Walter wrote: "Your rendition of our meeting is wonderful. You have captured the essence of what I attempted to convey about my experiences and my feelings for [James]." Similarly with Ronald: "You have quite correctly captured my life story—and done it very well." It took many weeks to contact Daniel after his narrative was completed. For reasons that I did not understand, he seemed to be avoiding me. After finally reaching him on the telephone, his only real words to me about his story were, "Use it." Neal had no suggestions, either.

Harry thought that what I wrote was "magnificent," but asked that I correct some historical facts. Changes in the stories of Peter, Luis, Glenn, and Pei also included correcting and/or amplifying historical detail and further disguising references to people and places. Although Mitchell was excited about his narrative, he wanted me to add more about familial relationships, clarify his response to Jay's coming out, delineate feelings, and contrast his ways of being a father over time.

Most dissatisfied was Marty. He was concerned that he was being portrayed as too much of a pushover and too prejudicial. Also, concerns were raised about parts of the portrayal of his son, Gary, specifically about his weight. He wanted to eliminate any suggestion that he had any preferences at all in his feelings for his two sons, emphasizing that everybody in his family was going to read it. Although I did temper the language a bit with regard to some of his concerns, we ended up striking a compromise. Some elements I took out; others I kept in. The overall design, the themes, and the impression created remain essentially intact. In the end, I think it was helpful for me to allow all of the fathers to be a part of this process. It gave me a chance to fine-tune my perceptions and to check for distortion. I think it also helped the subjects feel more like active participants, ones who were shaping, molding, and writing their own stories.

Other Thoughts on Trustworthiness

Becker (1967) notes that as we become intimate with those whom we study, "taking sides" (p. 239) becomes inevitable. Since we are telling others' stories, we will be greatly affected by the subjects themselves. As this may be unavoidable, how can we ensure that whatever distortion takes place is minimized so that our work can be useful? Given that many studies of a qualitative nature are "one-sided" (p. 247), Becker suggests that we attune to our own sympathies, investigate impartially, limit our conclusions, and be open to the possibility that others not so moved could contradict those issues that we resonate with most deeply.

Peshkin (1985) expands on this idea. He writes that subjectivity inclines a researcher to weave a particular story. Although it enables, it simultaneously disables. The only thing one can do is to try to be aware of not only the stories one is telling, but also the stories one is *not* telling. In writing specifically about the problems of narrative as a form, White (1981) says that "however seemingly 'full,' [it] is constructed on the basis of a set of events which *might have been included but were left out*" (p. 10). He might well be addressing the general problems of qualitative research. Kermode (1981) makes reference to the same thing when he writes: "a passion for sequence may result in the suppression of the secret" (p. 84), that secret being the other stories untold.

Mirvis and Louis (1985) go the next step. They observe that the research may have a therapeutic aspect. The chosen area of inquiry and the interpretations made may all be therapeutically self-serving, maintaining and legitimizing issues for the individual researcher in some pathological way. Despite the possible self-maintenance aspects, qualitative research also has the potential to illuminate something that is personally as well as universally meaningful.

THE INTERVIEW

In terms of the actual interview itself, I was interested in knowing about the subject's background, including his family of origin; his experience of expectant fatherhood—his hopes and dreams for his child; the quality of the father-son relationship during his son's early development and any particular events that stood out; whether or not his son seemed different early on; whether he ever considered that his son could be gay and how that possibility was experienced; when he realized or learned of his son's homosexuality; if he was actually told, by whom, and his reactions to that knowledge; the quality of the father-son relationship at that point and whether this moment had an influence afterward; whether this knowledge and experience shaped his development as a parent; whether it shaped his development as a person; and whether or not this experience has changed him overall in any way.

As the interviews progressed, I gathered much more information regarding the father's relationship with his own caretakers and, in the later interviews, tried to focus a bit more on the father's expectations of and his relationships with his other children. A temporal sequencing was observed, beginning with the past and moving to the present. Time was the central organizing component, in essence, "the substance of plot" (Connelly and Clandinin, 1990, p. 8).

Although this structure provided a basic foundation, I also tried to leave room for the subjects to use the interview situation in ways they themselves needed. Daniel, for example, freely discussed his conflicts around being gay and how this interfered at first with his role as a father. At this point in his life, however, he thinks his homosexuality may be a benefit for his gay son as well as for his heterosexual son.

REACTIONS: BEFORE AND AFTER

Prior to conducting the interviews, one of my thoughts was that the experience of talking about their sons would elicit profound feelings of disappointment and sadness for the fathers. This did not seem to be the case much of the time. The trend was for them to move away from powerful feelings, emphasizing positive aspects of their relationships and minimizing the negative. I was struck by the fact that most of them seemed to idealize their sons in many ways. It was hard to know if they were trying to protect their sons, protect me, and/or protect themselves. Both Peter and Luis told me that they would not have been ready to discuss their son's homosexuality and their response to it as little as a year prior to our meeting. They needed time to come to terms with all of the feelings that this event evoked. I think that their readiness to talk publicly about this was a signal that they as well as the other fathers had achieved a certain resolution of the idea of a gay son and about their part in it, if any. Of course, talking about feelings recollected as opposed to feelings experienced in the moment is very different. Perhaps the surprisingly muted quality to all of this was defensive. Was I seeing *isolation of affect* or a *reaction formation?* It all left me puzzled at the time.

I admit that some of these stories evoked strong feelings in myself, with some fathers more than with others. Walter's story was particularly heartfelt. Toward the end of the interview, he talks about his need to be close to his son, James—not wanting to be left behind by him, wanting "to be in the room with the . . . light with him." This struck a deep emotional chord in me. It was a culmination of an interview in which he was clearly struggling to get to the core of his feelings, some of which eluded him.

On the other end of the spectrum were feelings of shock and disgust. In one particular home, I saw massive disarray—clothes and newspapers strewn all over the floor, closets open, dirty dishes and pots all over the kitchen. It looked like a hurricane had torn through. This particular father was also drinking wine during the interview, although not enough to be inebriated. Perhaps he was anxious. Perhaps this allowed him to speak more freely. I do not know. Juan Miguel Jr. proved frustrating, too. Much of the interview I spent trying to contain and refocus him. Since he had recently suffered a stroke, it was not clear if his thought processes had been affected or whether there was a preexisting thought disorder. Some of his story was contradictory in places. In between these extremes, I sometimes came away with a sense of admiration for those fathers who were struggling so much with the fact of their son's sexuality. For those who claimed not to have been greatly affected, I wondered what they had to do to convince themselves that it did not much matter, what it was that had been split off from awareness. But perhaps, this was only my construction, my interpretation. That it was not within the parameters of my role to explore this as deeply as I might in a treatment situation also proved frustrating. Whatever feelings I had for the fathers had to be kept aside for the time being. It also had to be balanced with the reality that I was only going to be able to do a limited number of interviews and needed to be able to get to the heart of the matter fairly quickly. The initial contacts lasted about one and one-half hours. Telephone and in-person follow-ups were briefer. Referrals for treatment were not indicated.

Berg (1985) delineates the kinds of anxieties that might come to bear on one's research—personal, professional, and/or group level. Not that this is the only feeling that surfaces, but it is a predominant one. Mine centered mostly on the first—the personal—specifically in moving from a clinically oriented self to a research-oriented self. For example, doing the interviewing for the study involved the necessity of taking a more active stance than I am accustomed to as a clinician. I found this approach going a little against the grain. When to ask a question and when to reflect was not always clear—not that it always is in a clinical situation either. But it was even less so here. I had to provide enough structure while at the same time giving them enough breathing room to tell their stories. Eventually I found a style that seemed to work, but only after some practice. Also, as I indicated above, I had to accept what I was told as the fathers' reality. I could not challenge them in ways that I might with a patient. In general, I had to continually keep in mind that patients and subjects "are not the same" (Padgett, 1998, p. 377). On one hand, clinical intervention focuses on "problem identification, understanding, and resolution" (p. 377) accompanied by little in the way of self-disclosure on the part of the clinician; on the other hand, qualitative research focuses "on events and experiences." Self-disclosure by the researcher may be made and might even be desirable in certain situations as a vehicle for furthering the engagement process and building "trust" (p. 378). Given my experience and interests, the urge to turn this into a treatment situation was extremely powerful and one that I had to continuously resist. I had to remember that my job was "to describe, not fix" (Ely et al., 1991, p. 52).

Certainly I wondered what these fathers were thinking of me. I believe that most of them assumed that I was gay. Only one asked me directly. Others asked me related questions or inferred it. I cannot be too sure how this might have affected the process. If I were a father and therefore one of them, would they have been more open and revealed themselves in different ways? No doubt. Paget (1983) underscores that the interview is created by the interviewer just as much as it is created by the interviewee. The kinds of questions posed and the particular "perplexities" (p. 78) personally experienced by the interviewer in response to the answers by the interviewee shape the content of the material. Were they confused about why I would want to know about their experience, not being a father myself? If so, this was never voiced. I was always wondering if and what they were holding back.

Some of my other anxieties focused on the possibility that a few of them might experience a kind of negative transference reaction, making me the target of some of the negative feelings they harbored toward their sons. However, since our in-person contacts were comparatively brief, the possibility of this occurring was minimized. I had also thought it might be difficult for me to hear all of their feelings, that perhaps I was going to defend against listening and taking the story in, circumventing the process in some self-protective ways. However, most of the stories I heard were from fathers who were more accepting of their son's homosexuality, so there was little to defend against. Their disapproval and disappointment focused more on themselves as fathers rather than on their sons as gay. Either those feelings were more accessible to them or those were the feelings they were more comfortable revealing. However, many of them did say they felt they were learning how to make the best of a situation they neither anticipated nor wanted. In many instances, the results of their struggles were unexpected but gratifying in ways that they themselves could never have imagined at the time they learned of their sons' homosexuality.

I also had some concerns about digging up all this information on my subjects and then leaving them "high and dry." Although they seemed to welcome the opportunity to talk, I could not help but think that I was like a surgeon who opens the body, leaves the organs exposed, and then exits the operating room. Having contact with them after the interviews and giving them their written narratives, which I thought would sustain them until the study was finished, helped to ease the sense that I was abandoning them, but not completely.

DATA ANALYSIS

My primary sources of data included tape-recorded interviews, field notes/log, and analytic memos. The field notes/log included raw descriptions—impressions of my subjects and the interviews, thoughts and feelings about method, ideas about the analysis, and just about anything that occurred to me in the moment as I attempted to make order out of chaos. All of the interviews were recorded and then transcribed word-for-word by myself.

In considering ways to conceptualize the data, I wrote a narrative about each father, trying to capture something unique about him— his feelings, his modes of expression, his character—presenting "in miniature the essence of what [I as] the researcher" (Ely et al., 1991, p. 154) saw and heard. I was also doing a thematic analysis of each interview and a listing of all the themes that I thought were common to most of the fathers, if not all. The coding, categorizing, and hypothesis building were all done concurrently.

In a general way, it seems that what I was reaching for was some understanding of the *self* and its transformations, that configuration "of personal events into a historical unity which includes not only what one has been but also anticipations of what one will be" (Polkinghorne, 1988, p. 150). Mishler (1986) says that "whatever else the story is about it is also a form of self-presentation . . . a particular personal-social identity . . . being claimed" (p. 243).

In a grounded theory approach (Strauss, 1987), categories can be of two types—in vivo or psychological. The former is description-based, resonating with the subjects' experience; the latter is theoretically based (Strauss, 1987). I chose to think in terms of in vivo categories as these reflect more the personal nature of my work. Using the interview guide as a reference point, I constructed a matrix, arriving at the categories I used to separate out the data— Dreams, Beginnings, Wonderings, Disclosure, and Impact. Taken separately and together, these categories aim at giving a sense of the father and his perceptions of his son, himself, and their relationship over time, providing the foundation for Chapter 5. But first, who are the fathers?

Chapter 4

The Stories

MITCHELL

My journey isn't over.

Mitchell recalls that as a young boy, his mother owned a copy of the breakthrough novel, *The Well of Loneliness.* Although he read it, he did not discuss it with anyone. However, its very presence in their home sent the message to him that people of all kinds were to be treated fairly and respectfully. It was primarily his mother, now ninety-three, who shaped his liberal bent. She was careful to use "the proper words" in describing "people and . . . body parts." African Americans were always referred to as "Negro"; gay people were always referred to as "homosexual." Although his father, who died thirty years ago, "had his prejudices," he was much warmer emotionally than his mother: "he was a kisser; he was a hugger." In their own ways, both instilled in him an openness and a tolerance that he feels was unusual at the time. "I marched to a slightly different drummer among my peers," he says with pride.

Born sixty-one years ago into a "comfortable middle-class home" in a "middle-class neighborhood," Mitchell "was the baby." Years as well as emotional and philosophical distance separated him from his brother and sister. The brother, three years his senior, was a star athlete and professionally followed in their father's footsteps. The two never saw eye-to-eye on any issue. Despite their differences, Mitchell loved his brother, these feelings being generated by

---

Please note that all quotations in this chapter are taken directly from the original transcripts.

an emphasis on the "importance of family." The sister, ten years older, had already left the home when Mitchell was eleven years old.

Mitchell's great love was street sports. Jackie Robinson was his boyhood hero. Although "bright enough to get by," academics did not hold much interest for him at the time. However, he grew up to become a teacher and later a counselor, working summers at a progressive, interracial private camp, which he helped to develop. All of his professional life was spent in a nurturing capacity, which he attributed to being comfortable with his "feminine side." Perhaps this may have made him appealing to his wife, Amy. They met in college. Both were members of the folk-song club. They were engaged within a year and married shortly thereafter, but waited several years to have their first child and several more to have their second. Both are boys—Jamie and Jay, respectively.

The liberal spirit that pervaded his home in childhood did the same in his adulthood. Mitchell aligned himself with "all the right causes." He was an NAACP member, he was vocal in his protest against the Vietnam War, he was pro-union. "The homosexual factor," however, was an issue far from his consciousness. Any homosexuals he might have known were completely closeted: "they were like nonpeople"—until Jay, that is.

Although Mitchell describes his second son, Jay, as "absolutely beautiful . . . like a Gerber's baby," he acknowledges having been much closer with Jamie. The novelty of having their first child was exciting. After work, he would come home and play with Jamie, "spending every waking hour" with him. Not so with Jay. At the time of his birth, Mitchell was in graduate school and did not "have the time to put into him." They hired a nurse for the first week of Jay's life, as Amy felt exhausted attending to Jamie.

Clearly, Jay was different. Mitchell recalls that he was reading the newspaper at the age of three. He would sound out the title, the author, and the characters from the record jacket of *The Wizard of Oz* to refine his newfound skill. Beyond this, Jay "was a showman." He had the rather unusual habit of walking on his toes, much to the delight of whoever would watch. Mitchell experienced his second son as a very extroverted child—"always laughing, always smiling, always happy." Despite this, he was much more distant from him right from the start.

The causes of this distance had not only to do with Mitchell's being around less of the time than he had been during Jamie's early years, but also because Jay was the more difficult, "less malleable" child; "a bottomless pit," forever demanding and testing limits. Too, when Mitchell became aware of his son's greater ease with females—he connected more easily with his mother than with his father, with his aunts than with his uncles—he "pulled back" from Jay. "I couldn't get the bonding that I wanted," he says with some frustration. However, he affirms that the distance he maintained had nothing to do with Jay's difference or "his not being macho."

When Jay was in nursery school, the teacher told both parents that he spent all of his time playing with the girls. At first, Mitchell rationalized this by thinking that it was a good thing for children to be encouraged to explore behaviors and roles that were gender atypical. However, both he and Amy were concerned because of the exclusivity of their son's interest, that he *only* played with girls. In elementary school, however, Jay's social circle opened up to include some boys, but his closest connections were still with females. Because of Jay's good looks and his extroversion, he had girlfriends all through school, "one more beautiful than the next." Mitchell admits that "there may have been some stuff festering underneath . . . in my thinking." For the most part, however, any vague or fleeting thoughts that Mitchell may have had in relation to his son's developing homosexuality "went out the window."

Theater is Jay's life. Walking on his toes as a toddler, always being "a show-stopper," whetted his appetite for more. In high school, he was getting lead roles and "immediately started to shine." Mitchell boasts of his son's many talents—"he has a voice like an angel, he acts wonderfully and . . . he can move." He went to an out-of-town college that had a good theater program, but after one year dropped out. Mitchell was disappointed. This was not in the family tradition. Although he knew that Jay was making the right decision for himself, at the same time he encouraged his son to enter "some kind of school," which he later did. Jay enrolled in a dramatic arts academy and eventually graduated.

During this period, Mitchell and Amy would frequently travel to see their son, now twenty-one, perform in a small New England town. When they arrived for a summer stock production, it was clear that something was wrong. Jay seemed unhappy: "we couldn't put our finger on it." When they returned the following fall, Amy found a letter in Jay's room from one of the male actors in the company, breaking off their relationship. She became hysterical. Mitchell minimized it, trying to leave open the possibility that it may have been "a one-time thing," adding, "I guess I was in denial." They did not speak with their son about this at the time. When Jay moved back to the city, he continued to reside with his parents. One night when the three of them were returning home from a movie, Mitchell casually suggested that Jay, his close female friend, father, and mother "double-date" sometime. Jay remained silent for the rest of the ride home. Upon entering the house, he said to his parents, "I have to tell you something." Mitchell describes it as "a magnificent performance." Dry-eyed, well rehearsed, he announced, "Mom, Dad, I'm gay." Mitchell reflexively embraced his son. Amy was "devastated."

In the months that followed, Mitchell does not recall being that upset. His conscious concerns were related mostly to health issues, particularly AIDS, and to his son's physical safety. Fears of Jay being "gay-bashed and ending up in the emergency room [at] three in the morning" were uppermost in his mind. His desire to be closer to Jay was partially compensatory for his wife's withdrawal from him. He feels that his liberal bent did not make it "easy," but might have "made it easier" for him to accept this. Fighting for the "underdog" was familiar and natural. As a couple, however, he and Amy remained in "the closet for about seven years." That was to change dramatically, heralded by what Mitchell termed his "two . . . epiphanies."

The first of these took place at a New Year's Day party while he was conversing with a friend of his, a woman with "a wonderfully progressive background," one who supported every cause and "defended every . . . underdog." Upon seeing another woman enter the room, Mitchell's friend said, "You see that woman who just walked in? Her daughter's a lesbian." In the course of the afternoon, Mitchell had occasion to speak with this mother, who turned out to be an artist and firewalker. Their conversation was intriguing and exciting. The idea of reducing this fascinating person to just "the mother of a gay" sickened and appalled him. The second incident took place at a dinner party several months later. In conversation with a friend, the name Noel Coward came up. This friend, "another progressive," said to Mitchell, "You know, he's a fruit." That night he went home and "put the two incidents together." From that moment on he was determined that no one was going to reduce Jay like that and no one was going to reduce *him* to just "the father of a gay kid": "I'm more than that. I'm *much* more than that. . . . They're not going to do that to me and they're not going to do that to my kid." He was on fire. He was unstoppable. He was ready to take on the world. He was ready to come out.

So, "one by one, or couple by couple," he and Amy told most of the important people in their lives, except Mitchell's mother, then ninety-one. Upon reflection, however, he and Amy did not want her to die without knowing Jay. They also speculated that Jay might wonder if his grandmother would love him as much if she knew him for who he really was. As it turned out, she was surprisingly accepting, possibly based on the fact that she and Jay had a strong relationship already.

Over time, Mitchell became much more aware of deeper layers of feeling. The initial shame that he felt—more connected to societal prejudice—had given way to and was overtaken by his shame and guilt around not being "there" for his son, his shame and guilt around being "a nonprotecting father." The pain of Jay's struggle had eluded him: "the nights that he said he closed the door and went to sleep and he was confused and crying and I was in the other room, unaware of his torment. I wasn't there for him." The recognition of that reality shook him to the core. Part of Mitchell's response to this was to become an activist, to be "there" in a way that he had not been before—during the years following Jay's birth, the years prior to his son's coming out, and the years right after the disclosure.

Different stages and understandings mark Mitchell's description of his own coming out as a parent. The first has to do with accepting "the concept of gay." By this he means that a gay son is the same son who "walks in, kisses you hello, kisses you good-bye," the son that you have always known and loved, the son not yet in a relationship. Until that point, gay is still in a vacuum, still "an abstraction." However, once the words "I'm dating" are uttered, the situation begins to change. "Putting a face on gay" becomes even more of a reality. Getting used to the notion of two men in a relationship, two men "making love," "the graphics of sex," putting "two faces" on gay, has been more difficult for Mitchell. "Acceptance [isn't] such an easy thing," he admits.

In the beginning, "everything gay was good . . . if you were gay you were a great person." Mitchell relates that Jay's first boyfriend turned out to be distinctly "N.G., No Good." He was alcoholic and disloyal. Despite this, Mitchell felt a strong need "to be the accepting one," "to bend over backward" partially to compensate for his wife's unacceptance. The right to be discriminating and judgmental at certain times, about certain things, about certain people has been learned over time. "My journey isn't over," he reiterates emphatically.

Part of that journey has been helped along by being an active member of P-FLAG. Mitchell touchingly describes his first Gay Pride Parade two years ago as "the most moving experience [he has] ever had":

> as we came down Fifth Avenue and . . . made the turn around Washington Square Park and they were five and six deep and we were walking with a sign that said, "Proud Parents" . . . walking with our son in between us. And the response . . . of the . . . young people and old people whose parents had obviously rejected them; they came out, they ran into the street, they threw their arms around us, they hugged us, they kissed us. We were all crying; we were all weeping. It was such . . . a powerful, powerful moment.

Mitchell keeps a picture of that moment in his living room for all to see.

Also part of that journey was his helping to establish a "gay liberation Seder," the Passover ritual that commemorates the "coming out of Egypt," for him a metaphor for "coming out of the closet." He helped to write a Haggadah, the prayer book used at the Passover service, tailoring it to commemorate the liberation of gays and lesbians. His wife and his mother also contributed.

It seems that one of the more difficult parts of Mitchell's coming out as a parent has been telling his other son, Jamie, about Jay. Like Mitchell and his own brother, his two sons were estranged growing up, total opposites in both temperament and interests. Among the last to be told, Mitchell says that this was mostly "circumstantial" as

Jamie was living away at college around that time. Father took it upon himself to tell him during an extended stay home. The news came as no surprise. The two brothers are closer now, but not necessarily because of the disclosure. Mitchell feels that their better relationship has probably been more a result of Jay's affection for his sister-in-law, his feelings for her spilling over into and positively affecting the relationship between the brothers. Although his sons are now talking more to each other—"from coast to coast"—Mitchell describes them as "still worlds apart."

Mitchell admits that although he is *not* at a point where he wakes up each morning and "thank[s] God for a gay son," he does admit "that it's opened up new worlds" for Amy and him: "we see things . . . we didn't see before, we hear things we didn't hear before, we sense things we didn't sense before. . . . We are being admitted to a world we never thought existed." What he is thankful for is the fact that his son is who he is. Without that, Mitchell would not be the person *he* is: "we've impacted on each other." For him, the coming-out process has meant forging a closer relationship with his son, one that they never knew earlier in their lives. Part of this has resulted from Mitchell's coming to feel like the confident "protector" of his family, perhaps for the first time. He no longer feels "on edge" in a room full of people he may not know very well, no longer "afraid of the next gay joke." He now feels capable of defending himself and his son in a way that he did not before: "[Amy] and I are better people for this experience."

Although he does not claim to fully comprehend the process that Jay has gone through in coming out as a gay person, Mitchell feels that there is a shared sense of exhilaration that accompanies both of their journeys, a splendid emergence "into the sunshine." As he writes in the Liberation Haggadah (Calvani et al., 1996):

> My new-found freedom comes from the empowerment I feel as I once again can assume the natural role of parent-as-protector. As a modern day Moses, I can now set my energies to parting the turbulent waters of bigotry so that all of our sons and daughters can walk in safety on dry land each to his or her own promised land. (p. 23)

Amen.

JUAN MIGUEL JR.

> He was [Juan Miguel III], gay or not gay, he was [Juan Miguel III].

Juan Miguel Jr. has been no stranger to crisis. As a young boy growing up in Puerto Rico, he, his younger brother, his mother, and his father had to move to his grandfather's house after a hurricane demolished his father's medical factory, leaving them virtually homeless and penniless. There they lived until his father "came to be in the black." At that time, his grandfather, a "very large land-owner," gave the family a house: "it was a gift, [a] donation."

Both his father and his mother had dreams for their "genius" son. He was to follow in the footsteps of his mother's brother, who had studied medicine and graduated from a midwestern university. Off he went to major schools in Washington, DC, and Pennsylvania, his first stops before going to Europe to study medicine. He never finished. He had initially agreed to the plan "just to say yes to them." He had no interest in or talent for it: "memorizing all those books. . . . I just couldn't take it." The trip was not without its rewards, however. He did meet a girl, fell in love, married her, and moved back to Puerto Rico. But, tragedy struck a second time when his wife gave birth and their infant "was born dead." She left him, never to be heard from again.

After a seven-month stint in the Army in Central America, he returned to his native country, where he met his current wife. He lives there with her and three of their four children: two daughters and a son. Another son lives in the United States. "Half-retired and half-working" at age seventy, he still practices bankruptcy law—"the easiest career"—interesting in light of the fact that he had to declare bankruptcy himself twenty years ago.

Juan Miguel Jr. openly acknowledges his own homosexual activity as a preadolescent. He and two of his neighbors used to hide out "and masturbate each other. . . . There came a time when I didn't like that any more. I was after the girls." As a teenager, he would sometimes escort older men for the free drinks and the free dinners. He recalls on one occasion going to a man's room at the YMCA where he got two dollars for "a blow job." Things got a bit rougher on another occasion when he was almost raped by a German war veteran: "he locked the room and . . . was forcing me to act gay—kiss him, and he was taking off my pants. I . . . didn't like that." He pushed the man away, threatening to call the guard if he didn't stop. He says laughingly, "I just don't like men. It's that simple."

Juan Miguel Jr. feels that he answers to no one and does things his way. He does not use his mother's maiden name after his father's name as is typical of most Puerto Ricans and Spanish people, for example. Rather, he likes "the American way. I'm Jr." He is a staunch believer in facing life squarely, head-on, unencumbered by any organized system of thought other than his own: "I don't believe in God, or saints, church, no nothing." For him, it is "all cowardice . . . creat[ing] God to . . . hide . . . behind his skirts." The credo "if you can't do anything, leave it to God" is not for him. It is for the weak, the vulnerable. He will concede, however, that he does "believe in human . . . relations," that is, respecting others and not doing anything to harm anyone. He credits his four years in psychoanalysis with giving him the courage to look at things "realistically." One of those many things that he feels he has had to look at "realistically" has been the homosexuality of his oldest son, Juan Miguel III.

Despite his fierceness of independence, Juan Miguel Jr. does not feel different in all respects. One of the ways in which he feels similar to other fathers is a common need for immortality; "to keep on going with the [family] name . . . that's standard in almost every place." He was named after his own father and named his son after himself. To "keep on having [Juan Miguels] that would live forever" is a dream that will end with this son, however. If that was a source of disappointment for him, he was not willing to fully acknowledge it.

Juan describes his son, Juan Miguel III, as a person of many talents. He plays the piano and the organ. As a youngster, he studied privately and gave concerts at home. He also composes. In addition, he boasts that his son writes poetry and knows several languages: "I'm very proud of him." Early on, Juan did not see his son as different, not until "he was coming into his teens." Only then did he notice his son's "preference for boys." He never had any girlfriends, preferring to associate with two or three male friends. Although he wondered whether his son was gay, he only gave it "a small thought. It passed my mind and I forgot it." During those moments when he allowed this possibility to "pass [his] mind," he recollects a sense of sadness in considering his son "as an old man" and that "he'd be all by himself." As his son developed into manhood, however, it was obvious that all of his friends were gay men, confirming Juan's earlier "small thought."

One night about a year and a half before our interview when father and mother were in the bedroom watching television, their son, then thirty-two, came in and announced that he wanted to tell them something: "I immediately thought of it. I said he's going to say that he's gay." He had anticipated correctly. Despite their son's anxiety about this, Juan says that he and his wife were immediately accepting: "He was worried. We weren't worried." His son's attempts to come "out of the closet" to him seemed like an afterthought: "to me, he was never *in* the closet."

The worries Juan Miguel Jr. will acknowledge have more to do with his son's professional opportunities and how his being gay might impact on that. Although Juan Miguel III has completed his undergraduate degree, he has not found employment that is really satisfying. He completed one semester of law school, but did not have the interest or the aptitude for law. He now does clerical work. Juan has tried to get him other jobs, but has so far "failed to do so." His son expresses great anxiety over whether being found out at work will result in his being fired. Juan acknowledges that this is a strong possibility in his country, if he gets a job at all: "they find out he's gay, they'll give him another excuse, but he won't get it. I know that." His son's dream was to study music and earn his living that way. Juan refused to allow him to do that as he thought he "would be eating from the sidewalk," that is, there would be no money in it. He feels that his son now blames him for not having work that is steady and interesting: "I can feel it."

Juan claims that he is not interested in how his response to his son is the same or different from other fathers' reactions. He feels that he has always done the right thing: "I am myself." He says that his affection for his son "hasn't changed—up or down. Stays the same. . . . He was [Juan Miguel III], gay or not gay, he was [Juan Miguel III]."

He implies that his comfort with the issue has been influenced by the fact that he knew many people in his life who were gay: the other boys he had sexual experiences with as a preadolescent who he thinks developed homosexually; the young men he knew in the neighborhood when he was an adult; a roommate at the university; a first cousin who died of AIDS; and an uncle of his wife's. He also knows another father who has two gay sons, and they talk about gay issues together as they talk about anything else. He sums his attitude up by saying: "they happened to be born like that. . . . They're part of life. . . . They're human."

He also says that his relative ease with this has been marked by his *not* talking about it with his wife. He has told his mother, now ninety-two, a religious fanatic, who refuses to believe it. His other children responded with silence at the news, except for his oldest daughter, who has remarked to her father that she has seen her brother downtown "with his sweetheart." His own response to this has been to ignore her: "if you don't make any comments . . . she'll stop."

Juan Miguel Jr. prides himself in being different than some other fathers who have "a puritan response to having a gay child," whose lives are dictated by rules which "come from God," something he cannot make any sense of. He also prides himself in being able to go public. For example, if he hears others saying things about gay people he feels are not true, he would tell them that they "don't know what [they're] talking about." He has no patience for those who just parrot what others tell them. However, he is not necessarily at ease confronting others about this: "makes me nasty . . . like Hitler," thinking that they should be exterminated.

Juan feels that his son's revelation has made him feel closer to him. He expresses empathy for the discrimination that inevitably faces a gay Puerto Rican man. He wishes that attitudes toward gay people could be like they are in Europe where "they just don't worry about it. It's just not a problem." He is concerned about the harm that might come to his son if he makes himself too public too quickly. He tries to offset societal prejudice by being as understanding with him as possible. This sometimes takes the form of allowing his son to "think he's right" when the father knows he is not.

With a history of kidney failure and a recent stroke, Juan has worries about the precarious state of his own health as well as what will become of his son should he die. With no real way to fully support himself and with no "companion" yet, Juan would feel better knowing that his son were more settled: "I know I don't have many years to come." He is hoping that the same independence of mind and spirit that has pervaded his own way of living has rubbed off on his son. He feels that his role as a father is in giving his children the freedom to do things in their own ways: "you have to leave it up . . . to them. You might guide them, give them the basics of life as you think, but they have a mind of their own." This is his "realistic" philosophy of life. This is his legacy.

PETER

This [is] something that I have to face . . . this is the reality.

Peter's early life in Russia was marked by scarcity. When he was eight years old, his father was first taken away by the Nazis and later by the Communists. For five years he was left to fend for himself, which was complicated by the presence of an emotionally fragile mother. Trading, smuggling, and hiding became ways of life in the day-to-day struggle to survive. Upon his father's return from Siberia, the family moved to a town in Transylvania where Peter "was the only Jewish boy in high school." Although his family was financially better off after his father found a job, his mother became increasingly paranoid. At age sixteen, Peter moved out and went to Bucharest, living by himself in the school dormitory, returning home infrequently. He knew firsthand what it meant to be different.

The self-sufficiency that grew out of the persecutory environment in which he lived "sharpened certain . . . features." The capacity to be innovative and quick thinking has served him well in later life: "I decide very quickly what I want to do even in difficult times." It has also fostered a sense of compassion, a militant determination to stand up for the rights of others. However, not "growing up under normal circumstances" left him with a sense of confusion about "how people behave," in turn shaping unrealistic expectations of his own children. "I was not [an] easy father," he admits.

Peter, now sixty-four, met his wife, Sonia, in the chemical company in which they both were employed. The daughter of a doctor, "a bourgeois class," she was required to study *and* work. "I offered her a coupon for a free lunch so that impressed her very much," he says with some amusement. They were married within a year and a half. In 1963, a cousin brought the couple to Cleveland, where they lived for the next six years. After that, they moved to California for twenty-seven years and then to the East Coast.

The transition to life in this country was very difficult. Not knowing the language, not knowing the customs, they were out of sync: "I grew up in a mentality of the 'shtetl' [the ghetto] where everybody is very friendly and eager to share bread . . . because there is nothing else to share. . . . Everything that I considered normal was . . . reversed here." In Rumania, Peter grew up seeing "people on the streets," in Cleveland, they were "in the cars"; there when he went to the barber, he would be "facing the mirror," here he is "sitting against the mirror"; there "I'll see you soon . . . literally meant" just that, here it is merely an acknowledgment.

Despite his concern about irresponsibly bringing children into a world he considered still under the threat of evil forces, a world where he could possibly relive the hunger and deprivation he knew so well growing up, a world "half-crazy," his son, Richard, was born less than a year after they settled in Cleveland, around the time of his own father's death. His mother had died several years before. Concurrently, Sonia's father joined them, a man "full of life and great expectations." Hope remained alive for Peter.

Peter remembers his young son as a "very pretty child." In fact, his picture was so good that Sears used it and paid them some money. However, Peter feels that the physical resemblance between him and Richard "is almost nonexistent." While his daughter looks more like her father, he says Richard "looks more like my wife." Temperamentally, too, the father feels that his son is quite different from him. Richard was "stubborn . . . disorganized and sloppy and lazy. . . . He wasn't rough like I was . . . he was gentle," a boy who "very much needed his parents." The baby-sitters, none of whom lasted "too long," were not substitute-enough. His first day at school proved "almost traumatic . . . he wouldn't let go . . . we had to push him on the bus." Despite the fact that Richard called his father "Momma" at times, Peter did not feel that he was very patient with his son. "I didn't know how to behave to a child," he says with some regret. Punishment—sometimes through spanking, sometimes through ostracizing—was much more common with Richard than with his daughter, who is four years younger than her brother. Peter points to the experience he had with his own father, who would "beat [him] up" on occasion, as the model for how to discipline. Peter's expectations for his children ran high, partially revolving around his need for them to be "good Jew[s]," which meant that they should fully comprehend the lives of their predecessors, which he hoped would result in the continuation of their faith. Toward that end, father "pushed" Richard to go through Hebrew school and day school rather than allowing him to spend time with his peers engaging in sports-related activities.

Peter felt that it was Richard's need to please him that led to his request that he be allowed to attend an (all boys) yeshiva. He was fifteen years old at the time. Since they lived far from the school, Richard stayed with the rabbi and his family for a year and a half and spent six months in Jerusalem at the extension school there. Peter was hoping that this would "be a good influence." It was during this time that Sonia came across "sort of a love letter" that Richard had written to another male student. Confusion about this lingered for a while. But when Richard later became engaged and was ready to marry, Peter dismissed any thoughts he had about his son's possible homosexuality. The letter that Sonia had discovered a few years before Peter considered "a fluke, something that was of no importance." However, while Richard's relationship with his bride-to-be was going well on one level—he bought her a ring, the future in-laws met—Peter's confusion became reactivated when Richard would tell Sonia and him all about the male friends of the girl. The cycle was then repeated a few years later with another girlfriend until "everything went sour."

Although Peter continued to think of his son as "straight," his wife had an "inclination" otherwise. When Richard was in college and living in California, his mother showed up at his apartment unexpectedly. It took him a while to answer the door. When he did, another boy was present. His father dismissed this as well. A few more years elapsed until Sonia finally confronted her son and he acknowledged his homosexuality. She hid this from her husband for another year and a half. "She hoped that I'm going to die before," he joked. With mother and father now living on the East Coast and their son, now thirty-three, still living on the West Coast, the truth became easy to mask, that is, until Richard moved in with a partner. It was at that point that Sonia thought her husband would find out anyway, so she told him. As expected, Peter "was shocked." This was one year before our interview.

Growing up in Russia and Rumania, Peter's prejudice against homosexuality was deeply ingrained. Homosexuals were "ballet dancers" and men who "would congregate in the toilets." His one experience with another man, who made advances toward him at a public theater while he was on leave during his military service, left him "revolted." The idea of a Jewish homosexual was, for him, a contradiction in terms: "I was convinced that . . . a Jew cannot be a homosexual." The whole thing he considered "a laughing matter." After Richard's disclosure, however, it was anything but. He ordered his son back East so that they could look for a cure.

Frantically calling various universities and departments of psychiatry, "determined to find out more about this terrible thing that afflicted my family," Peter was told: "this [is] something that I have to face . . . this is the reality . . . there is nothing that can be done." The harshness of that reality resulted in sleepless nights and endless dialogues with Sonia, herself devastated. Richard tried to help his father understand that "he could live a life of lies . . . get married and have children . . . and make everybody unhappy." This did not ease Peter's pervasive guilt. He thought that perhaps the physical abuse he put Richard through somehow resulted in this "affliction." Then again, perhaps it was Sonia's fault. He did not understand how this could have happened. He still struggles. Attending various parent support groups has helped to ease his guilt to some extent; however, he still considers his son's sexuality "a problem." At this point in time, he is of the belief that it is something "in the genes . . . an orientation that is not chosen." Like others, he thinks that Richard was "born with this." Then again, maybe this is just a rationalization, he thinks at other times.

Peter describes his son's relationship with him as one characterized by "love and hate. . . . On one hand, [Richard] would do anything for me; on the other hand . . . he's impatient with me. . . . Maybe he doesn't have enough respect for me, maybe he does. I don't know." Peter acknowledges having a great deal of confusion and frustration about his son early on. His excessive demands on and high expectations for Richard fueled his perception that he was not growing into the kind of "hard-working and successful boy" Peter dreamed of. Simultaneously, this perception blinded him to the fact that Richard was, in reality, "a very, very loving . . . child," but was just having difficulties living up to his father's aspirations. "It was a very strange and unfortunate situation between us," Peter regretfully acknowledges.

Eight years ago, Richard asked his father if he could work for him at the company that the family owns and operates. Peter feels that Richard's need to please him was at the root of this request, similar in that respect to the one his son made years ago when he asked his father if he could attend the yeshiva. This seemed to have been a good move for Richard. From an impulsive and irresponsible boy, who would "spend money on things he didn't need," he has developed into a "calculated and organized" man. "He has matured quite a bit," Peter proudly acknowledges. He is also relieved that his son found a "friend," Matthew, whom he and Sonia are fond of. He is also pleasantly surprised that Matthew is going to convert to Judaism not only because Catholicism, Matthew's religion, negates homosexuality, but also because of his love for and devotion to Richard. "Finding somebody like this is . . . a blessing," Peter adds.

From a militant homophobe, Peter feels that he has changed into a much more understanding and compassionate parent and person. Although he would still like his son to "live a normal life" with a family and children, Richard's obvious happiness "counts a lot toward the compromise." He regrets that Sonia will not be a grandmother by way of their son, as she "would be fantastic." He does not feel that he would make a good grandfather, though, always being afraid of "bad things" happening: "my past is living with me now." Whether grandparenthood by way of their daughter remains possible or desirable for Peter and Sonia is unknown.

Despite his struggle with this issue, fears continue to plague him—bias, AIDS—all negative associations with homosexuality. Peter is all too aware of the persecutory environment in which he grew up and which he does not wish to replicate in his present relationship with Richard, something he feels he has done in their past relationship. Regrets continue to plague him as well—about not understanding his son's struggles, about not being able to help him make certain decisions in life, about not being "a better father."

What basically got him through this crisis is the belief that his son's homosexuality is "not a choice," but rather "a situation . . . a handicap" which he has been dealt. Because of that, Peter affirms, "He is what he is and therefore I am on his side 100 percent."

HARRY

I have hopes that he would marry and have children.

The year 1929 was catastrophic for Harry and his family. Not only did his father's silver business go bankrupt, but his mother passed away as well, necessitating that Harry, then five years old, and his brothers—one older, one younger—be placed in an orphanage, where Harry remained for the next fourteen years. His younger sister was brought up by their aunt, and his older sister continued to live with their father.

The monthly Sunday afternoon visits to the orphanage by various friends and family members "were happy times," but also "sad moments for everyone." Having "to say good-bye to their loved ones" time and time again proved difficult for the boys. When Harry was nine years old, his older brother died of double pneumonia. Five years later, he said good-bye forever to his father when *he* died. The few memories he has of his father, "a very good man . . . a very popular individual," are vague and mostly revolve around his playing the violin and the accordion. He does emotionally recollect, however, that his father was someone whom he felt "a lot of love for." Loss has been a constant companion for Harry.

Life in "the institution," as he calls it, "was a wonderful thing." It was a safe haven, a place to sleep, a place to eat, and best of all, a place to play—sports, that is, which he did very "aggressively . . . baseball, football, basketball, year in and year out, year in and year out." He lived for those moments. Appreciating what was available, learning how to make something out of nothing, became a way of life. The boys made their own softball, for example, by finding a sock, filling it up, then sewing it together. Although he felt that some of the caretakers, the Brothers and Sisters, were better than others, overall he thought they "did a tremendous job." The one week's vacation in the country during the summer when "everything was taken care of" seemed like heaven on earth. Harry recognizes how difficult life might have been had he not been placed. "I accepted it as a blessing," he said gratefully.

After graduating from high school and being discharged, Harry moved in with his older sister and her husband prior to finding an apartment in the vicinity. After serving in the Navy, he eventually settled in Venezuela for about thirteen years, working for a brokerage firm. His boss asked him to set up operations in Puerto Rico, expanding from "a three-man operation" ("two of the 'men' were actually women") to a staff of twenty-seven in the ten years that he was there. It was around this time that he met his wife-to-be, Rhonda. After a year's engagement, they married and eventually had four children. Prior to each birth, Rhonda would ask her husband what he was hoping for and he would always say, "A boy. That's what I would like to have." His prayers were finally answered with the birth of his last child, Harry Jr.

Harry recalls his son as "no problem at all." This was especially welcome after he was divorced from his wife in 1967 while the family was still residing in Puerto Rico. Although Rhonda received temporary custody of all the children, the tables turned as the mother increasingly got herself into "a few predicaments." Multiple addictions to alcohol and prescription drugs, freely mixed, resulted in suicide attempts and hospitalizations. He then received custody and was left alone with their children. Several years after the divorce, the police reported finding her body, which "had been thrown off the rooftop." With no evidence of "foul play," it remains possible that "she decided to take her own life." Harry is not sure of this. He never married again.

Father and children were not alone too long before Dolly, their live-in housemaid, came into their lives. From Saint Kitts, "she was the best thing that ever happened to us," he says. While he was out earning a living, she was taking care of the children—bathing, dressing, and feeding them, making sure they had their lunch boxes before going off to school. He vividly and affectionately recalls "this great big colored gal holding on to the small hand of little [Harry]" as the two walked together to where he attended kindergarten. The perfection of this arrangement ended abruptly after Dolly panicked, fearing that "the authorities" would catch up with her, as she only had a tourist visa. "She just left us one day," he says regretfully. Although they had other housemaids after her, none could take her place. Another important person in his life—gone.

Harry dreamed of having a son who would be as "sports-minded" as he was. Although certainly capable, Harry Jr. was less interested in team sports—his father's love—than in gymnastics. As a boy, he delighted in showing his father his back-flip technique—"standing erect and then throwing his body around backward and landing on his feet . . . with his head up in the air," a proud moment for father and son. These moments contrasted with others when Harry Jr. would actively engage in cross-gender behavior. On one occasion, a friend of Harry's came to the house, bringing a doll for each of the girls and a fire-truck for Harry Jr., who decided he did not like his gift and "wanted to trade" with any of his sisters for her doll. His father thought this "a bit unusual." On other occasions, the four children loved to dress up and put on skits. During these "festivities," Harry Jr. would don female attire "so that there would be four girls instead of three and one." It was "such a big hit the first time" that little Harry continued his display. Again, his father thought this "unusual but . . . didn't look into it any further than that." He has wondered in more recent years if there was "a message . . . being brought forth . . . in his behavior." He does not know.

With their return to the United States around 1970, the family tried to settle in. They had to live with Harry's sister and brother-in-law for a few months prior to finding a home to rent. Although the father's recollections of his son tend to be rather vague, he remembers him as a "fair" student, "nothing spectacular." He does recall, however, a relationship that his son had with Maggie, "a lovely young lady," who lived a few blocks away: "the two of them hit it off very well" for a couple of years. They saw each other daily. Harry recalls this being the only time his son has ever been "serious about a member of the opposite sex."

As the children grew a bit older, Harry seemed to become more distant from them. He feels that this grew out of financial necessity, as he was "bring[ing] in whatever [he] could to meet the incoming bills." They were left on their own for most of the day as he would work two, sometimes three jobs, anywhere from twelve to fifteen hours daily, sadly resulting in his "missing out on being at home with the children." He was losing touch with the son he so much dreamed of having so many years before.

The reality of this distance was made all too clear when his son, then twenty-one, came to him on a Sunday afternoon in the fall of 1985. (He remembered the day and the season. In a personal communication, Harry Jr. informed me of the year.) No one else was at home. "With a determined look on his face," he asked his father if they could talk. Harry never recalled any other time in their relationship that his son approached him with such intent seriousness of purpose. He remembers him being very direct and coming "right out with it," saying, "Dad, I'm gay." Harry Jr. made a strong case for himself, telling his father that "he had made up his mind and [that] he wanted to live that style and nothing I could say would persuade him." The father acknowledges being quite shocked by this disclosure, seeing "no indication whatsoever of that forthcoming . . . no trace of anything like that. . . . Everything else left my mind . . . just . . . that one thought. How? Why?"

After their initial discussion, Harry tried to think back on particular events that may have been significant, but nothing really stood out for him that might explain his son's "move in that area." Although he thinks that he probably discussed "the topic" with his son after that, it was "not to the extent that [they] had at that first meeting." The father's belief was that his son's homosexuality had developed out of his associations with others in "that particular . . . group," and he pleaded with him "to hold off and . . . try to change [his] lifestyle" so as to give the "[other] side a chance." He summarizes it this way: "I thought that it would be only fair to associate with others that didn't feel that way and . . . mix with them and mix with girlfriends . . . before he came to a final decision." He readily admits, however, that he had never met any of his son's friends at that point so he did not know for sure which "side" they were on. "Perhaps I was too presumptuous," he acknowledges. Harry feels that his wife would have fully supported their son's "making such a move," as she was always one to encourage others "to speak up and speak out."

Harry does not know how his own sisters feel about his son's gayness, as he has never spoken with them about it in depth in the twelve years since the disclosure. He has, however, addressed the issue with his daughters, but only after they brought it up first. "I was hoping that [he] . . . might change his mind," he says, still praying for the day when his son will "marry and have children." He thinks that Harry Jr. has the potential to be a very good father, if his relationship with his nephew is any indication.

Once his son moved to the city to attend art school, Harry is reasonably certain that "he fell in with that crowd . . . [and] became more involved . . . with that way of life." Living openly in a large city has its perils, however. He recalls an incident in which his son and a friend were walking in Greenwich Village and were attacked by a group of youths. Some of these boys were found and apprehended. Harry Jr. sustained some facial damage. Although Harry is worried that this could happen again, he is less concerned now that he sees his son making an effort to be "aware of his surroundings" and taking care of himself by not drinking or smoking and by exercising regularly. "He . . . has a magnificent physique," he says boastfully. Besides his disappointments about his son's sexuality, he sometimes feels that Harry Jr. "asks for more from others than he's willing to give of himself." This takes the form of his neither thanking his father for money he has sent to him nor paying it back, despite the fact that it was understood to be a loan, not a gift. Only more recently is Harry learning to deny his son's requests—"finally."

All of these have served as points of reference in reflecting upon his life as a father. Regretfully, he feels that he "did not do as . . . good a job with [his] children as [he] should have," that he did not act in their "best interest," feeling that they deserved more than he could give them. He was mostly gone from 7 a.m. until 7 p.m., necessitating that the children be on their own, even making dinner for themselves most of the time. He would even go so far as to further extend his day during those evenings when he tended bar— afterward playing shuffleboard or pool or just chatting with "the boys" before returning home.

At the very least, he feels that his absence negatively affected his son's (and daughters') attitude and performance at school. Whether it had any other effect, he is not sure. But he does acknowledge not knowing where his son was, whom he was with, and what he was doing during much of his adolescence and early adulthood. He is sad that his son cannot create professional opportunities for himself so that he can further develop his talent as a commercial artist: "I'm sorry that he can't find . . . a place in life instead of doing what he's doing now." Although Harry is talking about his son's career, he is also talking about his son's sexuality—his "liking," his "going one way." His need for Harry Jr. "to succeed" in life is linked to his own need to feel like a more successful father. Perhaps it is not too late.

LUIS

I understand and I accept my son because he's my son.

For Luis, now fifty-one, the middle child in a Jewish family, life in Argentina was reasonably comfortable. Although his father, a tailor by trade, was able to adequately meet his family's needs, nevertheless, he was a man who "was struggling all his life." Like father, like son.

Luis himself first came to this country at age twenty-seven for a Florida vacation. He decided to make the United States his permanent home at around the time his brother got married to an American woman whom he had met in Argentina. After a year in the United States, his brother divorced and moved back to their native country with the rest of the family, leaving Luis alone. As an immigrant—not knowing the language, having to earn a living at first washing dishes, cleaning motel rooms, and later as a cook—life evolved "slowly." Not one to dwell on the difficult times or on the discrimination he faced, he concentrates more on the fact that he "lived" through it, with some help along the way, much of it from Sue.

Sue was the next-door neighbor of his brother's wife's relatives: "I liked her at the first moment as I . . . saw her." Although she was recuperating from a car accident at the time they met, Sue showed Luis the sights and the sounds of her country and tried to make him feel at home here. She has been a major force in shaping his adult life, and he freely acknowledges that she is a "very good friend of mine—the best." Recognizing the importance of this relationship came slowly as well. The two got married, then divorced, then remarried. Although vague about what led to their separation and remarriage, he admits having some regret and confusion about this: "I thought it was the right thing to do. . . . I was wrong." He has done things in his life that he admits he does not completely understand, the reasons for his divorce being one of those. Something that he *is* sure of is his need to continuously "improve" himself, particularly in his work. As a head chef in a major restaurant, he is always looking "to develop new recipes . . . new systems." He looks to "improve" himself in a more personal way as well. An opportunity for this unexpectedly presented itself a year before the interview when his only child, Michael, then age sixteen, came out.

Luis fully acknowledges the expectations he had for his son prior to his birth. Of prime importance was his wish that Michael would eventually marry and have children, "dreaming that one day" he would be a grandfather. Also, he did not want Michael to have to work as hard as he has. "To work smarter, not harder," that is, to work with his mind rather than with his hands, was his father's hope. Sharing an interest in sports was also a dream. As a boy in Argentina, Luis enjoyed soccer, basketball, and spending time "with the guys." Sharing this with his son was not to be, however. Luis recalls taking Michael to the park when he was young to try to cultivate his interest, "but he was . . . never so thrilled about it." Michael was far more interested in other activities—dancing, for instance. The song "Flashdance" held him in its grip throughout much of his childhood: "for the longest time, he used to put . . . [on] that record and dance. . . . He loved that." Luis thought this obsession rather "cute" and did not feel concerned. Rather, he felt disappointed that he and his son could not share experiences that were so much a part of his own life growing up.

The only sport that Michael seemed to take any interest in at all was swimming. However, Luis recalls that his son would not swim "bare-chested," preferring instead to wear a T-shirt, something he thought "ridiculous." Luis always felt that he showed Michael that it was all right "to walk around" without a shirt, which he frequently did at home and outside. He continues to be confused about why his son was so self-conscious. He recalled that, as a young boy, Michael was "a little chubby," so he thinks that his son's reservations about his physicality may stem from that. He also thinks it may be tied in with Michael's homosexuality, but is unclear exactly how.

Any disappointment Luis feels about the distance between him and Michael is rooted more in his own lack of involvement in his son's life during those formative years. "If I could have done everything all over again, I would have loved to spend more time with my son," he says regretfully. Putting in "too many hours at work" took him away from cultivating a closer father-son bond. He concedes that Michael is more attached to his mother in the same way that Luis is more attached to his own mother.

Although Luis says he developed a close relationship with his own father while helping him in his store back in Argentina, he felt that the older man was "a little bit old-fashioned" and rather narrow-minded, more comfortable giving advice to his son rather than asking him about his feelings. It was his mother who would be more inclined to talk with him about personal matters. Similarly, Luis's wife, Sue, was responsible for introducing Michael to a broad range of cultural activities—art galleries, museums, movies, shows—as well as encouraging him to read—books, magazines, newspapers. Luis feels "very grateful" to his wife for providing their son with those opportunities, something that he feels he could not have done.

Given the closeness of the mother-son relationship, Luis was not surprised that his son told his mother first about being gay, during a car ride to school one morning a year before our interview. Sue promptly told her husband that same night after he came home from work. Luis was also not completely surprised. "Something inside of me . . . was telling me that something wasn't the way I expected from . . . him," as he observed in Michael a certain "feminine type of attitude," a particular way he has of "expressing himself." Luis recalls an incident when Michael, then age four, was caught playing naked with another boy in the neighborhood. The other boy's father prohibited Michael from further association with his son. "It bothered me a lot," Luis recalls. But he never thought it was that unusual given his son's age. Despite all of this, Luis still did not "expect [his son] to be gay."

Luis feels that at first, after disclosing his homosexuality, Michael was fearful of his response: "he was expecting me to be a little more harsh . . . expecting . . . I was going to . . . beat him up." Instead, Luis called his son up at his friend's house and told him that he would like him to come home. When he arrived, his father calmly reassured Michael, "You're my son. I love you no matter what." In addition to trying to be supportive, Luis told Michael that he was "a little disappointed," words which "just came out, just like that." While trying his best not to hurt his son, at the same time, he was trying to be true to his own feelings. He is glad that the issue has been opened up and thinks that Michael feels "better about himself" and that both mother and father "understand him . . . now." However, it is not a subject the family actively talks about, unless, for example, there is a related "article in the paper." However, both Sue and Luis are active members of two parent support groups. Luis feels that the "helpful" nature of the group experience has to do both with getting exposure to others who face "similar . . . situations" as well as providing a forum for more general concerns of parenting, not necessarily just those connected with a son or daughter's homosexuality.

Luis's recent attempts to come to terms with his son's gayness have been a struggle. In his native Argentina, homosexuality has always been a fact of life "since day one." As in other Latin countries, however, "people don't talk about it . . . they keep it to themselves." In that society, gay people are considered "weird." Furthermore, in his own family of origin, his father was "very stubborn" and close-minded, considering many subjects "taboo." Although Luis is trying to move away from that and be "more open-minded" than his father, all of this makes it that much more difficult for him to deal with Michael's sexuality. He feels he is trying hard to comprehend a situation he did not "expect," a situation that will now be a part of his life forever. Before he thought his son was just "a little confused." Now, he believes that his homosexuality is something that he was "born with." He says, "I understand and I accept my son because he's my son," but adds with resignation, "I'm not happy."

This is only one factor that he has had to deal with as a father of a teenager, a time in life when "everything is bubbling inside of you." Michael's irritability ("he's cranky in the morning, cranky at night"), his quickness to anger and to challenge authority ("he get[s] pissed off and . . . walks out") have more recently diminished. Now, he is more inclined to apologize and take responsibility for his actions: "we teach him well." Although not an A student, Luis says that Michael has an unusual blend of interests and talents. He knows a great deal about stones, ancient coins, antiques, and design. He also writes poetry and paints. "I'm a proud, proud father," he boasts.

As a child and as a teenager, Luis himself was always "the clown" in his group of friends. He told jokes about and ridiculed others who appeared different—gay people included. Now that his son has come out, he has changed "completely." Before, he would "go along with the guys." Now, he is more inclined to challenge the prejudices of others, particularly at work: "I make them understand that it might be a joke for them, but it's not a joke for me." He has grown more tolerant. He has "improved."

This new fact of his life has helped him feel a little bit closer with his wife. Alongside the "up[s] and downs" of any marriage, Luis feels that he and Sue now maintain a sense of "commitment" to go to their support groups and to continue to come to terms with whatever aftereffects this very recent event has brought and will continue to bring into their lives. He feels less removed, now closer to Michael as well. Although he continues to work long hours, his son is now more inclined to call him there just to "talk." Luis has not told anyone else in his family in Argentina about this yet, as his son has not given him "the green light." He says he is not that worried about how others will feel about this, making it clear that Michael is his priority: "I'm concerned about my son. Period."

Luis feels that his son is "still young," still very much in a state of transition. Although his sexuality has now been defined, the "moodiness," the turbulence of adolescence has, of yet, not quieted down. But he is quick to acknowledge that there is much he has learned from his son, much that he has "improved" about himself, and hopefully much that Michael has learned from him. "Kids learn from their parents and parents learn from their kids, too," he asserts.

Luis knows that he has come a long way from his home in Argentina and knows that there is still a long way to go.

DANIEL

He's like a trophy.

While Daniel was securely "tucked in [his] mother's womb," his father brought Daniel's fifteen-month-old brother down to the kitchen one morning, sat him in a chair beside the stove, and then proceeded to start it by pouring kerosene inside, immediately igniting the hot coals. His brother was badly burned and required surgery intermittently over the years, finally choking to death a decade later in the hospital after medical personnel failed to remove the gauze in his throat. Daniel's father, however, was immediately "vaporized," leaving his boys fatherless.

Now sixty, Daniel was then left with his maternal grandparents for the next four years in Maine while his mother moved by herself to another part of the state in an attempt to eke out a living as a schoolteacher. It was Depression time and jobs were few and far between. The "violently loud arguments" that would frequently break out between his grandparents, some of which were related to his grandfather's drinking, created the sense that Daniel was in the presence of two people who neither cared about nor liked each other very much. His mother periodically returned to visit and eventually took her boys with her.

Daniel's childhood and adolescence were spent scattered over small New England towns. His mother eventually remarried "a very nice man . . . a Buick salesman," who gave Daniel the money he had won as a gift for selling the most Buicks in his company, money Daniel was supposed to spend to buy clothes in preparation for college. An arthritic, his stepfather died shortly after the marriage, leaving Daniel fatherless for the second time.

Bright and academically oriented, Daniel got admitted to a good college, but "never really got engaged" with his classes or with the other students. The majors that he chose never seemed to hold much interest for him, he was not accepted into a fraternity, nor did he have "a big range of friends." He was preoccupied with a sense of "sexual confusion."

Awareness of homosexual feelings was not new for him. He was well acquainted with these as early as the age of eight, while playing "doctor attending to the young male patients." Although he attempted to date in high school, he was "never sexually successful." In college, he started actively exploring his gay feelings, seeking connection by way of anonymous encounters. At the same time he thought to himself: "if ultimately I got married and had sex I would be okay."

Daniel completed college and got a position as a schoolteacher for a couple of years, eventually going overseas to work. It was there that he met his wife-to-be, Betty. They married about a year later, relieving Daniel's "sexual worry"—for the moment anyway. Temperamental differences between him and Betty surfaced, however. His wife's timidity in many aspects of life contrasted with his own sense of curiosity and need for adventure; her desire for the comforts of the country stood in direct opposition to his desires for the excitement of the city. Coupled with this was his own sexual frustration. All during their fifteen-year marriage, he continued having "nonaffect, nonrelational type" encounters. One of these developed into something more. While attending a conference, he met and "just fell madly in love," awakening to the idea that a romantic relationship between two men was possible. Shaken by that realization, he knew now that he had to leave his wife along with their boys, Todd and Charles, who were ten and twelve respectively when he left the home. Daniel himself was then forty.

The birth of his first son, Charles, now thirty-two, was an event which he celebrated by coming home, taking out a recording of Handel's *Messiah,* and launching into, "For Unto Us a Child Is Born," which for him now held a new and deeper meaning. Little did he realize that he and Charles would be forever united, not only by blood, but also by the fact that both father and son are gay.

Although he never lost interest in his sons, his disinterest in traditional family life began to be more obvious during those early years of fatherhood: "I don't have a lot of patience with the . . . ordinary crap of everyday life." His refusal to go to Disneyland with the rest of the family was one of his "most notorious, antisocial acts." Summer trips to the Jersey shore, Betty's "perfect vacation," left him restless and bored. The prospect of baking on a beach "till you got cancer" held absolutely no interest. He ended up sitting on the porch, drinking gin and tonic, and maybe staring "at one solitary white crane standing in a marsh," while reading and sometimes reflecting. It was times like these that increased his sense of alien-ation, times like these that he "wanted to be somewhere else," perhaps "with some sweet man in a small but romantic garret in the Village." Daniel's continual sense of being out of place became increasingly heightened during the years of his marriage and early fatherhood. Preoccupation with his homosexual feelings as well as impatience and disinterest in the "crap" of day-to-day living fueled his sense of disengagement. Like that solitary white crane standing in the marsh, Daniel self-identifies as a man "on the edge."

Daniel recalls his older son, Charles, as a consistently "confident, successful" boy, who was not only easy to raise but also a fine student, socially accomplished, and "everyone's favorite." Al-though early memories of his son are vague, what was clear then and what remains clear now is Daniel's sense of difference from his son. While he considers himself very much "a loner," a man adrift at least for the first part of his life, Daniel sees his son as "a determined person . . . a real shit-kicker" by way of being an AIDS advocate, someone who has "assumed control of his life at a much earlier period," qualities he both admires and envies in Charles. Certainly the ways in which each has come out illustrates this.

It was only after Daniel left Betty that he went to visit his own mother to tell her about their separation and the reasons behind it. His disclosure about being gay helped his mother to then reveal a "secret" of her own—that she had to get married to his father because she was pregnant with Daniel's older brother. Although his mother tried to be supportive initially, she was ultimately rejecting, actively discouraging Daniel from bringing his Latino lover to her home. Her recent death has brought to light Daniel's realization that, sadly, much was still unresolved between them.

Charles' coming out occurred when he was sixteen, four years after his father moved out of the family home. Although his boys visited him on the weekends, Daniel never directly discussed his homosexuality with either of his sons up to that point. However, eventually it became clear to Daniel that his own son was gay, made obvious by the fact that Charles was "not dating" and "by his pushy interest" in his father's lovers. "I was careful not to leave him alone too long with any of them," he laughingly admits. After Daniel told his son that he was gay, Charles responded reflexively, "I know. I am, too." Daniel admits that when *he* was sixteen, he was not even fully conscious that there was such a thing as a gay person. And here was his own son, who was both aware enough and secure enough about it to reveal himself.

Charles chose not to tell his mother at that point, however, a decision that was fully supported by his father. Betty would continually ask her ex-husband if their son was gay and he would respond, "I don't know. Why don't you ask him?" knowing that she never would. Using Daniel as a guide and mentor, Charles informed his father a year later that he now felt ready to tell his mother and was going to do it that night. After Charles left his father's apartment, Daniel promptly telephoned Betty about what was about to occur. He emphasized the "unusual opportunity" that was being presented to her and with it, a chance to "be supportive" in the wake of hearing something difficult, yet "something important" about their son. Daniel felt a need to prepare Betty, partially "so she wouldn't fuck it up" and partially because he himself wished that someone important in his life could have done something similar for him. Although Betty became quite upset and "went down the whole litany," including her anticipated loss of being a grandmother, Daniel feels that at that moment, he was able to be helpful to both mother and son.

It also gave him an opportunity to do one of the things he feels he does best as a father—advise his sons in matters of sexuality, representing the voice of reason in the midst of their mother's hysteria. Another opportunity, although not as far-reaching as Charles' coming out, occurred when Todd failed to come home one night. Frantically, Betty called Daniel, wondering if their son was with his girlfriend. Immediately, Daniel called the girlfriend's home and calmly told Todd to call his mother and tell her that he would be back the next morning which, apparently, he did. Crisis abated.

Daniel feels that what he has offered as a father to both of his sons is the sense "that they could make mistakes . . . take chances." His "slightly strange, on-the-edge" persona, he feels, contrasted with the "unfailingly involved, kvetchy" presence of their mother:

"extreme verged with conventionality." Daniel's admittedly "perverse" preferences—bing-cherry ice cream, steaks that are "too rare"—sent a message that one could be different. He feels that this was especially important for Charles, who saw his father—another gay man—leading a "modestly happy" life, taking care of himself in the process. Professionally, too, Daniel seemed to come into his own subsequent to coming out. He is now retired after a successful career in publishing. In this respect, he was glad that he had the opportunity to be an example for his son. Both Charles and Todd, however, swiftly correct his sense of himself as "an undemanding daddy." He says that they both feel that he expected great academic success from each of them. Both boys attended the same university as their father. Daniel feels that his sons had better experiences and accomplished more there than he did in both the academic and social arenas.

Daniel describes his present relationship with Charles as resembling "very close friends." Both classical music buffs, Charles will sometimes call his father early in the morning and play perhaps some Vivaldi for him, knowing of his father's appreciation for this. They also share some rather intimate details of their own sexual lives, something which Daniel feels is "wonderful" and brings them closer together: "I'm not afraid of his humanity." At times, Daniel considers that he might like to see his son settled in an apartment "with some nice guy and . . . [having] brunch on Sunday," but only if Charles wants that for himself. All of this is in contrast to their relationship earlier, when Daniel feels that he lost "touch with his [son's] life" during adolescence after he himself moved out of their home. Even earlier than that, it was difficult for Daniel to remember sharing "intimate moments" with young Charles. There simply were not that many. Daniel was beginning his own struggles at that point and could not be fully present for his children.

In terms of Charles' relationship with his mother, Daniel feels that his son is quite sensitive to Betty's concerns, despite the fact that she can be "quite annoying" at times. In fact, Charles has been more a part of her life than has Todd, who is now married. Daniel thought that Betty had worries that Charles, because he was gay and had no family commitments, would "take off somewhere" as Daniel had done years before. Obviously, this has not happened. The brothers themselves "are extremely close," which Daniel feels was fueled by his own separation from the family "or maybe they just like each other." As far as he can see, Todd has been totally accepting of his brother's gayness.

Daniel did not tell Todd about his own homosexuality until a year after he told Charles. Todd said that he had "known it for a while." The fact that his father and brother are both gay may have made Todd feel jealous of their relationship. He once told his father, "I suppose you feel that you can talk more with [Charles] because he's gay and you're gay, but . . . I'm actually much more sensitive than [Charles] . . . and I probably can give you very good advice." Switching roles, Todd reassured Daniel at one point, "You should always . . . feel you can tell me things," something Daniel had always told his children. Reportedly, Todd was quite preoccupied with "AIDS worry" at one point, wanting to ensure that both his father and brother were taking care of themselves. This concern seems to have lessened over the years, however.

Although Daniel says that he cannot point to that many accomplishments in his life, he is admittedly proud of his "two happy, reasonably well-adjusted, successful sons" and proud of the part he has played in raising them. His relationship with Charles, however, holds a special place in his heart. Being gay and simultaneously having a son who is gay has created an unusual bond between them. With much left to do in his life, including writing a book and going off to Latin America to live with a family and learn Spanish, for him Charles remains his "trophy."

MARTY

Nothing would change my love for you—ever, ever, ever.

When Marty was eight years old, his father used to take him from their home in the Bronx to the Apollo Theater in Harlem to hear all the great black performers of the day—Fats Waller and Ella Fitzgerald, to name a couple. After the performance, father and son would sometimes go to the neighborhood bar to hear the more local talent. Marty did not tell his mother that he and his father did this. It was their little secret, an experience they shared together. So enthralled was he by what he heard that Marty came home one day and said to his mother, "I would like to be black." When his mother asked him why, he replied, "They always seem like they're having a good time."

The son of a milkman, Marty, now age seventy, was the second youngest of five children—all the rest girls. As a young boy, he readily admits to being "a champion baseball card tosser." Some of the kids in the neighborhood did not take too kindly to losing to a slightly built Jewish boy and would retaliate by pushing him around, taking back the cards he had honestly won. Always a quiet kid, he did not tell his parents about these incidents, preferring to keep it to himself—suffering in silence.

After graduating from high school, Marty enlisted in the Navy, never considering college as an option at that time. After serving for a year, he then worked as a civil servant. At twenty-one, he looked up and saw himself surrounded by middle-aged men, deciding that this was not his future. He was capable of more. Taking advantage of the GI Bill of Rights, he decided to send himself to college with a major in advertising. He had found his calling. His summers were spent working as a waiter in the mountain resort communities, meeting and befriending people such as Lenny Bruce. There, during one quiet summer, he met his wife, Susan, to whom he has been happily married for the last forty-four years.

After five years of marriage, living with her parents for a while and struggling financially, the couple decided to have a child. The infant lived for only six weeks after an aneurysm burst during the birth process—"all hell broke loose." It was a debilitating experience, one that took at least a year to recover from. Their son, Ian, whom Marty describes as "a beautiful baby," was born about two years later. Although now a public schoolteacher working on his master's degree, he evidenced minor learning problems early on and required tutoring and counseling to facilitate his development. Marty and Susan were relieved when their second son, Gary, came along twenty-two months later. He seemed naturally bright and "terrific in school." Gary is gay.

Marty describes feeling warmly connected to both of his sons during those early years of their lives. He lived for those moments when he would get home from work and they would yell, "Hey,

Daddy's here!" running to him, scooping them up into his arms: "the best years [are] when they're small, when you get all that love." A longing for those earlier times seemed painfully apparent. Although not athletic himself, Marty tried in vain to encourage his sons to be but, reluctantly, "didn't see any signs of talent there." He claims not to be disappointed by this, saying that he is "not that type either." Sometimes, father and sons would go off together leaving Susan behind, frequenting museums, parks, and Broadway shows. Although not artistic, Marty considers himself "cultural" and wanted to share with his children what was and is an important part of his own life.

Concerning Gary, Marty recalls that he was intellectually gifted, reading from the time he was three years old. At school, he was always actively involved in extracurricular activities. While he seemed to have friends, both boys and girls, there were few romantic attachments. Although Marty did not see Gary as different, he did feel that he was "lonely" at times, but attributed this to his weight problem: "he was always a chubby kid." He would have an occasional date with a girl, a few affairs, but never long-term involvement. Despite this, Marty never consciously suspected Gary was homosexual. Susan did, however. Around the time Gary graduated from high school, his mother asked him, "[Gary], are you gay? I don't see any girls around," to which Gary replied, "No, I'm just fat!" At the time, he was six feet tall and quite overweight.

Marty recalls that Gary, then age thirty-two, came out to him on Father's Day, 1993. Sitting around the table, having a cup of coffee together, waiting for Ian and his girlfriend to arrive so that they could all go to dinner together, Gary said to his father, "I have something to tell you." Given the seriousness of his son's tone, Marty's first thought was that Gary might be ill with "a terrible disease." Although he is not absolutely sure, Marty recalls that a split second before his son's pronouncement, he might have anticipated what Gary was about to say. Despite this, the words "I'm gay" shot through him like a thunderbolt: "it was . . . tremendous, like somebody socked me in the chest—BOOM!" Marty's first response was, "Are you sure? How long have you known?" Gary acknowledged only self-identifying as gay six months earlier, but admitted that he probably knew at some level since he had been a teenager.

Marty said that despite the initial blow, "within a minute . . . I grabbed him, hugged him, and said, 'I wish it weren't so. I can't lie to you. But nothing would change my love for you—ever, ever, ever.'"

Gary's disclosure came a few days before he was to go on a fund-raising campaign overseas for several weeks. Father and son agreed that they would wait for his return before informing Susan. However, unable to contain the secret, Marty told his wife right before the Fourth of July weekend. A state of crisis ensued. An all-night family meeting took place with Marty, Susan, and Ian. By the time Gary returned, the initial impact of the news had diffused to the point that everyone was able to more rationally discuss their feelings. Gary gave his parents information on P-FLAG. He also gave them a book specifically designed to impart basic information to parents about homosexuality. Within several weeks, both Marty and Susan were attending P-FLAG meetings and, since their son's disclosure, have both been active members. Marty acknowledges deriving comfort from his involvement.

Concurrent with Marty's show of support for his son, the sense of "what did we do wrong?" surfaced: "maybe there is something we could have changed; maybe when he sees how . . . difficult it is . . . being part of a gay life." Despite his thought that homosexuality might be "a genetic thing," regrets concurrently emerged that he did not push Gary "to be more athletic"; for not being "a discipline-type father"; for being "so easygoing and letting things slide sometimes . . . always want[ing] to be the good guy, to have them be my friend." Marty clearly saw his son's unhappiness while he was growing up, but did not completely comprehend all of its roots, citing his weight problem and not having a girlfriend as the primary causes. Reportedly, Gary told his mother that he was seriously considering not telling his parents at all, not knowing how they might react. Marty feels that that "would have been a terrible thing for himself and for us, too, because we would have drifted into a different relationship."

Marty prides himself on the fact that he has always had a good relationship with Gary, with only minor disagreements over the years, and feels that, on the whole, this revelation has brought father and son even closer together. "We now know him for what he is . . .

and he knows himself for what he is." Marty feels that acceptance of his son's homosexuality has been, in part, helped along by his own prior exposure to gay life. Working in theater advertising for the better part of his career, most of his assistants were gay men or lesbians. In that capacity, he helped launch many landmark gay productions over the years and maintained long-term affiliations and friendships with several prominent gay people within the theater community. Through these relationships, he has seen many facets of the lives of gay people: "not everyone is hanging out in the bars."

On another level, what also seems to have facilitated his acceptance is his identification with facets of his son's personality. Academically, Marty describes Gary as "very smart but . . . lazy," not studying for exams "until the night before. Maybe I did that, too," he laughingly admits. Marty's hope that his son would complete law school mirrors his disappointment in himself for not completely fulfilling his own professional capabilities and ambitions. Further, in describing himself as "never that athletic," as "a quiet kid," there emerges a sense of vulnerability, a trait that he also sees in Gary. Although Marty portrays his son as "very self-sufficient," he also sees him as "very temperamental" at times, "irritating" and quick to anger, someone who can impulsively "jump down your throat" should something be said not to his liking. Marty admits that he and Susan treat Gary "more gingerly" since his disclosure. He sees both himself and Gary as "underdogs."

Marty freely acknowledges that his son's coming out has contributed to changing many of the relationships in his own life. With his wife, things have changed between them "for the better." This event has helped them to maintain a sense of perspective about what is important and what is not: "if you can make that adjustment, you can make a lot of other adjustments." There is also a sense of greater risk taking. The summer following our interview, for example, they rented a place upstate, something that might have been unimaginable a few years ago. Marty feels that this was possible because his wife is being "more bendable."

Perhaps the biggest change is in relation to his oldest living sister, whose daughter felt that Gary should just "stay in the closet. Why upset the apple cart?" Marty staunchly defended his son's "right to live his life the way he wants to live." Although he claims to still be close to her, he will avoid the topic, circumventing any in-depth discussion relevant to Gary's homosexuality. Although Marty regrets the distance this has caused, he feels that his relationship with Gary "is more important."

Although Marty will concede some disappointment about aspects of Gary's academic and professional life, he did not readily acknowledge disappointments over ramifications of his son's homosexuality, except as it related to the possibility that he would never be a grandfather: "you have dreams and plans [of] what you expect your children to turn out to be and they constantly change." He hopes that his older son's recent marriage will result in the couple having a child or that, perhaps, Gary will adopt. Marty feels that he would be a wonderful grandfather, unabashedly acknowledging great affection for children. It would also help him to fill up the many hours of leisure time now afforded by his recent retirement.

In terms of his own development, this event has reinforced Marty's realistic approach to life. He feels that he has "learned to accept . . . and not to dwell on things," adding, if "you can't change it, get on with it." Even if he is lucky enough to have grandchildren someday, he willingly concedes "that they're not always around. They go home . . . you have to live . . . for yourself. I'm a firm believer in that. You just can't count on other people . . . to fill up your life." In wanting his sons and his wife to be happy, he is forever striving for his own happiness as well.

GLENN

It's a nonissue.

Glenn recounts that there had always been some distance between him and his own father. On his way to becoming a successful, established doctor, Glenn was determined to prove his self-sufficiency, which meant not accepting very much of anything from the older man or from anyone else, for that matter. However, on the way out of his parents' home on one occasion, his father offered him five dollars "for tolls." He took it. This simple gesture of acceptance signified to Glenn that he was better able to make room for his father's need to be a parent as well as to openly acknowledge his own role as son. The need to defensively "prove" himself was no longer so urgent. It all seemed to come together for him at that moment. Silently, unbeknownst to himself, Glenn had grown up.

Glenn's mother had a dream for her son—"to be a doctor, preferably . . . a surgeon," to live in the local New England town, to practice at the local hospital, and to drive a Cadillac. Part of that dream was fulfilled. Glenn, now sixty-three, grew up during the Depression. His father, now deceased, avoided military service because he had heart disease, working instead for a wholesale wine and liquor company, first in middle management, then in senior management. He describes his mother, a housewife, now ninety, as "a hypochondriac." Being elderly and having some real medical problems "hasn't helped her disposition," he says wryly. He and his sister, four years his senior, "were mortal enemies" growing up, but since the time that he was old enough to overpower her, "she saw the light" and they have been "friends ever since."

Academics were always a strength for Glenn. Although he considered a life as a musician, exposure to others who were more talented helped him to make what he feels was a wiser career move. Graduating from one of the top medical schools in the country, he has had vast experience in academic medicine as well as administrating in community hospitals in various locations. He met his first wife, Pam, when he was only seventeen, while working as a delivery boy for a pharmacist. The pharmacist was Pam's uncle. They "hit it off" after a blind date and married a few years later while Glenn was doing his internship in internal medicine. Adam, his first son, was born at the end of that year. "That was a great event," Glenn said proudly. It was also "a community event" in that the circumcision was done in the hospital itself and the ceremony was attended by many of his professors. He even got the afternoon off. Despite the fact that Glenn and Pam knew they would have a child at some point, Adam was, in fact, "an accident . . . [though] I was enough of a male chauvinist to be happy it was a boy," he says self-reflectively.

His sense of exhilaration about the birth diminished initially because Adam "didn't smile": "I don't think that I recognized him as being human until he was three months old." However, his own responsiveness increased in relation to Adam's responsiveness to him. "I used to . . . come home and get down on the floor and loved playing with him," adding, "he was a very good child." However, Glenn felt that Pam's failure to detach from Adam created problems for father and son. Although beautiful and sophisticated, Glenn also realized that Pam "was a very narcissistic woman," who reflexively blamed him for all the problems in their marriage. Arguments would frequently escalate into physical confrontations. Glenn's realization that he wanted to kill his wife led him to leave his family of fifteen years which, at that time, included another son, Dan, who is three years younger than Adam. During this time, he met another, younger, woman with whom he lived for about eight months while Pam fled to Europe with the boys. Upon her return, a reconciliation took place between husband and wife. The crisis abated—at least for the time being.

Glenn did not see his son as different during those first years. In fact, father describes Adam as "quite an athlete." Apparently, he holds his elementary school record for being the fastest runner "from one spot of the fence and back." Adam was thrilled at the prospect of joining Little League. Although Glenn reports that his son showed talent, this was displayed most prominently while he was "in the backyard." During an actual game with other boys, however, "he couldn't hit the ball." Glenn recalls an incident in which Adam's "team was losing 400 to 3." It was his turn at bat and the pressure was on, despite the fact that "it was not a winnable game." Adam "struck out and started to cry because he felt that he had lost the game for his team." Glenn consoled him, saying that he did not have to play if he did not want to. His impression was that Adam felt relieved and accepted by him at that moment. He never went back to baseball. Glenn reports feeling perfectly fine with this decision as he himself preferred a less organized, more spontaneous approach to team sports when he was growing up. The only perceived difference Glenn observed in his son was the fact that Adam was small: "in our family, we're all big." Dan, Adam's brother, is even bigger than Glenn, who stands over six feet tall. Pam's side of the family tends to be smaller. Adam received those genes.

Glenn's relationship with his son has been characterized by instability over the years. He felt that much of this was caused by the parental relationship. He seems to feel somewhat guilty about subjecting his children to so much conflict, feeling "that this had to be very damaging." During those early years, Glenn reports being "withdrawn . . . depressed," spending an inordinate number of hours working. At times, however, he enjoyed bringing his sons with him, watching as "they would play around the lab." Afterward, the three would go to the zoo, to a movie, or to a museum. Those times were special. They were offset by other times of irritability in which he "wanted to be alone . . . undisturbed." He knows he sent "mixed messages" to Adam about his emotional availability, but claims that this had nothing to do with Adam, who he felt "was perfect." It only had to do with him and his relationship with Pam, who was becoming increasingly unstable and who attempted suicide on several occasions over the years. Despite their affluence, Glenn feels that his sons were subjected to an upbringing that he describes as "traumatic."

Glenn did not think that Adam might be gay until he was a teenager. At that time, he was beginning to have some difficulties at school. When he asked his son what it was that was making him so uncomfortable in what seemed to be a perfectly good academic environment, Adam ducked the issue. It was clear to Glenn that his son was beginning "to avoid . . . social contacts." A close friend of Adam's tried to include him in social situations, but Adam "ran away from it." He was clearly not interested in girls. A transfer to another school setting, one in which there may have been fewer pressures to conform, proved more conducive to Adam's growth. It was at this time that Glenn thought in a more conscious way that his son was gay. He tried to soothe himself at first, saying that it was still early—"let's see what happens." Besides this, his sense of disappointment and shame alternated with a sense of empathy for Adam, who, he thought, may have been going through similarly alternating conflicts. Glenn never discussed any of this with anyone.

After completing high school and college with high honors, Adam entered a graduate program. This proved to be a disaster, and he remained steadfastly unapproachable about what had happened. Shortly thereafter, Glenn received a "tortuous . . . letter" from his son, confirming his earlier suspicions. In the letter, Adam acknowledged his homosexuality and the necessity of his being open about it. He reminded his father of the advice he had given to him concerning the importance of taking "risks" in life: "he had translated that into this." Adam was twenty-two years old at the time. Glenn had already left Pam after nineteen years of marriage and was remarried at the time this occurred.

Glenn's initial response was one of relief, as he felt that Adam had been so repressed that acknowledging any sexual feelings, homosexual *or* heterosexual, would be a sign of health. Further, he felt that Adam's "ability to come out of the very restrictive culture he was brought up in into a gay world and embrace it was very liberating." Glenn admits to only "ten minutes of . . . disturbance . . . well maybe it was two days . . . not more than that." He discussed it with his second wife, Barbara, who was unfazed by the news. A couple of days later, Glenn called Adam to tell him that he was glad he had written to him, that he had already suspected, and to offer him all the support he could. Besides the prospect of not having any grandchildren, Glenn says that Adam's sexuality "in all sincerity . . . doesn't matter." All of this seemed to provide the boost that the relationship needed after so many conflict-ridden years. Since that time, Glenn feels that Adam, who has now completed graduate school, is doing "splendidly." He talks about his son, now thirty-eight, a social worker treating inner-city youth and families, with great respect and admiration: "he's just a fabulous person," describing him as "sensitive and mature." Glenn is equally effusive about Adam's partner and is thankful for the joyful life they seem to have together.

At the same time, Glenn seems to continue to harbor much resentment toward Pam. Her possessiveness and seductiveness, he feels, contributed toward shaping their son's sexuality. While he does not suspect that there was any overt sexual abuse, he thinks that she encouraged incestuous wishes, implying that there may have been a blurring of boundaries between mother and son and that this could have been a "frightening experience" for Adam.

As far as others' responses in the family, Adam's brother, Dan, does not seem to have any difficulties with Adam's sexuality. However, Glenn acknowledges that it took time for him to tell his own mother and he never told his father at all, who was rather ill in his final years and who died three years after Adam came out. Glenn feels that his own mother is unresponsive to his children. "I don't think my mother has the grandmother gene," he says humorously. Continued feelings of animosity exist between his mother and Pam. Whether this has contributed to her disinterest in her grandchildren is unknown.

Glenn's present feelings about his son's sexuality have not changed much in the fifteen years since Adam came out. He feels that it "is irrelevant" to other more important "aspects of life." He does not go out of his way to discuss it: "I don't go around either praising or complaining that I have a gay son. It's nobody's business. If it comes up, it's not hidden . . . it's a nonissue." What he remains more disappointed in is the fact that neither of his sons wanted to follow in their father's professional footsteps.

Although father and son are closer now than they have been for many years, an element of distance is still present. He is unsure about what the cause of that might be, pointing to the schism that historically characterizes any father-son relationship. Whether Adam blames his father for contributing to the disintegration of their family remains unclear. Adam's holiday parties exclude his father and include his mother. Glenn claims to be just as happy not to be invited since he sees Adam on a fairly regular basis. He would like to be closer to his son and feels that the time will eventually come as it did with his own father, who he felt warmly connected to in the final years of the older man's life. Glenn traditionally invites Adam and his partner to all of his family celebrations with Barbara and his two stepsons. He is hoping that they will agree to come celebrate with him sometime in the not-so-distant future. As he did so many years ago, Glenn longs for that day when Adam will openly accept the five dollars "for tolls."

RONALD

I can't find anything good, bad, or indifferent about it.
It's just the way it is.

Change was a fact of Ronald's early life. He was born sixty years ago in Georgia. His parents divorced when he was three years old after his mother realized his father was an alcoholic. She remarried about a year later to a man who made the Air Force his career. He immediately went off to serve in World War II, with the result that

Ronald was raised during that time by his mother, her sisters, and her girlfriends. He recalls the fun they all had together—picnicking in the park, cooking marshmallows and hot dogs. Being the only child had its advantages as he could have their undivided attention, a situation he never found again.

Upon his stepfather's return, the family traveled widely, restationing to various parts of the country—a year or two in each town—until finally moving to Japan. After six months there, his stepfather was diagnosed with kidney cancer, necessitating relocation to Florida, where the climate would be conducive to rest and recuperation. He died shortly thereafter. His mother met another man a few years later, with whom she lived for another four decades, and who recently passed away. She now lives alone.

Despite the fact that there have been three father figures in his life, Ronald's connection to each of them was tenuous. After his parents were divorced, he spent one summer with his natural father when his stepfather was ill and hospitalized. Ronald was fifteen. Since their time together then was so brief, there was no real opportunity to develop a sense that they were, in fact, father and son. The older man seemed "like more of a buddy than . . . a father." The alcoholism that plagued him eventually "ate his liver out." He was found dead "in a gutter" at age forty-eight.

With his stepfather off in the service, obviously there was little chance of forming any kind of a bond during the time he was away. But even after his return home, things did not change much in that respect. After work, the older man routinely drank and then "gave it up for the night." Also, Ronald's mother and stepfather had another son together, creating a family within a family. One vivid memory of Ronald's was the morning after his half-brother was born. Ronald had been sleeping in the back seat of their car all night in the parking lot of the Air Force base hospital. After getting some food from "the chow hall"—his stepfather worked as a chef there—the two began the drive home. Prior to reaching their destination, his stepfather decided to stop at a bar. After coming back to the car "pretty well tanked," he realized he was not going to be able to make it all the way home and told Ronald to take over. "So I got behind the wheel of a '47 Chevy and drove," he recalls. He was nine years old at the time. Despite his excitement, this event served as a metaphor, reminding him that there was no one in charge, no one "behind the wheel."

His mother, "a dominant, cold, unemotional, unnurturing woman," left him to his "own devices" as well. A dime-store clerk, she worked about a half-mile from where Ronald went to nursery school. Since they had no car at that time, they depended on others to transport them. While his mother made sure *she* got to work, he was made to walk the rest of the way: "I always wanted her to take me." Because she worked long hours, six days a week, she hired a babysitter to watch him some of the time. But mostly he recalls being home on his own or spending time at the movies with friends. His mother soothed herself by thinking that he could "take care of [him]self." Ronald felt alone—motherless and fatherless.

"Phenomenal fears of abandonment" have plagued him since, wrecking havoc on his relationships in adulthood. After graduating college, he went into the Air Force and got interested in computers, the field in which he worked from that time through his retirement five years ago. It was in the service that he met Kathy, who agreed to get married "just to shut [him] up" after he "pursued the heck out of her." Ronald felt that her capacity for "warmth" and "nurturing" would somehow compensate for the lack of these in his own earlier life. Unfortunately, much of what she offered to him he felt unable to take.

From the start of their marriage, Ronald felt consumed with going "up the corporate ladder," at times working six or seven days a week. After a few years of living in different parts of the state, he spent time looking for and purchasing land, then building a house on it himself. He became increasingly self-absorbed. "By choice," he had little energy or interest left over for being a husband or a father to his three children—Andrea, Timothy, and Calvin. And the further he pulled away from them, the further they pulled away from him. The long and demanding hours at work and the frustrations of building a house, combined with the residue of feeling emotionally deprived that collected over his lifetime and which became exacerbated in the present, left Ronald unavailable at best, "a tyrant" at worst. Kathy was the "dumping ground" for much of his verbal abuse. So was Timothy, his gay son.

Now thirty-two, Timothy "was just a gorgeous baby and a gorgeous kid but . . . cried *all* the time." He and Kathy took him to doctors who could find nothing wrong. Given all of the pressures Ronald was under, sleep was a priority and no one was going to get in the way of that. So when Timothy would not "shut up" and stop crying, father put his son—crib and all—in the garage. He would handle this differently today, but is unsure exactly how.

By the time their house was finally built, Ronald was financially ruined and his marriage was on the verge of collapse. So was he. Although the family continued to live together, husband and wife "were no longer sharing the same bed." After their separation, Kathy and the children went their own way. The house that Ronald had worked so hard to build was eventually sold. It was the end of an era.

It was natural for Kathy to take the children with her. She had always been there to the extent that Ronald was not. The children connected to her "warmth." She was and still is the "anchor," holding the family together. But one person cannot do it all alone. She succumbed to the pressures of raising three children without the emotional support of her husband and, during one period of time, was bedridden with depression. She sought treatment, which had proven effective. At the urging of a mutual friend, Ronald embarked upon "intensive therapy," which was a turning point for him as well. Primal scream, bioenergetics, Gestalt, weekend retreats, he has done it all, breaking "through . . . the armored defenses," finally experiencing a sense of "relief" from all the pent-up hurt and anger.

Ronald's memories of his children are vague, increasingly so as he withdrew from family life, particularly after the separation. Certain things are clear, however. Andrea, the oldest, "was the perfect child," who got a great deal of attention. She "had long beautiful hair" that Ronald feels Timothy envied. As a toddler, his son would routinely take his Doctor Denton pajama bottoms and "pull the waist band over his head and let them hang down," pretending he had hair like his sister, hoping to get the kind of notice he perceived she got. Ronald feels that Timothy, like Andrea, did get much attention because of his good looks, but remained oblivious to it. Besides this, Ronald recalls that his son "tended to be on the quiet side," reluctant to "fight for himself," or "push himself into anything." It was difficult for Ronald to retrieve many recollections about Timothy: "I really don't know that he was there." He felt so absorbed with his own needs, he "was totally running blind."

When Kathy and Ronald separated, the arrangement was that the children could visit him anytime. As Andrea was already grown by then, the boys would come for the weekend or perhaps for a week in the summertime. Much as Ronald's mother had done with him, Timothy and Calvin were basically on their own for those few days while he busied himself with his friends and other activities. He realizes now just how little he knew his children during those early years. Sadly, he acknowledges that they were just "a nondescript group of little people whose faces I couldn't even see." He also realizes just how little he knew himself.

When Timothy was in his early twenties, he moved from country life to city life. His mother joined him there. She had wanted a change and ended up staying for a couple of years, studying, getting professionally licensed as a masseuse, and moving back to the area where she raised her family. But Timothy stayed. His dream was and still is to be a model.

Ronald is quick to point out how Timothy and his mother are "carbon copies" of one another: impractical; rigid in the sense that they have ideas that are "fixed" until proven otherwise by experience; emotional; health-conscious; "night people." In contrast, Ronald feels that he is none of those, but more concerned with the practicalities of life—"I tend to be very attentive to all those little nitpicking details"—and less emotional—"while I have emotions, I don't really show them." He does not feel that those real differences between him and his son had anything at all to do with the distance between them. Rather, he thinks that all of his children, Timothy included, kept away from *him*, fearful of continually getting "browbeaten." His common sense told him that one does not "mess around with grizzly bears too long. . . . You find another part of the woods to live in."

Given the closeness of mother and son, it came as no surprise when Kathy informed Ronald that Timothy was gay. It was the standard "mode of operation" that Ronald found out most things through her. This fact of life was no different. Father was unclear when that occurred, but thinks it was probably about twelve or thirteen years ago. He recalls hearing it and treating it like any other piece of information he learned about his children at that time: "I don't think I paid much attention to it." It was more of an interference, taking him away from whatever he was involved with at the moment. For many reasons, he has never spoken with his son about it directly.

On one level, it is not something he feels "particularly uptight about in general." His own mother's philosophy of "live and let live" has been something he has taken in and made his. On another level, he exempts himself from talking with others about their sexuality and their finances—the "two parts of a person's life that are considered very personal." He applies this principle to his friends and his family. On yet another level, the experience of homosexuality, he admits, is a foreign one: "I don't know what it feels like to be gay." The sense of something "unknown" makes him uncomfortable. It is an area of experience that he has not thought that much about because it is not something that he cares that much about. If his son is homosexual, "so what? . . . I can't find anything good, bad, or indifferent about it. It's just the way it is."

To be sure, Ronald does have some ideas of how his son's homosexuality developed, "a composite" of different elements including genetics, the wish to be a girl like his sister and to get the kind of attention she got, and the lack of his own presence in his son's life. Movingly, he describes himself as

> a father who hasn't been a good role model . . . a father who's never been there in an understanding way. . . . If I could have been a different father . . . if I could have been there and open and listening . . . then he may have wound up not being a homosexual.

Ronald feels that he missed out on the joys of fatherhood, missed out on getting what Timothy could offer as a son, missed out on giving to him what he might have as a father. If he had it to do over again, he might have chosen not to be a father at all, given that he thinks he is ill-equipped for the job. He feels this sense of inadequacy is based on a complex interweaving of many factors: being too self-involved; not knowing how to father since he himself felt inadequately fathered (and mothered); and fearing that he would not be able to meet whatever expectations he might have set for himself for fulfilling that role. Rather than dealing with any of those, he "basically ignored it all." Interestingly, his youngest boy, Calvin, now a father himself, is the kind of father Ronald might have aspired to be. He sees Calvin making every effort to be a part of his children's lives "and letting them be a part of his life." This brings up much guilt that he could not do the same for his own children during those early years.

However, with greater awareness sometimes comes change, at least for Ronald. Little by little, he has made "an attempt" to open up to his children: "I make an effort to be interested in their lives just a little bit." He now enjoys getting involved and being useful to them in whatever projects they are involved with. Being a computer professional, he is able to find information on a range of subjects. Sometimes they ask him for this, sometimes not. In the beginning, he admits this felt rather "contrived," but the more he does it, the "more natural" it feels. Timothy knows that one of his father's interests is building and designing, and encourages his father to come down to the city to see what he has done with his apartment, which Ronald *has* on occasion.

On a more emotional level, Ronald encourages his children to tell him when something he has done has made them angry. He has even offered to go to therapy with them if they would like. His own therapy has been life altering and he attributes whatever changes he has made in his relationship with his children to those experiences. He now feels "receptive" in a way that he did not before. Ronald says that it was Andrea who gave him "the best compliment" he had ever heard when she said, "You're not the man that we knew years ago." Although he knows on some level this is true, it is still hard to fully acknowledge.

In 1989, Ronald bought a house, after vowing for years that he would never want to own another one. He lives there today with Kathy. The two maintain quasi-independent lives now that they have been separated for twenty-two years, divorced for fourteen. They have come full-circle together. The house also serves as an "anchor" for his children, providing a sense of safety and stability that he never tried to cultivate before. Separately and together, it is a place where the family can gather on holidays or whenever they want. It is a place that they all now more easily can call "home."

NEAL

If that was the case, that's the case.

Neal's father, a tailor by trade, always made him feel special. For years, the older man kept a picture of his youngest child in his shop window. With "Buster blond hair and . . . a cane in [his] mouth," Neal thought he "looked pretty good." He always felt "uncomfortable," however, about this extra attention, thinking that his father "should have passed it around a little bit more evenly" among his older brother and his two older sisters. This remarkable outpouring of love—hugging, kissing, bestowing gifts—was confusing to him since Neal felt distinctly unremarkable.

Both of Neal's parents originally came from Eastern Europe. His father was from Rumania; his mother was from Russia. He remembers his father as a "hard-working man, who thought that education was a pretty good thing." He came to this country at the turn of the century to "make a little better life," settling on the Lower East Side of New York City. A socialist, his father joined organizations that "were striving to better man." *The Forward,* a socialist newspaper, "was his Bible." He "read it from cover to cover." Beset by what would now be considered routine medical problems—appendicitis, gallstones—the older man died at fifty-one, leaving his wife and his four children alone. Neal was seventeen then. It was the Depression, "a very trying time" when everyone was "hustling for a living." Now eighty-five, he remembers the close living quarters with no electricity. He did not question what today seems like a harsh reality. Rather, he accepted it because "that's how it was."

After finishing high school, he took "whatever kind of work [he] could get" in order to help pay the mortgage on the home his father had purchased. Employed in different capacities—at an insurance company, in a department store, by a furrier—these "odds and ends" eventually led to a successful business venture operating a training school for nurses. He has been retired for the past twenty years.

Musically inclined, Neal began studying the violin at the age of eight, which at first "didn't add up to much." But during the Depression he was able to get summer jobs in the Catskills, expanding his musical repertoire to include the saxophone and the clarinet. The fun that he had doing this only got better after he met Arleen. She was on the staff at one of the hotels, looking after her sister, a singer, who performed with the band. Together they put on "skits and bits," improvisations done vaudeville style. After a year or so of "a wild courtship," they married. He describes his wife as a "very vibrant person," a woman dedicated to looking after the home and giving their three boys—Andrew, Donald, and Daniel—"special care," much as his own mother had done. Arleen died about two years before our interview after recurring bouts with breast cancer, just short of their sixtieth anniversary.

Neal does not think he had any specific expectations for any of his sons. Rather, his goal was to ensure that they had "a good background," thus giving them the means to "find their way." His only hope was that first and foremost, they would all "be well." Neal acknowledges not being that close to any of his children while they were growing up, mainly because he spent much of his time working. However, he tried to compensate for that by ensuring that they were together on weekends, many times taking family trips. He and Arleen never went away and left them in the care of anyone else. Their children always went along: "they were a part of us." He speaks with pride about each of his sons, all of whom he feels are quite accomplished in their respective fields. He beams when talking about Donald, his middle child, now fifty, a gay man.

Neal recalls Donald as "much brighter than the average child." On one occasion, a teacher sent a note home expressing concern that Donald was sleeping in class and not paying attention. Neal thought his son "knew everything that was going on. He was just *bored.*" According to Neal, Donald's interests include just about "everything." His knowledge of music is far-reaching—"early music, late music, the names of people that collected music"—matched only by his knowledge of art—"past and present. He's an amazing person," Neal says boastfully. The only area in which he does not excel is athletics, which Neal claims is "no big loss" since he himself "was never a great athlete" either. "He has other great interests . . . which I admire," he counters. Donald was also a bit of an adventurer, having what his father describes as an "outward spirit." At nineteen, he traveled all over Europe by himself without much money. Neal thought this was a "crazy" idea; however, realized he had "a very bright fellow" on his hands who "wanted to see the world" and so did not interfere. This noninterfering stance has been characteristic of his approach to other areas of his son's life as well.

It was around this time that Donald moved out of his parents' home into his own apartment with a friend. Neal thought that his son had been feeling "uncomfortable" and wanted to be on his own. While visiting Donald, Neal came across a postcard addressed to a man in which he referred to the person affectionately as "dear." "Sounded a little odd to me," Neal admits. But, he did not "make much of it . . . hop[ing] it would go away." He admits that this was something he did not wish to face, and he never brought it up to anyone. Besides, even if his suspicions were true, he thought there was nothing he could "do" about it anyway, so why discuss it: "if that was the case, that's the case." Upon further reflection, Neal realizes that he had suspicions "earlier," but could not pinpoint anything specific—perhaps subtle mannerisms, perhaps a "remark" over the phone. "I wasn't definite about anything," he says, until finding the postcard, which served as "concrete evidence." When his son, now a psychologist, was about thirty-five, he settled down with Gene, whom Neal acknowledges as "a very warm, lovely person." They have been together since. They own a home and, within the last year or so, have adopted a Mexican child. They have "a regular relationship."

Consciousness about homosexuality was not what it is today, Neal considers. "We didn't think of it enough because we didn't know about it enough," he says. There was far less visibility. Coming across a gay person was rare in his experience, except if a man was obviously "a fairy." He admits he did not "know that women could also be gay." After the realization that his son was gay, Neal was not "too happy about it," given the difficulties that lay ahead for any person considered a minority. Being Jewish "has been a disaster to millions" he says with forceful conviction, clearly identifying with his son's situation. He feels that life is less complicated if one is part of the majority, if one goes with the current, if one "run[s] with the tide."

Over the years, the subject of his son's homosexuality has never been discussed with his son or with his wife when she was alive. He "accepted his living as normal." Making something out of nothing, that is, creating a problem where there was none, did not "seem like a smart thing to do at all." He felt that he did not "have any right to interfere." Besides, it was not such "a terrible thing." And if he had brought it up, what would he have said? This is "something that happens . . . something that . . . he was born with." Neal says he does not feel any responsibility for his son being gay. A part of him wonders, however, if perhaps he did not know any other way to approach it.

Although he has not discussed it within the context of his family, Neal has volunteered it elsewhere. Since his wife's recent death, Neal has looked for ways to fill the void left by her absence. Being an amateur musician, he finds others with whom he plays chamber music. He also visits places of interest. Last summer, he spent time at a camp for Jewish senior citizens. During a tedious group discussion in which everyone was getting up and extolling the virtues of their own children, Neal decided to take a different route. Apparently, two days before, Donald, his partner, and their son had come to visit him. The hugging and kissing were observed by many at the camp, generating some "behind the . . . back discussion." So, after the group leader asked him to talk about his own family and after some preliminary joking, he announced:

> My son is what they call gay and he represents about 10 percent of the people in this earth. And today, a lot of people are faced with that type of a problem and I was wondering how *you* deal with it . . . when you find out that your child . . . is gay or lesbian.

After the "sudden silence," he tried again. Disbelieving that no one "has anyone in their family" who is gay, he continued arguing that this is an issue that has torn others apart both individually and collectively, crescendoing into "it's a very important thing that people ought to talk about," prodding them more insistently than ever. No response. He could not even get the rabbi to debate it individually, someone whom he thought would have been a bit more "broad minded" and open to new ideas. The only thing louder than their silence was his own disappointment in them.

Although others approached him later in private applauding his courage, this failed to make up for the broader, more public discussion he had hoped for. He felt that the group's response to this issue had to do with "fear." If people claim not to know or be aware, then no one else can say that this was their fault, that they are not "the bear[er]s of this ill-tiding." If it remains unacknowledged, maybe it will "go away," which is not unlike the way *he* felt many years ago after finding his son's postcard. For Neal, saying what he thinks gets easier with age: "you have nothing to lose. Shock people. Do things. Let your ideas come forth. Nothing can happen to you."

Neal feels that his son's being gay has not affected him in the least. Although he would have preferred that he not be, he feels they "have the same loving relationship" they have always had. It has not caused any shifts "at all"; his affection has not changed "one iota." To be sure, they have had their differences over the years. At sixteen years of age, his son denounced him as "a fascist," feeling that he was not attuned enough to the social causes that were important. Neal strongly disagreed. If there was one thing he was not, it was a fascist. Besides wishing that Donald would be less "abrupt," less "sharp," Neal feels that his son is "ideal." He and his boys get together regularly. They even play chamber music together—Donald on piano, Daniel on oboe, Neal on violin. He is happy about having helped build the lives of his three successful sons and looks forward to sharing many more years together with them. "We're a great family," he concludes.

PEI

He's a complete person.

Pei was born sixty-five years ago in a farming village about sixty miles outside of Canton. As the oldest son in a family of seven children, the power he held was second only to that of his parents. Should they have died, he would have been expected to "take over." Pei remembers his mother as "easy to anger," never one to hesitate "to lash out" verbally or physically toward anyone in her path. "I cannot remember one day I receive a compliment from my mom," he says with some sadness. His father—a "passive . . . thoughtful . . . nonphysical" man—had a far different approach with him. A schoolteacher and artist, he "was much better educated" than the mother and treated his son "with regard." Although father and son stayed "at a distance," Pei remembers the sense of respect he held for him. However, his father would tend to "disappear" while his mother was on a rampage so as not to "create any more conflict" than was necessary.

When Pei was eleven, it was decided that he would come by himself to America, the "Golden Mountain." His mother was the force behind this idea, which reflected the weight of responsibility he was expected to carry, at least by her standards. His mission: to find his paternal grandfather and persuade him to return to China. The older man had left when his wife was pregnant with Pei's father. Pei was not to see his family again until many years later.

Coming by way of Seattle armed with an assumed identity and falsified immigration papers (he has since become a legal citizen), he was initially detained for about a month, but eventually made his way to San Francisco, to the church in which his grandfather had worked as a custodian for thirty years. "Presumably you are my grandson, but I didn't send for you. I don't know why you're here," was his grandfather's response, obviously shocked by his unexpected arrival. Insisting that there was "no room" where he was living, his grandfather found transitional housing for Pei in a place he shared with three others at a cost of $2.50 a month, which the grandfather paid, albeit reluctantly. The little money with which Pei had come to America was rapidly depleting. He had to find some way to make a living because his grandfather was "never really . . . around." Shining shoes, delivering newspapers, and washing dishes all became the means to survive what was a "dismal . . . lonely" early life. His mother also expected him to send money home. Two years after his arrival, Pei's grandfather died. With the rest of the family 10,000 miles away, he was on his own at thirteen: "I was thrust into being a man way before [it was] time for me to become one."

As a teenager, life continued to be all about survival. He envied anyone who had more than he did, which was just about everyone else he knew. At seventeen, he found the Air Force. Finally, he felt "safe." With food, clothing, shelter, spending money, and medical expenses all provided, he was now freer to apply himself differently and see parts of the world that were heretofore unseen—Japan and Korea, for example. The GI Bill afforded him the opportunity of finishing high school, attending a junior college, and eventually completing an electrical engineering degree from the University of California at Berkeley while working full-time driving a mail truck. He understood years later that electrical engineering was a profession that he chose based on the expectations of his own father, rather than one that held any personal meaning for him. Over time, he became increasingly disenchanted with the "inanimate . . . world," deciding to trade this in for one based on "human interaction" by going back to school to train as a social worker. This has proved more useful and more meaningful.

As a young man, Pei felt ill-equipped to deal with the opposite sex. Having received little "positive input" from his parents, particularly his mother, he came to those experiences never feeling "too good about [him]self." It always seemed as though he did not "blend well." He would "get too uptight and . . . critical": "it seemed like I scared all the girls . . . away." Despite the odds, he dated and had a girlfriend for three years after leaving the service. When that dissolved, a friend introduced him to his wife-to-be, Rita, who was engaged at the time. After the engagement broke off, Pei pursued her. Nine months later, they were married and subsequently had three children—Sharon, Chris, and Paul, now thirty-four, thirty-one, and twenty-eight, respectively. Chris, his older son, is gay.

Pei spent those first years of family life building "financial freedom." Coming "from the underclass," he thought that having money would provide a sense of "safety" and would be the answer to any and all problems: "I had this misguided thinking that . . . everything had to do with economics." He found out differently. It could not provide solutions for how to build relationships. While his expectations for himself ran high relative to providing things for his family that he had never received, they also ran high for his children. Regretfully, he acknowledges that the relationship he had with his mother parallels the relationships he had with his offspring, particularly with his boys. Since Chinese culture prizes males more than females, Pei unknowingly expected his sons "to perform" at their best at all times. If they did, nothing was said; if they did not, they heard about it. "Negative input" was never balanced with "positive input." He neither fully realized the message he was conveying nor just how "devastating" that message was until after the children were grown. Even recently, when asking Chris about how he managed to succeed so well academically in college without being pushed by Pei, Chris replied forcefully, "That's just what you think, Dad. . . . It's very difficult to be your son. . . . I felt . . . high expectation[s] from you all the time." Chris angrily said that it was fortunate that he was a good enough student to be able to fulfill his father's nonverbal demands, crescendoing into a fist-pounding, tearful: "You don't even know what you did!"

Pei realized early on that he had someone special in Chris. "On the skinny side," Pei recalls him as bright, quiet, reflective, likable, sensitive to the things around him, conscious of his own differ- ence—closer in temperament to Rita. Chris once confided in his father that even in nursery school, as he observed the other children in his class "running around" wildly, he felt himself as very much the "outsider . . . looking in." Like Pei, Chris never really felt like he was "part of the whole." Yet by others' standards, Chris fit in well. He was academically gifted, well-liked, and the leader of a select group of students, ones who were more interested in intellectual pursuits such as chess, science, and music. He was also a fine swimmer, but never pursued other types of competitive sports such as football or baseball. He rarely pursued girls either. Pei thought that perhaps his son, being "very tender, very sensitive," was more relationship-oriented and was not interested in just having sex. "Maybe the right girl never came along," was how he tried to reassure himself, while at the same time wondering whether his son was facing a "sexual identity crisis."

Hints of that came up time and time again when Chris was in college. Although Pei fully expected his son to be a leader in the corporate world, Chris would tell his father that he did not feel that he fit the mold, that he did not want to be responsible for the welfare of others, at least not in that way. And while he would occasionally talk about marrying, he would counter that with his sense that bringing children into the kind of world we live in might not be such a good thing. Pei thinks that his son was laying the groundwork for eventually coming out: "he was hinting and hinting and hinting." Despite all the hints, Pei "refuse[d] to be taken down that line," although there was a long period of time when he feels that Chris was not absolutely sure himself, when Chris thought he might be bisexual. After a great deal of "soul searching," after taking courses at school, and after getting some counseling at the university, Chris was finally ready to stop hinting and take a more direct approach.

When he was a junior in college, Chris was interested in learning more about the painting classes his mother was taking in the neighboring city. He visited the art room while she was there, accompanied by an obviously gay fellow student, who was "whizzing all over the place." The teacher registered a great deal of surprise that Chris would associate with someone like this. Rita started thinking. After coming back home that night, she confided in her husband about what had happened. Pei replied, "I always suspected." He in turn went to have lunch with his daughter, Sharon, to discuss the matter and learned later that Chris had already come out to her. After their meeting, Sharon called her brother to inform him of their father's concern. Chris then called his parents' home and spoke to his mother, telling her that he was gay. Pei received the news from Rita.

Although Pei admits that while he did not "go into a tailspin," nevertheless, his "imagination r[a]n wild." His first concern "was how can I protect that child?" Pei understood discrimination well. His way of protecting himself had been through "economic might." Since his son was not interested in making money and being part of the corporate world, Pei was unsure how he would defend himself. Pei admits that while he was not shocked by the news, neither was it something he was alert to or looking for: "you just go into denial for as long as you can." He thought that Chris imagined that telling his mother would be easier than telling him. Going "to the grave" without having ever informed his father was a very real possibility. Pei feels that his openness and his acceptance surprised Chris. Any lingering conflicts his son had about being gay were once and for all put firmly to rest.

Pei's respect for his son is obvious. Just as Chris was a leader at school, he was and still is a leader in their family. Everyone, his siblings included, admires and looks up to him. Although Pei is a trained counselor, he feels that Chris is more of a "natural" than he is, better able to listen, exercise good judgment, and approach problems logically. Because of these qualities, Pei found himself at one point in his life trying to extract "psychological support" from Chris, seeking from him what he should have sought from Rita. "One might say that I even committed some psychological incest," he realizes with regret. This has been one issue among many that father and son have talked about over the years. Those initial discussions about Chris's coming out served as a springboard for other unrelated but important matters. Pei deeply appreciates the openness the two now share.

Part of the pride he feels in his son is knowing that others recognize his specialness, too. One of those people is David, Chris's lover. The two met in college. Pei has watched them struggle and grow together for the last ten years as they define and redefine the parameters of their relationship. In observing their ever-increasing capacity to accommodate each other's needs, Pei has learned a thing or two about how to relate better to Rita. Their growth as a gay couple has also been a good influence on Chris individually. From a defiant young adult with a "funny haircut," who would wear clothing others might throw away, and whose attitude toward society could best be characterized by the words, "stick it," he has matured into "a conservative guy," who values the "good life" while "remaining very strongly connected to the world."

Part of the reason that he has been able to accept his son's sexuality is connected both to the fact that Pei has been completely "Westernized" and that he left the Catholic Church in his youth. Although he was baptized and was an altar boy, he ultimately found Church teachings "inflexible and overly dogmatic." A "do unto others as you would have them do unto you" philosophy is all that he feels he needs in order to coexist with others. He also thinks that Chris's homosexuality, which he considers "innate," is only a small part of who his son is as a person. "There's an enormous and total human being in him that . . . span[s] way beyond sexuality." At the same time, Pei acknowledges the losses that he will experience because Chris is gay. He is sad that there will probably be no natural grandchildren by him, although adoption remains a possibility. He would like his son to experience what it is like to be a father, given all his natural warmth and sensitivity as a human being. "He's a complete person," Pei says, sparkling with pride.

Pei has come out as the father of a gay man. He has gone public in many ways and in many forums. But he is selective about who he chooses to tell. Of the family that he left behind in China as a boy, most of his siblings along with his mother came to this country about twelve years ago. (His father died in the late 1960s.) He has not told them about Chris's sexuality because the values that they hold are more traditional, and it would be difficult for them to completely understand. Besides them and Rita's mother, now eighty-three, he has disclosed the fact of his son's gayness to nearly everyone else. Colleagues, friends, and neighbors all seem to have "no issue" with it. Some of them joke with him by saying, "If you don't want your son . . . we'll take him."

Watching Chris struggle with his identity and trying to find "his place in the world" has struck a deep chord in Pei. It has reinforced for him that life is not always just about being happy. It also involves being able to tolerate "pain and suffering." The two "go hand in hand." Both must be embraced. Pei willingly acknowledges that his son's sense of engagement with the world has been an inspiration. Chris's work in the gay community and with AIDS patients has given Pei the courage to give more of himself. When he sees his son doing what he does, he feels that he "can't do less." Indeed, Pei partially credits his son for his going back to graduate school to train as a counselor.

No one has been more surprised than Pei himself by the transformation that has taken place within him. He can now acknowledge and tolerate a greater range of feelings, accepting all of them as part of life, now able and willing to "make room" for and understand the pain, thereby lessening its impact, ultimately accepting it as neither "bad [nor] good." He has also let go of the idea that money is the be-all and end-all of one's existence. When in the early 1980s he lost much of his wealth in real estate, he went into years of depression. He no longer obsesses about those losses, nor is he driven by economic concerns. Money now takes a back seat to his physical health and his family relationships.

Pei reflects that "characters are built in . . . difficult time[s]." The tolerance he now feels for himself makes him that much more tolerant of others, despite their differences. He is confused and angered by others' prejudices, but thinks that the gay community has to claim some responsibility, because their own public portrayal of themselves is sometimes oversexualized.

In dealing with having a gay son, Pei feels that he was able to reach a depth of strength and experience he did not know was in him. "I didn't realize how capable [I was] of being a more complete human being." Chris has taught him well.

WALTER

I want to be in the . . . room with the light with him.

"Everything that came out of this was bad" is how Walter summarizes the events of his early life. Born fifty years ago, he was the oldest of five children, each about a year apart. When he was five years old, the fabric of his family was all but destroyed. His father, an alcoholic, was physically and verbally abusive to his mother, resulting in his parents' separation and divorce. The youngest three children, two brothers and a sister, were adopted—two together, one separately; another sister remained with their mother; and he was sent to live with his maternal grandparents. This arrangement lasted for three years. He never saw his father and his three adopted siblings again.

His own situation improved in the sense that his grandparents (and his aunt and uncle, who lived on another floor of the home) treated him well, although his grandfather, like Walter's father, was an alcoholic. However, when the older man was diagnosed with cancer, Walter was sent to live with his mother, her second husband, and his sister in the Midwest. His stepfather turned out to be alcoholic as well ("he was . . . very sneaky about it") and was verbally abusive to Walter. His sense of shame about this state of affairs pervaded his whole life at the time. He coped by withdrawing. Reading and running became tools for survival, ways to "escape." After he graduated from high school and went off to college, he "quit running but . . . kept reading. . . . The life of the mind was just so exciting, so interesting." He devoured tales of adventure—*One Day in the Life of Ivan Denisovich,* the Eddie Rickenbacker story. These captured his imagination: "men facing challenges and overcoming them . . . I could relate to that." He seemed hungry to find answers to the challenges that his own life presented.

In college, Walter began as a philosophy major and naturally "gravitated" to history and political science. He met his wife, Charlotte, when he was a junior and she was a sophomore. They married a year later. Working as a janitor and studying by day, he eventually completed his master's degree. He and Charlotte had considered joining VISTA, but their son, James, was born and they reevaluated this decision, choosing instead to take a teaching position on a Navajo reservation—a self-imposed challenge.

Walter had little preparation for what confronted him there. He did not anticipate the rampant alcoholism and extreme deprivation and understood little about "the cultural nuances" of the people. For example, looking others "in the eye," something which had been ingrained in him as a child, was taboo in this setting. In a very conscious way, he tried to adapt. The "disaster" of teaching Kafka and Shakespeare gave way to exploring other writers such as Tony Hillerman, for example, whose *Dance Hall of the Dead,* which takes place on a Navajo reservation, proved more accessible and enjoyable. His openness to trying to accommodate himself not only helped to reshape his teaching style, making it much less rigid and more fluid, but also seemed to help him prepare the way for challenges to come.

Feeling isolated, the family moved off the reservation and back into the mainstream of society. Walter taught at a college for about four years prior to pursuing his PhD, which took another four years to complete. His interest in reading and learning, which before had been ways to survive a difficult home environment, had now become a profession, a way of life. So the main expectation he had for James, now twenty-four, was that he become college educated. Walter still hopes for this. He feels this is the only part of his "script" for his son that he has not "torn up." The wording of that "script," however, has continuously changed over the years.

Walter wanted his son to have it easier than he did and feels he may have been "overly permissive" as a parent to compensate for this: "when I was a child, I was angry and . . . hurt and there was conflict in the home all the time." He did not want James to be subjected to that. Although Walter feels that he accomplished this, concerns about his son surfaced. Describing him as "gentle and kind," he feels that his son is introspective by nature: "there would be periods when . . . he was thinking very deeply about something, but [you] couldn't quite put your finger on it . . . you couldn't draw him out." Wistfully, Walter acknowledges that there was, and continues to be, a part of his son he will never know, which leaves him a bit frustrated and confused. That he and James do not "quite connect" has been a past, present, and painful reality.

Walter perceived James as being different from himself. While his own passions centered on sports and academics—history, political science, literature, philosophy—music was his son's passion. James studied the viola and played in the school orchestra. In junior high school, he had an all-consuming interest in Dolly Parton and in high school, Madonna was the center of his universe. Broadway show tunes were a never-ending source of pleasure, too. "I must have heard *Phantom of the Opera* about five hundred times," Walter says with some amusement and some exasperation. James also had "no interest in sports whatsoever." Walter put up a basketball hoop, hoping that that might be a point of connection for them, but to no avail: "I think he probably shot five baskets. That was it."

Unlike Walter, who spent some of his time "hell-raising" with other boys, James seemed to be more comfortable with females: "he always had a . . . tendency to gravitate toward girls in social situations instead of boys." His male peers had, obviously, observed this, too. In junior high, Charlotte found a pocketknife in his bookbag. When confronted by his parents about this, James said "he needed it for protection because he was being taunted." Walter thought that the other boys perceived his son as "a sissy." After that incident, James "changed radically." He began to smoke cigarettes, spiked his hair, and wore all black. Walter said, "That made him accepted." It was a way to "fit in," providing a sense of "group strength in facing . . . the rest of the community," not an easy thing to do in their small, Midwestern town, he suggests. Like the character of the *Phantom*, Walter was continuously confronted by the many sides of James and was never too sure how to comprehend them. When his son was a senior in high school, however, one of those sides which had always been in question, "if he . . . was more interested in boys than girls," became clear.

On one particular night, James failed to return home until 5 a.m., way past his 12 o'clock curfew. In fact, he had stayed out late on a number of occasions and was not accounting for it. The time had come for an explanation: "we said we're not getting up from here until we find out what's going on." James told his parents that he had been taking the car and driving around one street in particular. Walter and Charlotte realized that there was a gay bar around there and asked their son if that was where he was going. Evasively, he said that he was not exactly going to the bar, but was meeting "friends . . . outside of the bar." Walter realized that James meant meeting men and "having sex" ("probably oral sex," Walter thought). "I felt my heart sink," he recalls. He and Charlotte were "speechless." Panic about AIDS was his first concern: "God, that scared me to death." Then, "overwhelming" thoughts occurred about the kind of future James might have in terms of his education and what his relationship with the family might be. The "script" that Walter had written for James was being torn to shreds: "we didn't know our parts . . . there was no direction." He was left to improvise. Not surprisingly, Walter responded by reading "everything [he] could about homosexuality." That was the way he had coped with crises as a teenager and that was one of the ways he was coping with this. Information itself was important as a way to help him to understand a situation that made him feel so totally helpless: "all of a sudden, I had no grasp, I had no understanding." It also provided an escape, a way to collect himself and think. That was a beginning. Dialogues with Charlotte also helped. She was experiencing similar feelings. Guilt about causing their son to be gay was a preoccupation for both of them, particularly for her.

What was of broader concern to Walter was pervasive doubt about his capacity to be a father. Without "any great role models," he had little experience of feeling fathered so, consequently, had "a certain amount of insecurity" about fathering. This was magnified after James came out: "couldn't we have done this, shouldn't we have done that." For example, when they were made aware that their son's music teacher was paying him special attention, in retrospect, they think that that might have been a time to intervene. "I wasn't the father I . . . should have been" is a thought that has haunted him, although less and less as time goes by. Walter express-es the fact that he

> tried to interact with [James] on . . . a more emotional level. I showed him how I felt . . . quite often, hugged him a lot. . . . I just couldn't help it 'cause I loved him so much. But . . . maybe I could have done more. . . . I don't know.

Added to this was his regret about having remained in their community. Walter thinks that perhaps the rather conservative na-ture of the Midwestern setting made it even more difficult for his son to come out. However, at the time he was concerned that mov-ing around might have been too destabilizing for James and so opted for staying there until his son graduated from high school. After that, they headed East after Walter got a job offer at a small state school outside a major city. However, all of their guilt kept him and Charlotte in the closet for a year or so.

After their move and after James began college, he had a more formal coming out. He declared his homosexuality openly to his parents and told them that if they had any questions or concerns about this, he would give them any literature and information they needed. Puzzled at first, since James had already informed them that he was gay, Walter realized that his son needed to do this mainly "for himself." However, he also felt that James was trying to close the gap that potentially might have developed between him and his parents. Instead of using his coming out only as a way to declare his separateness, he was also trying to use it as a point of unification. Walter thought that this "was a really magnanimous gesture" on his son's part: "he was saying that we had to come out, too." Walter genuinely felt that James was trying to ease his par-ents' pain and forge a closer family bond: "he was moving us back together. . . . I should thank him for that." After this, Walter came out as a parent—"whole hog."

The primary area of conflict for him has been in the workplace. His nontenured status heightened his vulnerability. Concerns about who to tell, who not to tell, "outing your . . . own child" were all obstacles in developing relationships with others at school. Of course, he still wrestles with these issues. But after two years of agonizing, Walter said, "This is crazy . . . if the institution and my colleagues can't accept me for who I am, then [it's] not a place I want to work the rest of my career." With that thought in mind and after some discussion with Charlotte, Walter decided to offer a course titled, "Gay and Lesbian History of the U.S." Always one for a challenge, he "wanted to put all [his] reading and research to work" toward something new and personally meaningful. He feels glad to have taken that risk against the advice of other colleagues. It has transformed him in many ways.

Initial concerns about what to call the course and whether to attach his name to it proved fairly easy to resolve once he had really made up his mind to teach it. His commitment to changing the attitudes of those around him in his own individual way, "little increments at a time," fueled his determination. By way of teaching the course, he informed several of his colleagues about his son's homosexuality. Conversely, several of his students have come out to him, something that he feels very honored by, reinforcing his dedication to what he is doing. Easing their coming out while simultaneously not betraying their confidence is an issue to which he remains steadfastly committed: "society has to open up and give these kids a chance to be who they are." He does not want them to face the kind of difficulties that his son did. Walter feels that coming out was so fraught with problems for James that it interfered with his attending and finishing college. He wants to be there for his young students in a way that he felt he was not there for his son and in a way that other adults were not there for him.

There have been deeper changes as well. Walter feels that he can now express more of himself to others. The prospect of revealing that he is the father of a gay man had been something he felt he could never do—until recently. This experience has proved a powerful one. Further, his relationship with James, while he still feels the same amount of love for him is nevertheless a closer one than the two had when his son was younger. Walter is now able to say "I love you" more directly than he could before. "I really feel it when I say it. I hope he . . . knows that." Walter summarizes his personal transformation in this profound and moving way:

I feel as if I've stepped through a door and . . . it's a brighter room than before. . . . I could have gone through my whole life and not . . . even been aware of the . . . difficulties and the rewards and the joy of the lives of all those people that now are . . . accessible to me. Whereas before, they were in that other room and I . . . didn't go in. . . . My son's in that other room. . . . I want to be in the . . . room with the light with him. I hope that he feels . . . with my acceptance that I'm with him. He hasn't left me behind.

Chapter 5

Findings

It is joy to be hidden
but disaster not to be found.

Winnicott (1993)

In this chapter, I present the raw data using five categories: *dreams* or hopes and expectations the fathers had for their sons both in the past and in the present; *beginnings* of the early father-son relationships; *wonderings* or hints they may have had about their sons' sexuality prior to disclosure or clues they may have missed in looking back after disclosure; the *disclosure* itself, covering context, who, how, and the immediate responses the fathers had, including the issue of causation; and the *impact* all of this has made on the fathers, the sons, and on the two of them together. Note that all the quoted material comes directly from the transcripts.

DREAMS

You have dreams and plans [of] what you expect your children to turn out to be and they constantly change.

Marty

Fathers' dreams for their children occur at all points in life and change over time. Asking these particular fathers what those might have been before the births of their sons produced a range of responses. Representing one end of the continuum was Neal, who says, "Having expectations of children is such that it varies and changes to such a large extent that it really doesn't matter. I don't think I thought of that too often." He was confident that if he just gave his children "a good background, they would find their way."

Marty echoes this, saying that he is "not that kind of person that worries or . . . thinks too far ahead. I kind of live in the moment." Glenn does not recall giving "it very much thought," but "was enough of a male chauvinist to be happy it was a boy." Both Mitchell and Daniel had no clear expectations before the births of their sons either. And Ronald admits that at that particular point in his life, he "was totally running blind," totally preoccupied with worries revolving around building a career and a home.

However, other fathers were clear about what they wanted. These represented a wide range of interests and preoccupations. Before the birth of each of his four children, Harry would tell his wife that he desired a son: "that's what I would like to have." His prayers were finally answered with the birth of Harry Jr. Not only that, he wanted him to "be sports-minded." And not just any sport, but a team sport such as basketball, baseball, or football—all Harry's loves. Peter wanted his children to be "good Jews." He says, "I always wanted this more than anything." For him, being religiously observant is synonymous with compassion, goodness, and understanding. Being knowledgeable about the lives of his predecessors ensured continuation of their faith. Walter had many worries that his child "might be born with a birth defect or . . . retarded." His awareness of this possibility was heightened because of his wife's profession as a special education teacher. Walter thought if that happened, he was determined to "stay the course . . . whatever the outcome was." His other dream was that his child would "have a college education and not have to work as hard as [he] did." The latter was also a concern for Luis, the only father who acknowledged the expectation of marriage and grandchildren before the birth of his son. Other fathers talked about this expectation also, but identified it as occurring later in their lives. Juan Miguel Jr., for example, wanted his two boys to get married and give him "heirs," something he did not especially care about in relation to his two daughters. "That's what we call *machismo*," he concedes. Marty admits that he would love to be a grandfather: "maybe [Gary] will . . . adopt . . . a child one day. . . . I love children, just love children and I love playing with them." Glenn says that his son's gayness "in all sincerity . . . doesn't matter—minus the grandchildren." Pei, who recalls his past hope for young Chris to become "a corporate leader," is now aware of the "losses" he will experience by having a gay son: "I will probably not see any natural grandchildren from him." He entertains the possibility of adoption, though.

Dreams the fathers hold in the present may be clearer than they were in the past. Besides grandfatherhood, a range of other concerns is reflected. Peter hopes that his son will finish college someday. Eight years after leaving school, Richard "still has sixteen hours to finish." Walter would like his son James to resume his education as well. He dropped out after his first year, Walter thinks, because the coming-out process was fraught with too much conflict for him. Marty would like his son, Gary, "to make more money" and professionally rise "to his capabilities." Juan Miguel Jr. also sees his son as underemployed. The clerical work he does now is far below what he is capable of. Similarly, Harry would like to see his son "succeed" in the commercial art world, rather than have to work at a job at which he is competent but which holds no real meaning for him. Although his son has submitted his work for review and has gotten some notice in magazines, Harry says "those . . . who make the final decision" about these matters were not "as encouraging" as family members have been over the years. He hopes that one day his son will "find a place in life instead of doing what he's doing now . . . [as] he's far more capable."

Along with schooling and jobs that better suit their sons' particular talents, the fathers express a hope for them to be in a romantic relationship if they are not already. Mitchell wants his son "to be settled someday with the most wonderful, caring partner." Juan Miguel Jr. wishes "a companion" for his son, as does Daniel "if [Charles] wants it for himself." Marty thinks that his son is lonely, having never really met anyone special yet. In Harry's case, although his son does have a partner, he is still praying that Harry Jr. will marry a woman "and have children." Both Harry and Glenn want a closer father/son relationship. In Glenn's case, it was not until late in his own father's life that the two of them had what he calls "a rapprochement," something he wants between himself and his son, Adam. Glenn hopes for a time when they can open up to each other in a deeper way: "there's an open invitation every Passover, every Thanksgiving . . . those are always family events. . . . They're always invited, they're always welcome. That will stay that way."

BEGINNINGS

I wasn't *there* for him.

Mitchell

Marty fondly recalls the early years of fatherhood. "The best years [are] when they're small, when you get all that love," admitting that he had "to stand off" as his sons got older and began to make friends. But he feels he stayed very involved with them—trips to museums, to parks, to Broadway—with or without his wife. Although Marty says he is not particularly athletic, he made efforts "to go out and throw the ball" with both of his sons, but "didn't see any signs of talent there." As his gay son, Gary, got older, Marty became concerned because he gained a tremendous amount of weight, was socially isolated, and seemed unhappy: "you knew something was bothering him." Marty was at a loss to understand this.

Although Walter has now come to a sense that he "did a pretty good job . . . as a parent," he did not always feel that way. His own childhood was riddled with hurt and anger and he did not want his son to go through childhood like that. So he compensated, becoming "overly permissive, overly indulgent, too laid back in discipline." Beyond that, his son, James, now twenty-four, has always been a bit elusive to him, somewhat out of reach. Temperament and interests of father and son always diverged. Walter was drawn to sports, "hell-raising" with other boys, and academics. Music was his son's passion and socially he tended to relate better to girls. Walter is saddened and perplexed by his sense of never fully knowing James. He wonders whether or not knowing one's children is something that is a common experience or whether it has more to do with his own "insecurity," never having had "any great role models." He does not know the answer.

The birth of Glenn's first son, Adam, "was a great event." And even though it was "an accident," Glenn was "happy it was a boy." The early years of his son's life were difficult ones, though. Glenn was working hard and was "fairly depressed," mostly as a result of his marriage "going from mediocre to bad." His relationship with Adam was overshadowed by the unstable relationship Glenn had with his wife. His involvement as a father tended to be uneven. At certain times he "was very open and very available"; at other times he was "remote and short-tempered."

When he was open and available, Glenn would allow his sons to come to his medical lab and "play around," later taking them out for lunch and then on trips to the zoo or to the museum. He also helped Adam train for Little League. But adolescence was fraught with much turmoil for Adam. As he began to withdraw socially, Glenn had thoughts that this might be tied to the possibility that his son was gay. Glenn took a wait-and-see attitude.

"There was always a part of me that wanted to be somewhere else" was how Daniel describes his early experience of family life. He longed "to be with some sweet man in a small but romantic garret in the Village." The reality was that he had a wife and two sons who needed him. To be sure, Daniel has always been a nontraditional father. He celebrated the birth of his first son, Charles, but the pull of his needs and desires related to his own homosexuality were beginning to weigh heavily. He could not ignore them. After Daniel came out and separated from his wife, he saw his sons only on weekends, little by little losing touch with their lives and with a sense of who they were. "Intimate moments, shared moments . . . don't come to mind," he says sadly.

Harry's memories about his son are also vague. There was little about his character as a boy and as an adolescent that he could really describe. He accounts for this by way of the fact that he was not around enough, having to work multiple jobs to pay the bills. Regretfully, Harry says that when his son was a teenager, he did not know "what he was doing [or] who he was doing it with." Neal's recollections about his early relationship with his son seem a bit vague, too. He reports that much of his time was spent working "so [he] wasn't that close to" Donald or to his other sons.

Peter readily admits that having not grown "up under normal circumstances," he was left feeling confused about "how people behave." The inconsistent presence of his own father necessitated his taking care of himself in order to survive. When his father was around, he recalls the "physical punishment" that he endured: "he would hold me and . . . beat me up." With him as a role model combined with the high demands and expectations that Peter held for his own son, Richard, a boy who was quite different from him in looks and temperament ("he wasn't rough like I was"), Peter acknowledges that he "was not [an] easy father" to live with. When he became frustrated, Peter would spank or ostracize Richard. "I didn't know how to behave to a child," he says with regret.

"I wasn't *there* for him" was how Mitchell describes his own lack of presence in his son, Jay's, early life. Mitchell felt frustrated. Temperamentally, Jay "was unreasonable . . . impulsive . . . less malleable" than his older son, always testing limits: "he was a bottomless pit." These traits, combined with the fact that Jay related more easily to females than males, made Mitchell pull back emotionally. "I couldn't get the bonding that I wanted," he admits.

Ronald, too, is filled with guilt and regret about his lack of involvement in his children's lives. He feels that his was self-absorption carried to an extreme. Consumed with his job and building a home, he never allowed anyone else inside, despite the depth of his own neediness. Pushing his family away only compounded the problem, making him even more empty and rageful. Having never had enough reliability with his own caretakers, he feels that he did not know how to be a caretaker for others. If he had it to do over again, he might have chosen not to be a father at all. When asked to recollect about his son, Timothy, as a boy, Ronald says that's "an impossible question" to answer: "I really don't know that he was there. I hate to say that. It hurts to say that."

Unlike Ronald, who is not sure he would choose to be a father if given a second chance, Luis "would have loved to spend more time with [his] son," Michael. Luis's need to put in so many hours at his job took him away from knowing his son better and cultivating a deeper relationship with him. Luis made some attempt to share his love of sports, but Michael "was never so thrilled about it." Michael was more interested in things artistic. Luis assumed that his son would develop interests similar to the ones he himself had as a boy, but concludes, "it doesn't work that way . . . if I don't take him to the park and play soccer, I can't expect him to take *me* to the park." Luis says that he feels more disappointed with himself than with Michael for not being closer now.

Pei's high expectations for his children, particularly his sons, were based on the high expectations that his mother had for him. "Body language"—a look, a glance—was all it took for Pei to get his message across: "I expect my children to accomplish a lot of things that I was not able to accomplish myself." Certainly one of those expectations included stellar performance in the academic arena. His son, Chris, felt fortunate that he had the innate endowment to meet those expectations, but it was not without its pressures. "It's very difficult to be your son," he forcefully told his father once.

WONDERINGS

> It's something that, as a father . . . you don't look for . . . you just go into denial for as long as you can.
>
> Pei

The myth that mothers intuitively "know" their sons are gay but fathers "don't" may be one we can partially dispel. Of those with whom I spoke, five of the fathers saw clues at different points in their sons' lives. Walter was putting the pieces together early. He observes that James "always had a . . . tendency to gravitate toward girls in social situations instead of boys," "liked to play with dolls," had "no interest in sports whatsoever," and "was perceived as being a sissy." Through all of this, he "would occasionally wonder if . . . [his son] was more interested in boys than girls."

The possibility of homosexuality was more commonly considered while their sons were in mid- to late adolescence. When Glenn observed his teenage son, Adam, isolating himself, being subjected to pressures at school, and not dating, Glenn thought at the time that Adam was probably gay. This was accompanied by a sense of shame and disappointment, but he told himself, "Let's see what happens . . . it's still early." Juan Miguel Jr. also considered the possibility that his son was gay "when he was coming into his teens." Having "never had any girlfriends" and only a small circle of male friends, he "wondered," giving it "just a small thought," admitting, "It passed my mind and I forgot it." This was accompanied by a sense of sadness as he pondered his son's future: "he'd be all by himself." Daniel, the gay father, "knew" that his adolescent son was similarly inclined by the fact that Charles was "not dating," and "by his pushy interest in [his father's] lovers," saying with amusement, "I was careful not to leave him alone too long with any of them." Neal found a postcard that his nineteen-year-old son was sending to another man with the words, "dear, will you do this?" It "sounded a little odd to" him, but he "didn't make much of it," hoping "it would go away." Never discussing it with his son out of a sense of embarrassment, he says, "I couldn't do anything about it anyway."

In another category were five other fathers who did not consciously consider the possibility that their sons could be gay but who, looking back later in life, in trying to put the pieces together, realized there had been clues. They just had not been fully aware of them at the time. For example, Harry reports that when his young son cross-dressed to entertain guests "so that there would be four girls instead of three and one," the other girls being his sisters, Harry thought that there was something unusual about this, "but . . . didn't look into it any further than that." After his son came out, Harry wonders if there was "a message that was being brought forth . . . in his behavior dressing like a . . . female."

In a similar vein, Luis recounts an incident in which his four-year-old son, Michael, was caught playing naked with another boy in the neighborhood and was forbidden by the other boy's father to associate with his son from then on. Later on, Michael tended to be physically self-conscious ("he didn't like to be bare-chested") and displayed a "feminine type of attitude," a certain way of expressing himself. Given all of this, Luis says that "something inside" was telling him that "something wasn't the way" it was supposed to be.

Mitchell says, "I guess my first time I was aware of concern was around nursery school, preschool—[Jay] must have been four or five—and the teacher said to my wife, he plays a lot with the girls, he plays in the doll's corner with the house." He continues, "Any ideas that we may have had that [Jay] was gay, if we had them at all, [and] we certainly weren't conscious of them, probably went out the window . . . and we never thought of it," acknowledging that "there may have been some stuff festering underneath . . . in my thinking, but . . . I wasn't aware of it." When Mitchell and his wife discovered a letter to their twenty-one-year-old son written by a man, who had in effect broken off their relationship, Mitchell "was in denial . . . looking for all kinds of rationale why [Jay] was into this." He reports that it "stayed in the back of our mind for a while, but we kind of pushed it out" because Jay had resumed what to his parents looked like a heterosexual social life after that point.

Peter reports that when he looks back, he did have a sense "that things [were] not 100 percent" with his son, Richard. His wife had found a letter addressed to another boy at the yeshiva he attended as a teenager, sending Peter into a state of confusion. Later on as a young man when Richard got engaged, it was easy to dismiss that letter as "a fluke, something that was of no importance." But to Peter, this engagement "was not a normal affair." Apparently, Richard would frequently talk about his fiance's male friends with some interest. After this engagement and a second one "went sour," Peter's confusion continued.

Pei recalls conversations in which his son would try to tell him that there was a "tremendous responsibility" in marrying and raising children, one which Chris did not feel he was up to. When he was surer of his homosexuality, Chris told his father that he was bisexual, thinking that this might be easier for him to accept: "he was hinting and hinting and hinting." But Pei steadfastly "refuse[d] to be taken down that line."

Both categories of fathers—those who consciously acknowledged the possibility of their sons' homosexuality prior to disclosure and those who did not, but who recollected clues when they looked back after disclosure—all had some degree of what DeVine (1984) calls *subliminal awareness* (pp. 11-13). The difference between these two groups is subtle but distinct. What binds them is the use of denial as the primary defense in coping with what they perceive as a threat: the possibility that their sons might be gay.

DISCLOSURE

This [is] something that I have to face . . . this is the reality.

Peter

Context

In looking at the context of the act of disclosure, Harry, Marty, Ronald, Glenn, Luis, and Juan Miguel Jr. all attribute their sons' declaration as solely precipitated by the internal processes in the sons themselves. They report no event or external trigger that might have led to the decision their sons made to come out to them at that moment in time. In other cases, whatever the sons were going through was compounded by family pressures in varying degrees of severity. In Mitchell's situation, that pressure was rather benign. Driving home after a movie one night, he suggested that Jay, a close female friend of Jay's, his wife, and himself might "double-date" sometime: "that remark . . . probably sent him over the edge and gave him the strength to come out to us." Pei's situation was a bit different. After an episode in which his son, Chris, brought an obviously gay man into his mother's art class, Pei and his wife discussed their worry that Chris might be gay. Pei spoke with his daughter about this, who then called Chris to register their father's concern. Chris in turn called his parents and came out to his mother. She in turn told Pei.

Sometimes pressures were less benign, more insistent. After Walter's son, James, stayed out until 5 a.m. one night, not the first time he came home past curfew during that particular period, both Walter and his wife jointly confronted him: "we said we're not getting up from here until we find out what's going on." James confessed. Other pressures were more obviously direct. Peter's wife, Sonia, asked their son, Richard, if he was gay after a series of clues she put together over several years—a letter he wrote to another boy when he was a teenager, two failed engagements, find-ing another young man in his apartment. Daniel's case was a special one. After revealing his own homosexuality to Charles, his then sixteen-year-old son responded reflexively, "I know. I am, too."

Who was told? Neal's son, Donald, represents one end of the continuum. He never disclosed his gayness to either parent. And Neal never asked. Neither did his wife when she was alive. It was "just an understanding" that existed among all of them. Ronald's son, Timothy, disclosed to his mother, who in turn told Ronald. However, father and son to this day have never talked openly about it. Telling their mothers first was also the option Peter's son, Luis's son, and Pei's son chose. The wives then told their husbands. Adam, Glenn's son, told his mother individually and then told his father. The reverse was also observed, although less often—sons telling their fathers first. Marty was informed by his son. Marty then told his wife. Although Daniel was informed first by his son, Charles, Daniel did not tell his ex-wife. Rather, Charles waited to tell his mother about a year later. Walter's son, Mitchell's son, and Juan Miguel Jr.'s son told their parents simultaneously. Finally, there was Harry's son, who only told his father. His mother had passed away years earlier.

How were they told? All of the sons chose to disclose verbally to their parent(s) except for Adam, who informed his father by way of a letter. Many of the fathers vividly remember their son's sincerity and/or anxiety at the moment of disclosure. For example, Harry recalls "a determined look on his [son's] face that indicated that he was very sincere and not pulling [his] leg." Marty "knew by [Gary's] tone that this [was] serious." Juan Miguel Jr. thought his son seemed worried. Peter's son, Richard, "explained to [him] that he . . . could live a life of lies and he could get married and have children and then still be a homosexual and make everybody unhappy." Mitchell says that Jay had his coming-out speech "rehearsed very well." Glenn recalls the "torturous . . . letter" that his son, Adam, sent to him, detailing his need to "take some risks" in life. The fathers saw these as grave matters for their sons.

Immediate Responses

Five of the fathers report shock. Marty describes it as "like somebody socked [him] in the chest." Harry claims he saw "no indication whatsoever of that forthcoming." It was sudden, unexpected. He could think of nothing except that: "everything else left my mind." Luis also did not expect his son to be gay, despite his "feminine type of attitude." Walter was "speechless." Peter admits to being "shocked and in disbelief . . . determined to find out more about this terrible thing that afflicted [his] family." His determination took the form of seeking a cure for his son. After a point, it was obvious that no cure was going to be found. He was told that this was something he was going to have to face: "this [was] the reality."

Three fathers were panic stricken. Pei's first concern was how he was going to "protect" his son from discrimination. Mitchell's initial anxieties were "about the health issue [i.e., AIDS] and about . . . physical safety." Walter was also "scared . . . to death" about AIDS as it was "the height of the epidemic" at the time his son came out at age seventeen.

Harry was quietly desperate. He "pleaded" with his son to "try to hold off and . . . try to change [his] lifestyle" in order to "give [the other] side a chance," arguing that only by "associating with others who were of the same belief . . . he was missing out on . . . the other type of life." In his shame, he also did not want to divulge this secret to others. Luis told his son that he was disappointed. Walter recalls his sadness as well as his disappointment—"I felt my heart sink"—combined with a sense of helplessness: "all of a sudden, I had no grasp, I had no understanding." The "script" that he had written for his son's future was being "torn up" before his eyes: "we didn't know our parts. We didn't know what words to say, we didn't know where we were to sit, where we were to stand . . . there was no direction."

Not all of the fathers, however, reported shock, panic, desperation, shame, sadness, disappointment, and/or a sense of helplessness. Ronald avoided all of it, claiming, "I don't think I paid much attention." Glenn acknowledges a sense of relief, glad that Adam was "something," thinking that it was more important that his son be a sexual person with less emphasis on what his sexuality actually was. Better this than a life of unhappiness and sexual repression, the state he felt Adam was in at the time. Juan Miguel Jr. reports dealing with it matter-of-factly. After his son went into his bedroom to tell him and his wife that he was gay, his only response was, "That's fine." He thinks his son was more worried than he himself was. Whether in fact these three fathers only reacted in those ways at this stage or whether other responses were blocked from awareness, we will never know. In addition to denial, other defenses such as isolation of affect or reaction formation could possibly be operative here as well.

Causation

In many cases, these initial reactions were followed by feelings of guilt and regret, usually dominated by a sense of abdication of the fathers' role, sometimes, but not always, culminating in self-blame for their sons' homosexuality. Two fathers think in retrospect that they exercised too little discipline. Marty, for example, wonders

if pushing his son "to be more athletic" might have made a difference. On a deeper level, he thinks that had he "been more a . . .
discipline-type father rather than so easygoing and letting things
slide sometimes," and "always want[ing] to be the good guy," needing his son as his "friend," perhaps that would have changed the
course of his son's sexuality.

Walter echoes Marty. Because of all the conflict he went through
growing up, Walter did not want his son to experience anything
similar. So he became "overly permissive, overly indulgent, too
laid-back in discipline," although he is unclear about how that could
have shaped the outcome of his son's gayness. All his vulnerabilities as a father then became exacerbated. He had ongoing discussions with his wife about "things [they] did and . . . didn't do" and
experienced tremendous feelings of guilt. For example, when they
became aware that their son's music teacher in junior high school
was paying special attention to him, Walter thinks now that perhaps
they should have intervened then; perhaps he should have inter-
acted with James on "a more emotional level"; perhaps his neglect
contributed to his son's sexuality, or so he thought. However, for
Walter, all of these worries are intimately tied to a larger issue—the
degree to which he feels capable of being a fathering presence. Not
being the father he "should have been" is a thought that haunts him;
less so, however, as time goes by.

On the opposite end of the spectrum was Peter, who feels that
perhaps the physical abuse he subjected his son to might have
contributed to his homosexuality. He was quick to blame himself:
"maybe I made terrible errors." Acknowledging that he "was not
[an] easy father" to live with, he thinks his background as a Holocaust survivor no doubt played a big part in the expectations he had
and the demands he made on his children.

More common, however, was a pervasive sense of neglect. Most
of the fathers reported that they were not present in their sons' lives
in ways they thought they should have been. Mitchell regrets that he
"wasn't aware of the pain of [Jay's] struggle" while he was growing
up: "the nights that he said he closed the door and went to sleep and
he was confused and crying and I was in the other room. I wasn't
there for him." Much of his guilt revolved around being "a nonprotecting father." Glenn acknowledges sending "mixed messages"

to his son, at times being emotionally accessible, at other times being completely self-absorbed. Ronald, too, admits being more concerned with satisfying his own needs and was much less concerned with the needs of his wife and three children. He played "a one-person gig." Admittedly, he made little room for anyone else, including his gay son, Timothy. This was particularly true after Ronald separated from his family. He wonders what Timothy would have been like had he been "a different father," one who was "there and open and listening."

Daniel never got fully engaged as a "family man" either, always wanting "to be somewhere else," always "on the edge," forever "a loner." Luis wishes that he had spent more time with his son earlier on so that they might have developed similar interests, resulting in more of a relationship now. Harry acknowledges that he "did not do as . . . good a job with [his] children as [he] should have." They were either cared for by a housekeeper or, when they got a bit older, were on their own for most of the day. Pei goes as far as to admit "psychological incest," turning to his son, Chris, for "psychological support" and "relying on him" in ways that he thinks he should have relied on his wife.

Let me emphasize here that even though some of the fathers may have felt they were abusive and/or neglectful, it did not mean that they all considered themselves necessarily the cause of their sons' homosexuality. This was only obvious in the cases of Marty, Mitchell, Peter, Ronald, and Walter. But Harry, Luis, Daniel, Glenn, and Pei only say that their actions caused a rift between themselves and their sons for which they were remorseful and guilty. They did not go the next step and say that their actions were necessarily causative.

To summarize all of this, a range of factors was offered for causation. Ten of the fathers now consider the role of genetics as primary in the formation of their sons' sexuality, although they did not all arrive at that in the same way. Marty, Mitchell, Peter, and Walter initially blamed themselves and only later considered genetic factors as key. Others—Juan Miguel Jr., Luis, Daniel, Neal, and Pei—report always considering genetics to be primary. Ronald gives weight to his own absence, the role of genetics, and the rivalry between his son and his daughter. Harry blames it on his son's association with other gay people. Both Peter and Glenn thought their wives could have been partially responsible. Glenn is convinced that his first wife's dependency on their son was formative, saying, "She would literally carry him around with her everywhere. She wouldn't . . . detach from him. I didn't think anything of it when he was an infant, but I do blame her." He feels that she was seductive toward their son as well.

Prior to interviewing the fathers, I anticipated that this event would have been considered a crisis by most if not by all of them. This was not the case, however. Luis even objected to my use of the term, saying, "I never [said] it was a crisis." Only Walter and Peter seem to describe their responses to their sons' disclosure in that way. For both men, a sense of helplessness and confusion ensued (Rapoport, 1965), creating almost a suspension of reality marked in their cases by obsessive preoccupations with self-blame. Although both had become subliminally aware of clues about their sons' homosexuality over time, when confronted with the truth, each of them seemed to fall apart, albeit temporarily. Clearly both went through "a period of disequilibrium" (Parad and Caplan, 1965, p. 56) in which they were pressured to find alternative solutions to problems which seemed "insoluble" (p. 66) at the time.

IMPACT

I want to be in the . . . room with the light with him.

Walter

In examining the impact of the disclosure and the unfolding of the processes connected to it, I will look at the fathers' perceptions of their sons past and present and any changes they see in them since, any changes that have taken place in the father/son relationship, and any changes the fathers now see in themselves.

Son As Feminine

In describing their sons, nine of the fathers see them as being partially identified with the feminine in different ways. For example, Harry remembers that when his son was perhaps two or three years old a friend visited, bringing dolls for Harry's three daughters and a fire truck for his son. Harry Jr. did not like this particular distribution and wanted to trade his truck for a doll. Father thought this "a bit unusual." His children frequently entertained, putting on skits for the guests or just for themselves. During those times, Harry Jr. would be inclined to "dress up as a girl so that there would be four girls instead of three and one." In nursery school, Mitchell's son, Jay, played exclusively with girls "in the doll's corner" and was never interested in anything athletic. Walter observes that his son, James, "had . . . a tendency to gravitate toward girls in social situations," which, in retrospect, he realizes now is "pretty typical of gay men." When he was growing up, most of James' friends were female. He also "had a tremendous interest in Dolly Parton and . . . Madonna" in junior high and high school, something that both intrigued and confused Walter, keeping him wondering if his son was gay or straight. Also, James was never interested in anything remotely athletic. At one point Walter put up a basketball hoop, hoping to find some common ground between them, but this was not to be: "he probably shot five baskets. That was it." Ronald recalls that when Timothy was a toddler, he used to take his Doctor Denton pajama bottoms and place them over his head, pretending that "he had long, beautiful hair" like his sister, whose attention from others he envied. "I think [Timothy] would like to have been a girl," he concludes. Perhaps the most dramatic example of a father who obviously identifies homosexuality with femininity comes from Neal. He never discussed Donald's homosexuality with him because he thought it did not seem like the right thing to do: "like ask him why . . . don't you have the . . . organs of a girl?"

Two of the fathers see their sons as more resembling their mothers in physical appearance. Peter observes that his son, Richard, "looks more like my wife." Glenn notes that most of the men in his family are "big"—himself, his younger son, his wife's father and brother. But his gay son, Adam, "is a small man," those genes coming from his wife's mother's side of the family. Two other fathers see their sons resembling their mothers in temperament. Pei observes that his son, Chris, is closer to his wife than to him in their mutual need to be liked by others and their more feeling-centered approach to life. Ronald views his son, Timothy, and his ex-wife as "carbon copies" of each other and everything that he himself is not. Both mother and son want to be "rich and famous"; both are impractical, emotionally expressive, health conscious, and "night people."

Four of the fathers feel that their sons have historically been emotionally more connected to their mothers. Mitchell's son, Jay, was more obviously at ease with females right from the start. Mother and son were at home together during those early years. Both loved music. She is a musician and Jay began "poking at the keys" early on. Luis acknowledges that his son, Michael, has spent more time with his mother than with him. Mother and son go to art galleries and museums, things that Luis is not much interested in. She has also encouraged Michael to read and to develop the creative and intellectual sides of himself. Ronald said that during his marriage and after, he depended on his now ex-wife to maintain "the connection with the children." He got all of the information about them through her. Glenn observes that during holiday time, his son, Adam, only invites his mother (Glenn's ex-wife) to family get-togethers. He is conspicuously left out.

Son As Special

Along different lines, all of the fathers tend to describe their sons in idealistic terms. Ten of them spontaneously speak about their high intelligence either in the academic arena, in their idiosyncratic knowledge of a particular subject, or in their common sense. Marty, for example, says that Gary "was terrific in school . . . always got into the best classes, always had the best marks, always read from the time he was three years old." Similarly, Mitchell relates that his son, Jay, "was an unbelievably early reader." Apparently from "the age of three, he was reading the [newspaper]," not understanding what he was reading necessarily, but "sounding out all the words," nevertheless. Jay used to practice this skill using the record jacket of *The Wizard of Oz*. Glenn characterizes his son, Adam, as "very, very bright" and "was convinced that he was a genius all along." Pei says that when Chris was in elementary school, tests showed that "he had [a] tremendous IQ," and he was placed in the gifted class. As a young adult, his performance in college was equally impressive.

Daniel also considers his son, Charles, "a brilliant student." Neal thinks that Donald "was much brighter than the average child." According to Ronald, Timothy "came through high school without even hardly opening a book and made straight A's." Luis's son, Michael, while not "an A student," is "very, very bright in other areas" including a broad knowledge of ancient coins and antiques. While not particularly academic either, Peter thinks that Richard is "a very smart man" in the way he handles his gayness, neither flaunting nor denying it. Juan Miguel Jr. considers his son "very smart" in his understanding of the dynamics of prejudice.

Nine of the fathers highlight their sons' creative and artistic endeavors, several of them doing so in idealistic ways as well. Juan Miguel Jr. describes his son as a kind of renaissance man who plays the piano and the organ, has composed a number of piano pieces, writes poetry, and knows a number of different languages. "I'm very proud of him, very proud of him," he says. Mitchell's son, Jay, has always been "a showman." His habit of walking on his toes as a young boy, always "a show-stopper," prepared the way for what was to come. Mitchell boasts of his son's many talents: "he has a voice like an angel, he acts wonderfully, and . . . he can move." Mitchell reports unashamedly, "I cry every time I see him. I take such delight in his talent. He's a wonderfully talented person." Walter's son, James, studied music and played the viola in the school orchestra.

From the beginning it was clear that Luis's son, Michael, was interested in music and dance. The song "Flashdance" took him by storm as a young boy. As a teenager, he has branched out into different forms of creative expression, mostly writing and painting. He also has an interest in antiques. "I'm a proud, proud father," Luis says. Glenn's son, Adam, has a degree in fine arts; Pei's son, Chris, is an art broker; and Ronald's son, Timothy, is pursuing a career in modeling. Harry's son is striving to be a commercial artist. Although he feels sorry that his son has not been quite able "to make a go of it" in the commercial art world, he admires his willingness to keep working at it. Neal boasts that his son, Donald, in addition to being an amateur pianist, has vast knowledge about various art forms: "he knows everything about early music, late music, the names of people that collected music" and "seems to know all about art," concluding that "he's an amazing person."

In contrast, the fathers' own involvement in this area was less prominent, although Neal is a violinist, Glenn a pianist, and Daniel a writer. Marty spent the better part of his career in theater advertising and Luis is a chef by profession, all creative endeavors. On the whole, though, creative/artistic expression appears to be more central in the lives of the sons than in the lives of the fathers.

Besides intelligence and creative/artistic talents, five of the fathers describe the physical appearance of their sons in idealistic terms, also. Mitchell says that when Jay was born, "he was absolutely beautiful." Ronald says that Timothy "was just a gorgeous baby and a gorgeous kid." Harry boasts of his son's "magnificent physique." Peter also thinks that his son, Richard, was a "very pretty child." Apparently he was good-looking enough to receive a prize for his picture when he was about three years old. Neal's son, Donald, was also a child model.

Nine fathers consider the characters of their sons unsurpassed. Mitchell describes Jay as always having had a social way with the girls, who apparently all wanted him, requiring that he beat them off "with sticks." Mitchell claims that he would not want to change anything about his son because "he's great the way he is." Marty talks about Gary as "the good son, wonderful son. . . . He was a terrific child . . . a wonderful man." Luis describes Michael as "a wonderful person, terrific human being . . . if you know him better, you know how . . . kind and how nice he is." Walter also considers his son, James, "gentle and kind" and overall "a wonderful person." Daniel describes Charles as "always confident, successful, very easy kid to . . . raise . . . always was the . . . one who people . . . loved and wanted to have as friends." He admires his son's sense of activism, his determination, and his overall sense of engagement with life, qualities that Daniel feels he himself lacks. He also says that Charles is considerate of his family: "he's a nice person." Peter thinks Richard is "very able and very nice." Neal considers his son, Donald, very well-rounded and "ideal." Glenn thinks of Adam as the "perfect" child and a "fabulous" adult. Pei sees his son, Chris, as "just a very warm, sensitive human being [who] very few people dislike," someone who is "incapable of doing things that inflict pain on other people." Pei says that Chris has been a kind of teacher to him, one who has shown him the value of helping and the value of struggle.

Six of the fathers have observed that since coming out, their sons seem better adjusted. For example, Glenn notes that Adam has "a very full and . . . joyful life" and that "things are going just splendidly." Peter says that his son, Richard, has gone from being "quite disorganized and sloppy and lazy" to "a very calculated and organized person," and is amazed at the difference in him. Walter is grateful that his son, James, "is so committed to having a relationship." Neal thinks that Donald has adjusted wonderfully to his gayness. He has been living with another man for the last fifteen years, they have a home together, and they have adopted a child. Luis thinks that Michael "feels better about himself." Perhaps most dramatic was Pei. He describes his son, Chris, as a kid with a "funny haircut," who would wear "atrocious . . . clothing," who was constantly telling the world to "stick it," and who has now transformed into "just a conservative guy," one who remains "very strongly connected to the world." Pei feels that his son is now "a complete person."

Son As Vulnerable

In contrast to the fathers' idealistic perceptions of their sons was a sense of them as extremely vulnerable. Seven of them had ongoing concerns about possible physical harm and discrimination that their sons might be subjected to as a result of being gay. After Jay came out, Mitchell recalls that AIDS and physical safety were uppermost in his mind. About the latter, he says, "I've heard of so many cases of kids getting gay-bashed and ending up in the emergency room [at] three in the morning." Walter remembers that "worry about AIDS" surfaced quickly when his son told him about his homosexuality. Peter, too, admits being gravely concerned about AIDS and about bias: "there is so much ignorance in this world." As a volunteer, Pei has worked with AIDS patients and has "seen the horror of it." Harry recalls an incident when his son and a "buddy" were attacked in Greenwich Village by a couple of kids and "took a beating." Harry Jr. suffered some minor facial damage. Although Harry acknowledges that his son now "takes good care of himself," he still thinks that another attack could occur. Juan Miguel Jr. has worries about his son not being able to find work because of discrimination. In Puerto Rico if it is known that someone is gay, that person may be more prone to harassment and getting fired. He compares this to the discrimination he himself might experience applying for a job as an elderly person. He thinks that the employer would look for another reason not to give him the job: "it's like age—gay and age, the same." Neal also observes that if you are gay, "life becomes a little more difficult." As a Jew, he understands this fact of life firsthand.

Fathers and Sons Now

About the current relationships with their sons, ten of the fathers—Marty, Mitchell, Peter, Daniel, Walter, Luis, Neal, Ronald, Juan Miguel Jr., and Pei—say that their relationships with their sons may be the best they have ever been in their lives, at least in their adult lives. Examples of this abound. Daniel began to reconnect more with Charles after his son revealed his homosexuality at age sixteen, acting as a kind of advisor, mediator, and mentor for him. Daniel feels good that he could serve as a role model for his son, helping him to see "that someone could lead a gay life and be at least modestly happy." Now he and Charles are "just very close friends." He rejoices in Charles, saying, "He's like a . . . trophy." Peter says that he loves his son now "more than ever." Neal acknowledges that he and Donald "love each other very much. . . . he has a lot of respect for me [and] I have a lot of respect for him." Mitchell says that he and Jay "are closer than we've ever been."

The types of support the fathers sought both formally and informally obviously helped to improve their relationships. In the cases of Marty, Luis, Peter, Mitchell, Pei, Walter, and Glenn, husband and wife turned to each other. This seemed effective not only emotionally, but also as a vehicle for sharing information about homosexuality. In addition, Walter turned to books to help him understand, resulting in his feeling less helpless and more in control.

Although Ronald did not seek therapy to help him deal specifically with his son's gayness, nevertheless, he reports that those experiences were crucial in assisting him to become aware of and express the hurt and anger of his childhood which so much affected the relationships that followed. But while he is closer to his children at this point, he still finds it difficult to really give of himself to

Timothy or to anyone. However, he now takes more of an interest in what his son is doing, particularly the ways in which Timothy is designing his apartment. He also enjoys the company of his son's boyfriend—Harry's son—when the two come for a visit. Ronald feels good that he tries to find some common ground between himself, Timothy, and his other children.

Seven of the fathers—Marty, Luis, Peter, Mitchell, Pei, Walter, and Juan Miguel Jr.—sought help from Parents and Friends of Lesbians and Gays (P-FLAG). With the exception of Juan Miguel Jr., who has only been marginally involved, the other six are mostly active in the organization. Walter's participation is more inconsistent. Of the seven who enlisted help through P-FLAG, six fathers attended a meeting sometime during the first year and a half after they learned of their sons' homosexuality. Marty attended as early as a month after his son, Gary, disclosed. Mitchell was the exception. He claimed that since his wife was not ready to come out as a parent, they did not really begin to deal with the issue until seven years after their son's disclosure. Additionally, three of those actively involved with P-FLAG are also members of a subgroup, New Jewish Voices. Daniel, Neal, Ronald, Glenn, and Harry have never attended any parent group.

Juan Miguel Jr. says that although he has always felt close with his gay son, now more than ever because of an understanding of "what he's going through" with his homosexuality, more recently he has had a sense of having failed him. He would like to leave his children an inheritance, but he has nothing substantial to offer. He is still working, despite his ill health. His son has no real money either, making a living doing "very basic clerical work." Juan Miguel Jr. told him that he would try to find him other work, but he has so far "failed to do" that. At thirty-three years old, his son still lives at home—no companion, no apartment, and no job that uses his creative and intellectual talents. Juan Miguel Jr. worries about what will become of his son after he dies.

Four of the fathers report that their sons' homosexuality made no long-term difference in their own lives either positively or negatively. Glenn says that even though Adam's coming out initially provided a boost to their relationship after so many conflict-ridden years, an element of estrangement still exists between them. Glenn feels that this has more to do with himself than with his son. In the early years of his marriage and career, he "was too much into [him]self" to develop a relationship with Adam or with anyone. Although he "would like to be closer," it is not meant to be—not now anyway. Glenn points to a historical schism that is characteristic of most father-son relationships, wishing for the same "rapprochement" he had with his own father in the later years of the older man's life. He feels that for himself, his son's homosexuality is "a nonissue."

In some ways, Harry seems to be in a class by himself. While he acknowledges his son's homosexuality, nevertheless, he refers to it and to gay people in ways such as "lifestyle," "his making such a move," "that way of life," "that style," "his liking," "going one way," "this liking toward the male sex," "others who were of the same belief," "that crowd." He only used the word *gay* in the context of what his son said to him when he came out. He says that he still hopes and prays that his son will "marry and have children" someday and that Harry Jr. would be a fine father. A residue of denial still lingers. Although Harry acknowledges that he loves his son, their relationship "has not been as strong as it had been in years gone by." He feels that his son is unappreciative, "has the answer for all cases," and "must have his own way at all times." Like Glenn, Harry hopes for a better relationship in the future.

Neal reports that his son's gayness "hasn't affected [him] at all actually." Ronald "can't find anything good, bad, or indifferent about" his son's gayness. "It's just the way it is," something that he can intellectually understand, but cannot relate to emotionally. "I don't know what it feels like to be gay," he says. Although he is aware that it probably has had some effect on him, as it is "another ingredient" in his experience in life, he is hard-pressed to pinpoint exactly what that effect could possibly be. It should be observed here that these last four fathers—Glenn, Harry, Neal, and Ronald—those who claim to have been the least emotionally affected by their sons' homosexuality, are also the ones who have never sought any formal supports such as P-FLAG.

Most of the fathers, however, not only experienced a changed relationship with their sons, but also now see themselves as changed parents and changed human beings as a result of their sons' disclosure. These changes took many forms, all resulting in a more expansive self. Peter says it this way: "from a militant homophob[e], I became an understanding and compassionate person not only to my son but to the . . . community." Because he grew up in a persecutory environment, Peter does not wish to replicate that any longer. He hopes that involvement in this study and with his parent support groups can contribute to a lessening of "ignorance." Similarly, Luis now feels a greater compassion. On his job, he will challenge others who ridicule gay people, whereas before he would just "go along with the guys." His son has taught him something about tolerance of others' difference. Juan Miguel Jr. also says that he is more inclined to challenge prejudice and now has "stronger feelings [about] helping gays." Although Mitchell waited seven years after his son came out to really begin his "journey," he and his wife now have new lives: "we see things . . . we didn't see before; we hear things we didn't hear before; we sense things we didn't sense before." Although very vocal about his own absence earlier in life, Mitchell now feels that he has assumed the role of "father-protector," a role that he had abdicated. Through a process of graduated steps, Mitchell feels he is now "there" for his son in a way he has never been. His son's coming out presented an opportunity to recast their relationship, resulting in a sense of rebirth.

Walter now says that he is "really comfortable with the fact that [James is] gay." But this has not always been the case. He struggled long and hard: "the introspection and the questioning we [he and his wife] went through, the dialogues we had—couldn't we have done this, shouldn't we have done that, and tremendous feelings of guilt over things we did and we didn't do." After much soul-searching, Walter has arrived. He says that any guilt he suffers now has more to do with his questions about his competency as a parent than about his contributions to his son's homosexuality. The ultimate test came when, as a teacher, he proposed a course in gay and lesbian history at his school against the advice of his wife and his colleagues. After his proposal was accepted, he had some initial concerns about what to call the course and the possible ramifications of being associated with it. Despite this, Walter feels that he made the right decision in going ahead with it, now helping others to come out in a way he could not do for his son. Those others are now "open . . . accessible" to him in ways that he never would have dreamed possible. The world is now "a brighter place." He has changed. In weighing who to tell about his son's gayness and when to tell them, concern about other's reactions, and "accidentally out-ing" colleagues and students, Walter is clear that his own coming out as a parent was parallel in some ways to the one his son had to go through, an idea that Mitchell echoes as well.

Marty feels that he is now more flexible as a person. He says that his son's coming out "was a big adjustment," continuing, "if you can make that adjustment, you can make a lot of other adjustments." Pei says, "Coming out to me is a never-ending process." In that process, he has been able to find a capacity for tolerance he did not know he had. Through the example of his son, Chris, he has learned to withstand pain and suffering, seeing them as part of the panorama of life. He now has no need to run. He is safe from himself. Chris has inspired him to just be "satisfied with little victories." He rejoices in those victories.

Chapter 6

Discussion

I would know my shadow and my light,
so shall I at last be whole.

Michael Tippett
A Child of Our Time

In this qualitative study, using a grounded theory approach with accompanying narratives, I document the multiple reactions of twelve fathers in their coming to terms with their sons' homosexuality. In this chapter, I will conceptualize the data, placing the findings in a theoretical context, with an emphasis on developmental considerations mostly drawn from an ego psychological perspective. The limitations of the study, the implications for future research, some implications for practice, and a personal note bring all of this to its conclusion.

ACKNOWLEDGMENT/ACCEPTANCE

Acknowledgment and acceptance of a child's homosexuality represent two points on a wide continuum. Ben-Ari (1995b) differentiates between them. She says that the former is merely "recognition of a fact"; the latter "includes an affective component" (p. 107). It is possible to acknowledge without accepting; it is not possible to accept without acknowledging. Of the twelve fathers, Harry appears to be the only one who just acknowledges his son's homosexuality, hoping and praying that a change to heterosexuality is still possible for him.

Acceptance is an ambiguous concept, not an easy one to define or measure. Griffin, Wirth, and Wirth (1986) remind us that acceptance is an ongoing, dynamic process characterized by three progressive *levels of understanding* (pp. 138-154). These levels begin with parents' concerns about themselves as they attempt to ease their own inner conflicts. As those abate, they become more available to then focus on the concerns of their gay or lesbian children. Finally, universal concerns about all parents and all gay children together ultimately prepare the way for full acceptance.

Acceptance is not a one-dimensional concept either. It has different tints and shades. The fathers in my study seem to fall into three distinct categories. The first is what I call *resigned acceptance.* Marty describes this best with his own advice: "if you can't lick 'em, join 'em." Luis says, "I understand and I accept my son because he's my son," acknowledging, "I'm not happy." Peter is "not happy" either, but counters with the fact that his son *is,* "so this counts a lot toward the compromise," meaning that Richard's happiness helps him to reconcile and accept his homosexuality in a way he might not be able to do otherwise. Neal, Glenn, Juan Miguel Jr., and Ronald have a "that's the way it is" philosophy. There is nothing they feel they can change about their situation. They, too, are resigned. A second, less usual type I call *narcissistic acceptance,* one based on the son filling a narcissistic need and being a narcissistic extension of the parent. Only Daniel represents this. As a gay man with a gay son, Daniel describes Charles as his "trophy." The third type I call *unconditional acceptance,* which is represented by Mitchell, Walter, and Pei. Mitchell describes this best when he says that his son is "great the way he is."

My impression is that most of these fathers, whether they accept resignedly or unconditionally, are trying to defend against collective shock and disappointment by doing whatever they can to accept "the reality of change" (Neugarten and Gutmann, 1968, p. 62), perhaps at the cost of denying their own strong feelings about it and, at the same time, trying "to find new bases for intimacy in the new situation" (p. 62). They knew they were up against forces with which they could not compete and felt they had no other choice but to either accept their sons or lose them. Fear of being abandoned, as many of them had been earlier in their lives by their own caretakers, and the narcissistic vulnerability that results from that fear were movingly voiced by Walter: "I hope that he feels . . . that with my acceptance . . . I'm with him. He hasn't left me behind."

In looking at some of the external factors that seem to have facilitated acceptance, the fathers' exposure to gay people prior to their sons' disclosure was important, a conclusion drawn by Griffin, Wirth, and Wirth (1986) as well. For example, Marty estimates that during his career in theater advertising, 90 percent of his assistants were gay men. As a doctor in laboratory medicine, Glenn also worked with gay people. Juan Miguel Jr. knew young gay men in his town, a roommate in school, a first cousin, an uncle of his wife, and another father who has two gay sons.

Exposure to gay people and to other parents with gay children after disclosure helped Mitchell, Luis, Peter, Marty, and Pei. The seven fathers who are involved with P-FLAG—the five just mentioned as well as Walter and Juan Miguel Jr.—clearly have the most open relationships with their sons. (The only exception is Daniel, who himself is gay.) Harry, the father who just acknowledges, claims that he knows no other gay or lesbian people or parents struggling with this. He also has strong religious convictions. Those two variables—lack of exposure to others affected by homosexuality and adherence to religious beliefs—separately and in combination, might work against acceptance, although I cannot substantiate this further with more evidence from any of the other fathers. In looking at some of the intrapsychic dynamics that came to the fore, identification, idealization, and internalization are key in helping the fathers move toward a more accepting stance. They also serve as unifying themes throughout the rest of the chapter.

IDENTIFICATION

In summarizing the history of the concept of identification, Bronfenbrenner (1960) observes that Freud's use of this term continuously changed over the years—as did many of his other clinical ideas—referring to it as both process and product. First used explicitly in "Mourning and Melancholia" (1917/1959), Freud later defines identification in *Group Psychology and the Analysis of the Ego* "as the earliest expression of an emotional tie with another person" (1921/

1971, p. 46), making it central in the resolution of the Oedipus complex. Simply stated, since the boy cannot *be* the father, he assumes the position of being *like* him, taking his father "as a model" (p. 47). In this context, identification has an ambivalent quality—love tinged with hostility.

Freud also indicates that identification "may arise with any new perception of a common quality shared with some other person" (1921/1971, p. 49). Attitudes, feelings, values, and characteristics of another who is "loved, admired, feared, or hated" (Goldstein, 1995, p. 79) can all provide a basis. While Freud's other writings (1923/1962, 1924/1959, 1927/1959, 1928/1959) mostly emphasize the boy's identification with his father, there is a passage from "On Narcissism" (1914/1959) in which he speculates that the reverse might also be true, that there is an identification of the father with his son. About this, Freud writes: "[t]hat which he [the father] projects ahead of him as his ideal is merely his substitute for the lost narcissism of his childhood—the time when he was his own ideal" (p. 51). The child representing the parent's idealized past self stands juxtaposed with the child representing the parent's hope for the self-to-be. The theme of mutual identifications is also one taken up by ego psychology, notably by Benedek (1959) and Jacobson (1964). What is it that these fathers seem to identify with in their gay sons?

Many of the fathers have encountered and overcome tremendous obstacles over the course of their lives. Although dealing with their sons' sexuality has been a unique challenge, it did not seem to be the most difficult one they have had to face. Loss and abandonment, danger and adversity were some of the predominant themes in their stories. Many struggled early on to deal with the presence or absence of their own caretakers—mothers, biological and stepfathers, grandparents. Many of them lived through difficult, sometimes tragic, beginnings. How they took care of themselves, survived, even thrived despite adversity seems critical to our understanding of these men and how they have faced crises. Three of them—Peter, Luis, and Pei—were immigrants to this country. Their struggle to accommodate themselves to a different set of values, one that includes a more open attitude toward homosexuality, was and continues to be a challenge. Several struggled in their work—finding what interested them, or having to involve themselves in further academic training, and/or putting in long hours on the job to support their families. Many of them were witness first-hand to the hardships of the Depression, and this was certainly operative in shaping their everyday work lives. More recently, retirement has presented its own set of difficulties for many of them after long years of productivity. The struggle to deal with marital conflicts, other family-related crises, and questions about their own identities were also evident.

Highlighted was the struggle over how to parent and not feeling good enough as a father. Too much or too little discipline and lack of involvement with their sons early on were regrets that were voiced over and over again. Tied to this was the struggle to connect with a son who may have appeared different in certain ways earlier in life, as well as the struggle to accept his homosexuality. For many, what resulted from some combination of these factors was a sense of distance from their sons.

Their acknowledged preoccupation with their own individual struggles earlier in their lives left little room for discovery of who their sons were. They were too busy finding out who they *themselves* were. Although self-preoccupation lessened their physical and emotional availability, the experience of struggle also seemed to have resulted in an identification with their sons in their struggles. Like themselves, the fathers see their sons challenged in many ways: deciding whether to go to college or finish it; securing work that is creatively satisfying; finding a love relationship; earning enough money to live on; protecting themselves from attack and discrimination; and/or a combination of any of these. Without exception, these fathers see their sons' gayness as placing those younger men in an extremely vulnerable position. A powerful need to protect them came through in ways that the fathers felt they themselves were not protected. The process of uncovering who their son actually is creates opportunities for the fathers to see more clearly those parts of the son that are like or unlike those parts of themselves. In so doing, a real relationship is born.

Further, because their sons are gay, the fathers now become parents of a gay child, a shared stigma or, as Goffman (1986) refers to it, a *courtesy stigma* (pp. 30-31) or *stigma by association* (Neuberg et al., 1994).

Whatever one calls it, this becomes another point of identification between father and son. The parallel process of coming out as gay and coming out as a parent of a gay or lesbian child is an idea well-documented in the literature (Aarons, 1995; Baker, 1998; Bernstein, 1995; Borhek, 1979, 1988, 1993; Dew, 1995; Fairchild and Hayward, 1989; Fricke and Fricke, 1991; Griffin, Wirth, and Wirth, 1986; Shyer and Shyer, 1997).

IDEALIZATION

"The overvaluing of another person . . . beyond what is realistic" (Goldstein, 1995, p. 82), or *idealization,* can facilitate identification. As I reported in Chapter 5, the fathers idealized their sons along a number of different lines—intelligence, creative/artistic talents, physical appearance, and character. Freud (1920a/1961) writes that a tension exists between the unrestricted pursuit of pleasure versus the maintenance of its repression in the service of achieving higher aims. Developing this idea, Manninen (1992) observes that "the search for . . . paradise lost" (p. 2) or the total and complete unity with the mother invariably involves a relinquishment. The tension between "the fantasy of phallic supremacy" (p. 4) and the illusion of magical powers which this brings exists side by side "with the ideals of genitality" (p. 8) or "the oedipal reality" (p. 25), that is, acknowledgment of one's limitations and the rewards that *this* brings. Efforts around trying to resolve this tension take "the rest of our lives" (p. 2). Might their gay sons as both idealized and imperfect objects embody the fathers' quest for that state of bliss and merger, an attempt to recapture "fusional love" (Diamond, 1986, p. 455) on one hand—the "lost narcissism of his childhood" (Freud, 1914/1959, p. 51)—and the confrontation and recognition of their own limitations, i.e., reality, on the other? Might they be trying to have with their gay sons what most of them did not have with their own fathers? How might identification and idealization link up and coexist with other larger developmental issues?

INTERNALIZATION

In *The Seasons of a Man's Life,* an examination of the lives of forty men all between the ages of thirty-five and forty-five, Levinson and his colleagues (1978) ambitiously attempt to find an analogue in adulthood akin to the developmental sequencing of childhood and adolescence. What they found in their study was that the *individual life structure* (p. 317) evolves through an alternating series of "stable, structure-building" and "transitional, structure-changing" periods. The tasks of the former relate to creating stability and usually last from six to eight years; the tasks of the latter relate to reevaluating what already exists and usually last from four to five years. These tasks are all connected to aspects of love and work. Biological, psychological, and social components are all considered equal in importance. Although they were studying men entering midlife, some of the issues they delineate have relevance for the older man as well.

Their conceptual framework takes Erikson's (1963) ideas as a starting point. His *eight ages of man* (pp. 247-274) are built on the notion of opposing forces within the person and how these get resolved vis-à-vis the external world, ideally resulting in a sense of well-being. The notion of a life structure (Levinson et al., 1978, p. 317) incorporates these, but gives equal weight to the external forces as well. Self and world are one: "[t]he self is in the world, [t]he world is in the self" (pp. 46-49). The metaphor of seasons is used to connote the idea that there are unique qualities of each phase of the life cycle as well as to highlight the inevitable comings and goings. Each season plays its part in the whole of life; each as important as the one that precedes it and the one that follows it; each "linking past and future and containing both within itself" (p. 7). During those "transitional, structure-changing" (p. 317) periods, times when one is reevaluating who one is and what one wants and needs, Levinson and his co-workers note that a number of different polarities surface simultaneously. I will begin with what they call the *masculine/feminine.*

From Masculinity to Femininity

In the course of his discussion of the developmental process, Jung (1933) observes that as a man moves through "life's noon" (p. 107), a gradual and imperceptible physical and psychic revolution begins to occur in him—"a reversal into the opposite" (p. 107)—incorporation of the feminine in himself. In looking at what has traditionally been considered masculine and feminine, Levinson and colleagues (1978) observe that central masculine qualities have to do with activity—*doing, making, having* (p. 233), that is, establishing one's place in the outside world vis-à-vis competition with others. Diametrically opposed are those feminine qualities that have to do with passivity—softness, dependency, feeling. Transitional periods afford the opportunity to further integrate the feminine with the masculine. In this way, a sense of wholeness is achieved. Both the psychoanalytically oriented literature and the empirical literature (Neugarten and Gutmann, 1968) support the notion that as a man ages, he becomes less defended against and more receptive to the feminine part of himself, his *anima* (Jung, 1956, 1964), a part that may have been split off and out of his psychological reach earlier in life.

Important in the fathers' descriptions of their sons was seeing them as being connected with the feminine. This took many forms: cross-dressing; doll play; greater social comfort with females; resembling their mothers both in physical appearance and temperament as well as being emotionally closer with them. In associating his gay son with the feminine, my hypothesis is that through the act of acceptance, the father is internalizing or "taking in" (Goldstein, 1995, p. 80) the feminine part of his son, making it his own. That part, which may have gone underdeveloped in the father, he now needs in order to feel whole and complete his own development, simultaneously furthering a sense of identification with his son.

From Destruction to Creation

Alongside the masculine/feminine polarity is its sister, *destruction/creation* (Levinson et al., 1978). The task here is to understand the place that destruction has had in terms of its effects on relationships both with others and with oneself. Drawing on a greater capacity for introspection and self-knowledge, a man must seek to reflect on how, through his rage and hatred, he has damaged others and in turn been damaged by them, coming face to face "with his grievances and guilts" (p. 224), clearing the way for the creation of relationships that are deeper in meaning and richer in fulfillment. Power, heretofore used to destroy, can now be exercised with compassion to create. Increased awareness of one's uniqueness as well as one's finiteness (Gould, 1978; Neugarten, 1968b) facilitates this process.

In addition to admiring the creative/artistic gifts of their sons, most of the fathers exude a respect for the struggles their boys have had to endure in order to come out and shape their own identities. Glenn expresses this idea best. He had always told his son, Adam, that it was important "to take some risks" in life. He had no idea that Adam was going to translate those words into maintaining the importance and the necessity of living his life as a gay man. Glenn says of Adam: "his willingness and his ability to come out of the very restrictive culture he was brought up in into a gay world and embrace it was very liberating for him." Like the feminine part, the process of accepting a gay son becomes a vehicle through which the father internalizes the creative part of his son, finally making it the father's own.

FROM SEPARATENESS TO ATTACHMENT

As a man ages, he begins to move away from his role solely as provider. In so doing, he may become less authoritative and directive (Bozett, 1985). "[A] lessening of the parental imperative" (Cohler and Boxer, 1984, p. 178) makes room for other "[p]reviously suppressed communalistic and narcissistic needs," opening up an increased capacity for relationship with self and other. In their study of transitions over the life cycle, Lowenthal, Thurnher, and Chiriboga (1975) found that the men in the preretirement stage, whose mean age was sixty-one—close to the mean age of the fathers in my study—describe themselves as less controlling and less driven than their younger counterparts, coupled with a greater emphasis on their need for close interpersonal relationships, concurrently experiencing a greater comfort with other people and with themselves. This desire for greater relatedness, also a factor in the fathers' acceptance of their sons and their sexuality, ties in to Erikson's (1963) concept of *generativity*, defined as both an "investment in the future through one's children and creative achievements" (Bozett, 1985, p. 48) as well as "the concern in establishing and guiding the next genera- tion" (Erikson, 1963, p. 267). As Datan and Thomas (1984) ob- serve, later adulthood is characterized by "an enlarged personal vision no longer focused upon the self . . . but upon the species and its well-being" (p. 210). Peck (1968) terms this *ego transcendence.* A gradual shift away from the need for power (Gould, 1978) toward a position of greater influence (Sheehy, 1998), greater sensuality and affiliation (Zube, 1982), and greater nurturance and introspec- tion (Neugarten, 1968a) are all central motives in the development of the adult male.

The polarity of *attachment/separateness* (Levinson et al., 1978) invariably involves a balancing act between one's obligation to oneself and one's obligation to family and society. If one can suc- cessfully move beyond the needs of the self, there is more of a chance that one can be more responsive to the needs of the other. With less focus on acquiring specific skills and knowledge with which he can compete in the world, a man can now focus on fostering relationships both inside and outside of his family. In so doing, "[h]e can be more loving, sensual, authoritative, intimate, solitary—more attached and more separate" (p. 243). The older father then may be the better father (Peskin and Livson, 1981). In asking the fathers why they decided to participate in this study, the answer I invariably received had to do with making contributions to the gay movement. Involvement in P-FLAG clearly served this function for some as well.

With a diminishing of pressures to succeed in the world outside come compensatory needs to nurture. The pervasively vague sense of their boys earlier in life was not only because of the fact that the fathers themselves remained unavailable. The sons, too, were elu- sive for reasons of their own. In addition to finding a missing piece of their sons' puzzle—homosexuality—the developmental thrust toward new levels of relatedness and intimacy facilitate a greater interest in their sons than they previously had, now getting to know them as individuals in their own right despite, in some cases, wide geographical separation.

Although the stage of generativity (Erikson, 1963) typically refers to younger fathers than my subjects, this concept has relevance for some of these fathers, too. Their descriptions of their present relationships with their sons in many cases had a sense of freshness about them, as if they were experiencing their sons in new and different ways. Many now feel like fathers for the first time. Most have moved "from competing to connecting" (Sheehy, 1998, pp. 147-149), a central task for men beginning in midlife and continuing through late adulthood.

FROM ILLUSION TO REALITY

Gould's (1978) examination of adulthood takes us on a journey from illusion to reality. In his hands, life is a series of false assumptions that must be challenged and overcome in order to grow, a reconciliation of seemingly contradictory forces within the self. In the final phases of the life cycle, we come to the realization and the acceptance that the person we are is the person we are going to be. Relinquishing the competitive other world, we begin to create more of our own world. From a "made-to-order self" (Sheehy, 1998, p. 34), we move toward a "more authentic self," one more capable of intimacy between self and other. No longer an innocent, we can then move about in that world with more freedom, toward a sense of "inner-directedness" (Gould, 1978, pp. 309-310), toward a sense of claiming our whole self. It is in this way that one achieves what Erikson (1963) calls *ego integrity,* an adaptation "to the triumphs and disappointments adherent to being" (p. 268) and a final acceptance of all that one has done and an integration of all that one is; in a word, *coalescence* (Sheehy, 1998, p. 218). Acceptance of the self now prepares the way for acceptance of the other.

In further discussing the tasks of adulthood, Levinson and colleagues (1978) address the importance of the Dream in a man's life, something which "may be modest or heroic, vaguely defined or crystal clear, a burning passion or a quiet guiding force, a source of inspiration, strength, and corrosive conflict" (p. 245). It is through the Dream that life takes on meaning. "[S]elf and world" (p. 246) are one. However, that Dream may not be realistic or may exercise an "excessive hold" (p. 331). In reexamining the early expectations they had for their sons, it appears that some of these fathers have had to "modify the Dream" (pp. 245-251, 331-332), now learning to live with less. In the process of learning to live with less, however, they seem to be getting more.

In addition to the developmental thrust toward intimacy, idealization comes into play. If what one hopes and dreams of does not fully come to pass, one's narcissism may become threatened. It is through idealization of their sons that the fathers' narcissism becomes restored and strengthened. In acknowledging their sons' intelligence, talent, physical attractiveness, and specialness, their homosexuality becomes of lesser importance and thereby neutralized in the process. In idealizing their sons, the fathers can also idealize themselves. They can now see their own reflection in their sons' eyes. This in turn serves to further strengthen the relationship between father and son. As I previously noted, ten of the fathers report that their relationship with their sons is now the best it has ever been in their adult lives, findings that complement those of other researchers and writers (Cramer and Roach, 1988; Holtzen and Agresti, 1990; Muller, 1987) who have studied the parent/gay child relationship.

The act of coming out has given many of these fathers access to their sons and to other parts of themselves in ways they did not previously have. In turn, their acceptance has created a chance to reshape and carve out a new relationship, one that most of them did not feel they had with their sons earlier in life. The crisis of homosexuality, perhaps first a *danger*, now an *opportunity*, represents a second chance, a rebirth for each of them separately and both of them together. On a deeper level, reshaping and recasting themselves to accommodate to the reality of a gay son, a situation that most of the fathers did not want but who are doing their best to endure, seems to describe what Hartmann (1958) terms *autoplastic adaptation*, changing oneself in order to adapt to the environment. This then furthers ego integrity (Erikson, 1963), "the acceptance of one's one and only life cycle as something that had to be and that, by necessity, permitted of no substitutions" (p. 268). Like a puzzle, all the pieces now fit together: idealization and internalization further identification; identification furthers attachment; attachment furthers adaptation.

In discussing *narcissism* as a developmental line separate and apart from object love, Kohut (1966) observes that transformation or "redistribution of . . . narcissistic libido" (p. 244) culminates in the capacities for creativity, empathy, contemplation of transience, humor, and wisdom. Elson (1984) suggests that these transformations come into play in parenthood, specifically the parent's *"ability to respond to the child as a center of perception and initiative . . .* without unempathic intrusion of their own conflicts" (pp. 298-299). Part of this may take the form of relinquishing whatever cherished goals a parent may continue to have for the child as well as the centrality of the parental position in the child's life. Relinquishing oneself in favor of one's child is a primary task of parenthood throughout life. Elson writes: "Parental narcissism matures in the forging experience of expanding and deepening tolerance of differences and the ability to reconcile these where reconciliation and resolution are crucial" (pp. 301-302). In working toward acceptance of their sons' homosexuality, these fathers are relinquishing some of the dreams they may have had for them and are now living with the dreams the sons have for themselves. This is not an easy task, but one which has reaped its own unique rewards for some.

LIMITATIONS AND IMPLICATIONS FOR FUTURE RESEARCH

All studies have limitations. This one is no exception. As with most qualitative studies, whatever data is accumulated and whatever findings are made are usually based on a relatively small sample. My research involved interviewing only twelve fathers, all of whom were willing to speak with me. As I observed in Chapter 3, what about those fathers who were not so willing? What about fathers who think that their gay sons are mentally ill, going against religious doctrine, or are the personification of evil? Since I could not get access to fathers who believe that, I could not factor them in. The most I could do was to work with those whom I did get. So whatever findings come out of this study must be applied with caution. They do not necessarily generalize. They describe certain fathers with certain experiences, all of whom at least acknowledge their sons' homosexuality, most of whom are working toward full acceptance. These subjects and this study are only representative of that experience, not the experience of *all* fathers.

What is obviously needed is a study with those who are not only in a different stage of the process, but who also reflect a different point of view, that is, those who do not see acceptance as necessarily the goal. It would be important to find ways to help them express their ideas. Perhaps much could be learned. The few opportunities I almost had with what I would call more rejecting fathers did not materialize. One of them told his son that he thought he would not feel free enough to express how he really feels on the subject, that no one could possibly understand the depth of his pain. Granted, it would probably be difficult to find men who were rejecting of homosexuality who would talk to a researcher, since the shame and guilt for them would probably be immense. If one is shameful and guilty, all efforts go toward hiding, not exposing.

Another question that arose during the course of the study was the degree to which the fathers' relationships with their sons were also characteristic of the fathers' relationships with their other children. Did they feel as neglectful, as absent with them as some recalled feeling with their gay sons? Some did. Harry says that he "did not do as good a job with [his] children as [he thinks he] should have." Ronald thought of his two sons and his daughter as "a nondescript group of little people whose faces [he] couldn't even see." Others did not. Mitchell was admittedly more attached to his older heterosexual son than he was to his younger gay son when they were children. Pei acknowledges that his expectations for his two sons—one homosexual, one heterosexual—were higher than his expectations for his daughter and that he had been more invested in the boys' futures than he had been in hers, attributing this to cultural values. Marty and Neal both seem more connected to their gay sons than to their heterosexual sons. Glenn describes being equally distant from both his homosexual and heterosexual sons while they were growing up. Daniel is definitely more connected to his gay son than he is to his heterosexual son, but then he himself is gay. Walter and Luis only have one child. From what I was able to glean, no trends emerged around the fathers' relative presence or absence vis-à-vis his gay child versus his other heterosexual child(ren). As this was not the primary focus of my study, a more intensive investigation should be done. It would also be interesting to look more thoroughly at other dyads in the family—the mother/son, the sibling relationship—to see what emerges there. Complicating all this is the fact that these relationships and the perceptions of them change over time.

Another consideration would be how much the fathers' improved relationships with their sons results from their own development and how much can be attributed to the fact that we live in a political climate which, in general, has become somewhat more tolerant of homosexuality. Although there is no way to really answer that, it is something that must be taken into consideration as we look at the whole picture.

Another connection that became apparent was that those fathers who are involved in parent support groups such as P-FLAG appear to have the most open relationships with their sons. In light of that, it would be important to look at both the kind of parent likely to join such organizations and the kinds of benefits derived from their involvement. Since some of the fathers I was interviewing already had a history of participation, it was difficult to know exactly what effect their participation had on them. Did P-FLAG help them achieve a greater level of understanding and acceptance? Did they have those prior to their involvement? Was it a combination of both that made the difference?

The fathers' ideas on the causes of their sons' homosexuality open up other questions. Initially, four of them blamed themselves, wondering what they could have done differently to prevent this from happening. This is a common occurrence when faced with a crisis of one sort or another—our own illness (Kübler-Ross, 1969), the illness of a loved one (Chodoff, Friedman, and Hamburg, 1964) or a catastrophe (Lindemann, 1965). Self-blame might be the first step that some people go through in trying to cope with a loss, or it may be a learned response, or it may be more common for people with certain character styles. In reviewing the literature, Wortman (1976) suggests that accepting blame may be adaptive in the sense that it gives the illusion that events that occur are under one's control. The idea that things occur randomly makes all of us vulnerable. That may be too frightening to contemplate.

All of the fathers who initially blamed themselves then moved on to consider genetics as the primary cause, joining six other fathers who said they always held that belief. It would be important to understand more about how and why this shift occurred. Wortman and Brehm (1975) underline that relinquishing a sense of control or a sense that one is responsible in situations that are in fact uncontrollable is ultimately the more adaptive response. In this scenario, attributing causality to one's genes represents, if not a relinquishing of control, then a loosening of it in the sense that they themselves are not to blame for their sons' sexuality. It is less threatening than attributing causality to one's behavior, allowing the fathers to buffer possible narcissistic injury and maintain their self-esteem. Off the record, one father said to me that the gene theory was probably some attempt to rationalize his guilt. Perhaps it was for others as well.

This study also raises the question of how the phenomenon of crisis might intersect with development. Some of the fathers say they resolved the immediate impact of their son's disclosure rather quickly. Marty indicates that within a month of his son's telling him about his homosexuality, he and his wife were attending P-FLAG meetings. Peter sought a change for his son, but soon gave that up and focused more on getting help for himself. This might relate to either the character style of the father and/or the developmental push toward intimacy, both superceding and predominating over the immediate crisis, thereby lessening its impact.

About *self as instrument* (Mirvis and Louis, 1985, pp. 230-232), how my being a gay man and not a father of a gay man shaped the interview is impossible to say, but it must have in some indefinable ways. If I were a father, undoubtedly my subjects would have revealed themselves differently. They would have told me another story. It would be interesting to do the same study, only researched this time by a father, to see how it might compare. However, this might pose other problems, such as overidentification with subjects, sacrificing objectivity in the process. The identity of the researcher poses a problem either way.

One final point: as with any individual researcher working in isolation, I may have been prone to construct the story along certain lines. Even though I feel I substantiated what I found as it emerged directly from the interview material, my own sensibilities probably led me to emphasize certain things over others. No doubt someone else would see something different had he or she analyzed the same material using the same method. To be sure, the one I constructed is not the only story. This is an important issue to keep in mind when working within a qualitative methodology. Try as we might to be as objective as possible, we are, in the end, subject to our own selves. I would argue, however, that these very sensibilities are what give qualitative research life.

IMPLICATIONS FOR PRACTICE

When parents try to understand their gay children, they often see their sexuality as foreign in some way, as outside the realm of their experience, as ego-dystonic, as something unlike anything in themselves. On some level that may be true. In this spirit, it would first be important to assist them through the process of mourning. Part of that would be to help them think more broadly about the source of their discomfort and then, if possible, assist them with locating anything in their own experience and their own selves that might facilitate identification, helping them to resonate with their gay child. Some parents will not be able to get to this, at least not right away. Like anything else, it would be a slow process, if it occurs at all. If this event has been a crisis, as it clearly was for Peter and Walter, their child's homosexuality represents first and foremost a danger. Only later does it become an opportunity. In seizing this as an opportunity, learning to respect and develop a greater awareness of and appreciation for others' difference, as many of the fathers proudly told me, eventually resulted in a more expansive sense of self. In the process of coming out as a parent, some of them were able to go beyond what they thought was possible, finding strengths they did not know they possessed.

For some of the fathers, there was a sense that even though it was difficult reconciling to the fact of having a gay son, in the end their love transcended sexual orientation. This was expressed time and time again. Juan Miguel Jr. says that "gay or not gay," his son is still his son. Luis echoes this: "I understand and I accept my son because he's my son." Peter expresses it in this way: "he is what he is and therefore I am on his side 100 percent." Marty said to Gary after he came out, "I wish it weren't so. I can't lie to you. But, nothing would change my love for you—ever, ever, ever." These fathers have "modified the Dream" (Levinson et al., 1978).

OTHER THOUGHTS:
RESEARCH VERSUS TREATMENT

When the father started to be noticed as an important figure in family life, not just from the point of view of economics but of psychology, what was observed most was his absence (Biller, 1968, 1969, 1970, 1974; Biller and Bahm, 1971; Blanchard and Biller, 1971; Santrock, 1970). This theme has been pervasive in the writings about homosexual men and their families from Freud (1905a/1965, 1910/1964) to the present (Isay, 1987, 1990, 1997; Silverstein, 1981). In exploring the position of the gay son in the life of his father, I was curious about what the fathers would have to say, how they would describe their sons, themselves, and their relationship over the years.

From the fathers' perspective, I did find confirmation of their absence, but *not* necessarily for the reason presently in vogue—that the gay son poses a threat to the masculinity of the father, resulting in his pulling back defensively from the relationship, which in turn causes the son to retreat, resulting in a mutual estrangement (Green, 1987; Isay, 1987, 1990, 1997). This is a formulation based on the treatment of gay men, *not* the treatment of fathers of gay men—an important distinction. I am not saying that this could not have happened in certain cases. I am just reporting that this is something that did not surface in quite that way. Perhaps it remains too buried for some. For others, it may not have happened at all. I do not know. The closest I came to this scenario was in Mitchell's case. He says that he felt wounded that his young son, Jay, seemed better con-nected to his mother than to him, emphasizing that this was only one reason why he did not feel as emotionally connected with Jay as he had with his first (heterosexual) son. Other factors had to do with Jay being extremely demanding and a "less malleable" boy. Mitchell was also physically less available than he had been earlier in his own life. He emphatically states that whatever distance was between them had *nothing* to do with his son not being "macho."

Let me state the obvious: this is research, not treatment. What fathers report to a researcher is going to be what they remain most aware of. It was not my role to probe beyond a certain point. Had I done that, I might have lost most or all of my subjects. Although dynamics uncovered by way of the treatment process are probably the closest we can get to reality, I think that what these fathers have told me by way of this method is important and must be considered as part of a very complex picture.

Clearly, many factors took the fathers physically and emotionally away from their sons. Whatever distance existed was multidetermined. In Walter's case, for example, he reports an awareness of the possibility of his son's homosexuality in childhood or in early adolescence. In other cases, including Glenn, Juan Miguel Jr., Neal, and Daniel, it was not until mid- to late adolescence that this possibility was consciously considered; in still other cases, such as Ronald and Marty, it was not considered at all. So the notion that the fathers kept their physical and emotional distance from their oedipal child out of anxiety and narcissistic injury remains, at best, speculative.

FROM CHILD TO ADULT

Because this is a qualitative study, I think that ending on a personal note is in keeping with its character. When one spends time conducting a study or writing a book, the question should be asked: why am I choosing this topic? Besides this examination probably being some attempt to alleviate my guilt about coming out and the real (or imagined) effects this had on my family, my interest in fatherhood extends back many years. Because I am not a father and probably never will be, perhaps writing about the fatherhood experience will be my contribution. Certainly, the processes of writing a book or any other creative endeavor are akin to nurturing a child and watching it grow. Both start with an idea, a seed, needing the right conditions for optimal growth. There were times in the writing of this that I almost felt it was being taken out of my hands. It took on a life of its own.

There is another dimension. Much of my professional life, before social work education and after, has been spent thinking and writing about the problems of children (Gottlieb, 1996). This is where I felt at home. This is where I was emotionally safe. The adult world has been more frightening. I have moved into that with much anxiety and trepidation. But as difficult as this has been, it is where I need to go next. Perhaps if I were to have done a study ten years ago, I might have researched the gay son's experience of his father. My own needs would have been different then.

Perhaps exploring this area was my attempt to learn more about how adults cope in the world, how to deal with events beyond our control, how to reshape our dreams and survive, "better people" for it, as Mitchell told me. Perhaps in giving voice to the fathers, I am also trying out my own adult voice. In helping them emerge "out of the twilight," perhaps I, too, emerge.

Appendix A

Consent Form

If you sign below, you are choosing to participate in this research project, which seeks to explore the experiences of fathers who have learned of their sons' homosexuality. Your participation is voluntary. You may choose to withdraw at any time without penalty or repercussions of any kind. This study fulfills a requirement for my PhD in Clinical Social Work from the Shirley M. Ehrenkranz School of Social Work of New York University.

There will be one or two audiotaped interviews conducted solely by myself, lasting in duration from one to two hours each. These tapes will be given a number known only to me. These tapes may be reviewed by you. I will honor your request that any or all of the contents be destroyed should you have reservations or be dissatisfied in any way. I will also request other kinds of materials which you may have in your possession—letters, diaries, for example—which might add another dimension to what you tell me. If you have any of these, allowing me access would be solely at your discretion. Your name and other identifying information will be altered in the write-up. No monetary compensation will be offered. However, you will be given a summary of the results.

Your willingness to talk about your experience may be important to others. However, this process may be emotionally difficult for you. Should any discomfort arise or you feel a need to continue talking about the issues that are raised, I will discuss this with you further and a referral for counseling may be offered and arranged with your full consent.

If you have any further questions before, during, or after you have completed your participation, you may call me at (___) _____ or write to me at: _____.
You may also call my faculty advisory, Dr. _____, at (___) _____.
Thank you very much for your interest.

_____   _____
Participant   Investigator

_____   _____
Date   Date

Appendix B

Statement to Subjects

If you would like to participate in my study, I will explore with you your past and present relationship with your son and in what ways, if any, this experience has impacted on your own development. I have nothing that I am looking to prove or to disprove. Whatever ideas develop will come solely out of what you and the other fathers tell me. I will try to see if there are any common themes, perhaps a collective experience underneath the individual experiences.

To the best of my knowledge, a study such as this has never been done before. Much of what has been written in the psychological literature about fathers of gay men comes from the perspective of the son and his therapist. This is your chance to tell what you have experienced, a chance to speak for yourself, in your own words.

Appendix C

Semistructured Interview Guide

The interview covers a number of different areas. I begin by inquiring about the father's background and his family of origin, particularly his relationship with his parents. I then move into what expectant fatherhood was like—his thoughts, feelings, hopes, dreams for his son and for himself vis-à-vis his child. I want to know about the early years of his son's life, specifically as these related to the father-son relationship and if there are any particular events that stood out. I ask if the son seemed different to the father in any way and, if so, how. If there was a sense of distance from him, how did he understand what contributed to that? Had he ever thought that his son might be gay? If so, when was that and what was that like for him? I want to know in great detail when the father realized that his son was gay; if this was a gradual awakening or if he was told very specifically and by whom. What were his reactions and how was this handled in terms of family and friends? What was the quality of their relationship like up to that point and did it change after the father's knowledge of his son's sexuality? What is the quality of the current relationship? Did the knowledge of his son's homosexuality shape the father-son relationship? Did it shape the father's development as a parent? Did it shape his development as a person? And did the experience of being a father to a gay son change the father overall in any way?

Appendix D

The Fathers at a Glance

Mitchell, 61, Russian-Polish/Jewish, retired high school teacher and guidance counselor: "My journey isn't over."

Juan Miguel Jr., 70, atheist, born and living in Puerto Rico, lawyer: "He was [Juan Miguel III], gay or not gay, he was [Juan Miguel III]."

Peter, 64, born in Russia, Jewish, entrepreneur: "This [is] something I have to face . . . this is the reality."

Harry, 72, Polish Catholic, supervisor of a maintenance department: "I have hopes that he would marry and have children."

Luis, 51, born in Argentina, Jewish, chef: "I understand and I accept my son because he's my son."

Daniel, 60, Canadian/Methodist, gay, retired from publishing: "He's like a trophy."

Marty, age 70, Russian/Jewish, retired from theater advertising: "Nothing would change my love for you—ever, ever, ever."

Glenn, 63, Polish/Jewish, medical doctor: "It's a nonissue."

Ronald, 61, Irish-English/Protestant, retired manager for a computer company: "I can't find anything good, bad, or indifferent about it. It's just the way it is."

Neal, 85, Russian-Rumanian/Jewish, businessman: "If that was the case, that's the case."

Pei, 65, born in China, born Catholic, retired electrical engineer and social worker: "He's a complete person."

Walter, 50, English-Scotch-Welsh/Agnostic, college teacher: "I want to be in the . . . room with the light with him."

References

Aarons, L. (1995). *Prayers for Bobby: A mother's coming to terms with the suicide of her gay son.* New York: HarperCollins Publishers.

Abelin, E. L. (1971). The role of the father in the separation-individuation process. In J. B. McDevitt and C. F. Settlage (Eds.), *Separation-individuation: Essays in honor of Margaret S. Mahler* (pp. 229-252). New York: International Universities Press.

———— (1975). Some further observations and comments on the earliest role of the father. *International Journal of Psychoanalysis, 56,* 293-302.

Anderson, D. (1987). Family and peer relations of gay adolescents. *Adolescent Psychiatry: Developmental and Clinical Studies, 14,* 162-178.

Anthony, E. J. (1970a). The reactions of parents to adolescents and to their behavior. In E. J. Anthony and T. Benedek (Eds.), *Parenthood: Its psychology and psychopathology* (pp. 307-324). Boston: Little, Brown and Company.

———— (1970b). The reactions of parents to the oedipal child. In E. J. Anthony and T. Benedek (Eds.), *Parenthood: Its psychology and psychopathology* (pp. 275-288). Boston: Little, Brown and Company.

Apperson, L. B. and McAdoo, W. G. Jr. (1968). Parental factors in the childhood of homosexuals. *Journal of Abnormal Psychology, 73* (3), 201-206.

Baker, J. M. (1998). *Family secrets: Gay sons—A mother's story.* Binghamton, New York: The Haworth Press.

Becker, H. S. (1967). Whose side are we on? *Social Problems, 14* (3), 239-247.

Bell, A. P. and Weinberg, M. S. (1978). *Homosexualities: A study of diversity among men and women.* New York: Simon and Schuster.

Bell, A. P., Weinberg, M. S., and Hammersmith, S. K. (1981). *Sexual preference: Its development in men and women.* Bloomington, Indiana: Indiana University Press.

Ben-Ari, A. (1995a). Coming out: A dialectic of intimacy and privacy. *Families in Society: The Journal of Contemporary Human Services*, 306-314.

———— (1995b). The discovery that an offspring is gay: Parents', gay men's, and lesbians' perspectives. *Journal of Homosexuality, 30* (1), 89-112.

Benedek, T. (1959). Parenthood as a developmental phase: A contribution to the libido theory. *Journal of the American Psychoanalytic Association, 7,* 389-417.

———— (1970a). Fatherhood and providing. In E. J. Anthony and T. Benedek (Eds.), *Parenthood: Its psychology and psychopathology* (pp. 167-183). Boston: Little, Brown and Company.

———— (1970b). Parenthood during the life cycle. In E. J. Anthony and T. Benedek (Eds.), *Parenthood: Its psychology and psychopathology* (pp. 185-206). Boston: Little, Brown and Company.

Berg, D. N. (1985). Anxiety in research relationships. In D. N. Berg and K. K. Smith (Eds.), *Exploring clinical methods for social research* (pp. 213-228). Beverly Hills, California: Sage Publications.

Berman, P. S. (Producer) and Minnelli, V. (Director) (1956). *Tea and Sympathy* [Film]. (Available from MGM/UA Home Video, Inc., 10000 W. Washington Blvd., Culver City, California, 90232)

Bernstein, B. E. (1990). Attitudes and issues of parents of gay men and lesbians and implications for therapy. *Journal of Gay and Lesbian Psychotherapy, 1* (3), 37-53.

Bernstein, R. A. (1995). *Straight parents, gay children: Keeping families together.* New York: Thunder's Mouth Press.

Bieber, I., Dain, H. J., Dince, P. R., Drellich, M. G., Grand, H. G., Gundlach, R. H., Kremer, M. W., Rifkin, A. H., Wilbur, C. B., and Bieber, T. B. (1965). *Homosexuality: A psychoanalytic study of male homosexuals.* New York: Vintage Books.

Biller, H. B. (1968). A note on father absence and masculine development in lower-class negro and white boys. *Child Development, 39,* 1003-1006.

———— (1969). Father absence, maternal encouragement, and sex-role development in kindergarten-age boys. *Child Development, 40,* 539-546.

———— (1970). Father absence and the personality development of the male child. *Developmental Psychology, 2* (2), 181-201.

———— (1974). Paternal deprivation, cognitive functioning and the feminized classroom. In A. Davids (Ed.), *Child personality and psychopathology: Current topics* (Vol. 1, pp. 11-52). New York: John Wiley and Sons.

Biller, H. B. and Bahm, R. M. (1971). Father absence, perceived maternal behavior, and masculinity of self-concept among junior high school boys. *Developmental Psychology, 4* (2), 178-181.

Blanchard, R. W. and Biller, H. B. (1971). Father availability and academic performance among third-grade boys. *Developmental Psychology, 4* (3), 301-305.

Blos, P. (1967). The second individuation process of adolescence. *The Psychoanalytic Study of the Child, 22,* 162-186.

———— (1970). *The young adolescent: Clinical studies.* New York: The Free Press.

———— (1985). *Son and father: Before and beyond the Oedipus complex.* New York: The Free Press.

Blum, H. P. (1990). Freud, Fliess, and the parenthood of psychoanalysis. *Psychoanalytic Quarterly, 59,* 21-40.

Bogdan, R. and Taylor, S. J. (1975). *Introduction to qualitative research methods: A phenomenological approach to the social sciences.* New York: John Wiley and Sons.

Bolen, J. S. (1990). *Gods in everyman: A new psychology of men's lives and loves.* New York: HarperPerennial.

Borhek, M. V. (1979). *My son Eric.* Cleveland, Ohio: The Pilgrim Press.

———— (1988). Helping gay and lesbian adolescents and their families: A mother's perspective. *Journal of Adolescent Health Care, 9,* 123-128.

_____ (1993). *Coming out to parents: A two-way survival guide for lesbians and gay men and their parents* (Revised and updated edition). Cleveland, Ohio: The Pilgrim Press.

Boxer, A. M., Cook, J. A., and Herdt, G. (1991). Double jeopardy: Identity transitions and parent-child relations among gay and lesbian youth. In K. Pillemer and K. McCartney (Eds.), *Parent-child relations throughout life* (pp. 59-92). Hillsdale, New Jersey: Lawrence Erlbaum Associates.

Bozett, F. W. (1985). Male development and fathering throughout the life cycle. *American Behavioral Scientist, 29* (1), 41-54.

Bronfenbrenner, U. (1960). Freudian theories of identification and their derivatives. *Child Development, 31,* 15-40.

Burlingham, D. (1973). The preoedipal infant-father relationship. *The Psychoanalytic Study of the Child, 28,* 23-47.

Calvani, D. et al. (1996). A liberation haggadah for lesbian, gay, and bisexual Jews and their loved ones. New York: The Jewish Community Center on the Upper West Side.

Caplan, M. (1996). *When sons and daughters choose alternative lifestyles.* Prescott, Arizona: Hohm Press.

Chang, J. and Block, J. (1960). A study of identification in male homosexuals. *Journal of Consulting Psychology, 24* (4), 307-310.

Chodoff, P., Friedman, S. B., and Hamburg, D. A. (1964). Stress, defenses and coping behavior: Observations in parents of children with malignant disease. *The American Journal of Psychiatry, 120* (8), 743-749.

Churchill, W. (1971). *Homosexual behavior among males: A cross-cultural and cross-species investigation.* Englewood Cliffs, New Jersey: Prentice-Hall, Inc.

Cohen, R. S. and Balikov, H. (1974). On the impact of adolescence upon parents. *Adolescent Psychiatry: Developmental and Clinical Studies, 3,* 217-236.

Cohler, B. J. and Boxer, A. M. (1984). Middle adulthood: Settling into the world—person, time, and context. In D. Offer and M. Sabshin (Eds.), *Normality and the life cycle: A critical integration* (pp. 145-203). New York: Basic Books.

Colarusso, C. A. and Nemiroff, R. A. (1979). Some observations and hypotheses about the psychoanalytic theory of adult development. *International Journal of Psychoanalysis, 60,* 59-71.

_____ (1982). The father in midlife: Crisis and the growth of paternal identity. In S. H. Cath, A. R. Gurwitt, and J. M. Ross (Eds.), *Father and child: Developmental and clinical perspectives* (pp. 315-327). Boston: Little, Brown and Company.

Colichman, P., Davimos, J., and Harris, M. R. (Producers), and Marks, R. (Director) (1996). *The Twilight of the Golds* [Film]. (Available from BMG Entertainment, 1540 Broadway, New York, New York, 10036.)

Connelly, F. M. and Clandinin, D. J. (1990). Stories of experience and narrative inquiry. *Educational Researcher, 19* (5), 2-14.

Corneau, G. (1991). *Absent fathers, lost sons: The search for masculine identity.* L. Shouldice (Trans.). Boston: Shambhala Publications, Inc.

Cramer, D. W. and Roach, A. J. (1988). Coming out to mom and dad: A study of gay males and their relationships with their parents. *Journal of Homosexuality, 15* (3/4), 79-91.

Datan, N. and Thomas, J. (1984). Late adulthood: Love, work, and the normal transitions. In D. Offer and M. Sabshin (Eds.), *Normality and the life cycle: A critical integration* (pp. 204-229). New York: Basic Books.

D'Augelli, A. R. (1991). Gay men in college: Identity processes and adaptations. *Journal of College Student Development, 32,* 140-146.

D' Augelli, A. R., Hershberger, S. L., and Pilkington, N. W. (1998). Lesbian, gay, and bisexual youth and their families: Disclosure of sexual orientation and its consequences. *American Journal of Orthopsychiatry, 68* (3), 361-371.

Demby, S. (1990). The role of the father in the son's pre-oedipal development. *Issues in Ego Psychology, 13* (2), 147-156.

Devereux, G. (1953). Why Oedipus killed Laius: A note on the complementary Oedipus complex in Greek drama. *International Journal of Psychoanalysis, 34,* 132-141.

DeVine, J. L. (1984). A systemic inspection of affectional preference orientation and the family of origin. *Journal of Social Work and Human Sexuality, 2* (2/3), 9-17.

Dew, R. F. (1995). *The family heart: A memoir of when our son came out.* New York: Ballantine Books.

Diamond, M. J. (1986). Becoming a father: A psychoanalytic perspective on the forgotten parent. *The Psychoanalytic Review, 73* (4), 445-468.

Disney, W. (Producer), and Shapsteen, B. and Luske, H. (Supervising Directors) (1940). *Pinocchio* [Film]. (Available from Buena Vista Home Video, Dept. CS, Burbank, California, 91521.)

Eliot, T. S. (1935). *Murder in the cathedral.* New York: Harcourt, Brace, and Company.

Elson, M. (1984). Parenthood and the transformations of narcissism. In R. S. Cohen, B. J. Cohler, and S. H. Weissman (Eds.), *Parenthood: A psychodynamic perspective* (pp. 297-314). New York: The Guilford Press.

Ely, M., Anzul, M., Friedman, T., Garner, D., and Steinmetz, A. M. (1991). *Doing qualitative research: Circles within circles.* New York: The Falmer Press.

Ephron, H. (Producer), and King, H. (Director) (1956). *Carousel* [Film]. (Available from CBS/Fox Video, 1211 Avenue of the Americas, New York, New York, 10036.)

Erikson, E. H. (1963). *Childhood and society* (Second edition). New York: W. W. Norton and Company, Inc.

Evans, R. B. (1969). Childhood parental relationships of homosexual men. *Journal of Consulting and Clinical Psychology, 33* (2), 129-135.

Fairbairn, W. R. D. (1952). Endopsychic structure considered in terms of object-relationships. In *Psychoanalytic studies of the personality* (pp. 82-136). London: Routledge and Kegan Paul LTD.

Fairchild, B. (1979). For parents of gays: A fresh perspective. In B. Berzon and R. Leighton (Eds.), *Positively gay* (pp. 101-111). Millbrae, California: Celestial Arts.

Fairchild, B. and Hayward, N. (1989). *Now that you know: What every parent should know about homosexuality* (Updated edition). New York: Harcourt Brace Jovanovich, Publishers.

Fenichel, O. (1945). *The psychoanalytic theory of neurosis.* New York: W. W. Norton and Company, Inc.

Fineberg, B. L. (1986). Structure and defense in the therapy of little Hans. *Bulletin of the Menninger Clinic, 50* (5), 440-446.

Freud, A. (1958). Adolescence. *The Psychoanalytic Study of the Child, 13,* 255-278.

―――――― (1966). *The writings of Anna Freud, volume II: The ego and the mechanisms of defense* (Revised edition). New York: International Universities Press, Inc.

―――――― (1967). About losing and being lost. *The Psychoanalytic Study of the Child, 22,* 9-19.

Freud, A., Nagera, H., and Freud, W. E. (1965). Metapsychological assessment of the adult personality: The adult profile. *The Psychoanalytic Study of the Child, 20,* 9-41.

Freud, S. (1905a/1965). *Three essays on the theory of sexuality.* J. Strachey (Ed. and Trans.). New York: Avon Books.

―――――― (1905b/1977). *Case histories I: Fragment of an analysis of a case of hysteria,* A. Richards (Ed.), A. Strachey and J. Strachey (Trans.), (pp. 29-164). New York: Penguin Books.

―――――― (1909/1977). *Case histories I: Analysis of a phobia in a five-year-old boy,* A. Richards (Ed.), A. Strachey and J. Strachey (Trans.), (pp. 165-305). New York: Penguin Books.

―――――― (1910/1964). *Leonardo da Vinci and a memory of his childhood,* J. Strachey (Ed.), A. Tyson (Trans.). New York: W. W. Norton and Company, Inc.

―――――― (1914/1959). On narcissism: An introduction. In E. Jones (Ed.), J. Riviere (Trans.), *Collected papers* (Vol. 4, pp. 30-59). New York: Basic Books, Inc.

―――――― (1915/1959). Instincts and their vicissitudes. In E. Jones (Ed.), J. Riviere (Trans.), *Collected papers* (Vol. 4, pp. 60-83). New York: Basic Books, Inc.

―――――― (1917/1959). Mourning and melancholia. In E. Jones (Ed.), J. Riviere (Trans.), *Collected papers* (Vol. 4, pp. 152-170). New York: Basic Books, Inc.

―――――― (1920a/1961). *Beyond the pleasure principle.* J. Strachey (Ed. and Trans.). New York: W. W. Norton and Company, Inc.

―――――― (1920b/1968). The psychogenesis of a case of homosexuality in a woman. In J. Strachey (Ed. and Trans.), *The standard edition of the complete psychological works of Sigmund Freud* (Vol. 18, pp. 145-172). London: Hogarth Press.

―――――― (1921/1971). *Group psychology and the analysis of the ego.* J. Strachey (Ed. and Trans.). New York: Bantam Books.

―――――― (1923/1962). *The ego and the id.* J. Strachey (Ed.), J. Riviere (Trans.). New York: W. W. Norton and Company, Inc.

―――――― (1924/1959). The passing of the Oedipus-complex. In E. Jones (Ed.), J. Riviere (Trans.), *Collected papers* (Vol. 2, pp. 269-276). New York: Basic Books, Inc.

———— (1927/1959). Fetishism. In J. Strachey (Ed.) *Collected papers* (Vol. 5, pp. 198-204). New York: Basic Books, Inc.

———— (1928/1959). Dostoevsky and parricide. In J. Strachey (Ed.), *Collected papers* (Vol. 5, pp. 222-242). New York: Basic Books, Inc.

———— (1951). Historical notes: A letter from Freud. *The American Journal of Psychiatry, 107* (10), 786-787. Copyright 1951, the American Psychiatric Association. Reprinted by permission.

Freund, K. and Blanchard, R. (1983). Is the distant relationship of fathers and homosexual sons related to the sons' erotic preference for male partners, or to the sons' atypical gender identity, or to both? *Journal of Homosexuality, 9* (1), 7-25.

Fricke, A. and Fricke, W. (1991). *Sudden strangers: The story of a gay son and his father.* New York: St. Martin's Press.

Friedman, R. C. (1988). *Male homosexuality: A contemporary psychoanalytic perspective.* New Haven, Connecticut: Yale University Press.

Gerzi, S. and Berman, E. (1981). Emotional reactions of expectant fathers to their wives' first pregnancy. *British Journal of Medical Psychology, 54* (3), 259-265.

Goffman, E. (1986). *Stigma: Notes on the management of spoiled identity* (First Touchstone edition). New York: Simon and Schuster, Inc.

Goldstein, E. G. (1995). *Ego psychology and social work practice* (Second edition). New York: The Free Press.

Gottlieb, A. R. (1996). John: Some thoughts on mourning. *Clinical Social Work Journal, 24* (3), 271-283.

Gould, R. L. (1978). *Transformations: Growth and change in adult life.* New York: Simon and Shuster.

Graves, R. (1955). *The Greek myths.* New York: George Braziller, Inc.

Green, A. (1993). Analytic play and its relationship to the object. In D. Goldman (Ed.), *In one's bones: The clinical genius of Winnicott* (pp. 213-222). Northvale, New Jersey: Jason Aronson Inc.

Green, R. (1987). *The "sissy boy syndrome" and the development of homosexuality.* New Haven, Connecticut: Yale University Press.

Greenacre, P. (1966). Problems of overidealization of the analyst and of analysis: Their manifestations in the transference and countertransference relationship. *The Psychoanalytic Study of the Child, 21,* 193-212.

Greenberg, M. and Morris, N. (1982). Engrossment: The newborn's impact upon the father. In S. H. Cath, A. R. Gurwitt, and J. M. Ross (Eds.), *Father and child: Developmental and clinical perspectives* (pp. 87-99). Boston: Little, Brown and Company.

Greenson, R. R. (1978). Disidentifying from mother: Its special importance for the boy. *Explorations in psychoanalysis* (pp. 305-312). New York: International Universities Press, Inc.

Greenspan, S. I. (1982). "The second other": The role of the father in early personality formation and the dyadic-phallic phase of development. In S. H. Cath, A. R. Gurwitt, and J. M. Ross (Eds.), *Father and child: Developmental and clinical perspectives* (pp. 123-138). Boston: Little, Brown and Company.

Griffin, C. W., Wirth, M. J., and Wirth, A. G. (1986). *Beyond acceptance: Parents of lesbians and gays talk about their experiences.* Englewood Cliffs, New Jersey: Prentice-Hall, Inc.

Gurwitt, A. R. (1982). Aspects of prospective fatherhood. In S. H. Cath, A. R. Gurwitt, and J. M. Ross (Eds.), *Father and child: Developmental and clinical perspectives* (pp. 275-299). Boston: Little, Brown and Company.

Hartman, A. A. and Nicolay, R. C. (1966). Sexually deviant behavior in expectant fathers. *Journal of Abnormal Psychology, 71* (3), 232-234.

Hartmann, H. (1958). *Ego psychology and the problem of adaptation* (D. Rapaport, Trans.). New York: International Universities Press, Inc.

Herzog, J. M. (1980). Sleep disturbance and father hunger in 18- to 28-month-old boys: The erlkönig syndrome. *The Psychoanalytic Study of the Child, 35,* 219-233.

——— (1982a). On father hunger: The father's role in the modulation of aggressive drive and fantasy. In S. H. Cath, A. R. Gurwitt, and J. M. Ross (Eds.), *Father and child: Developmental and clinical perspectives* (pp. 163-174). Boston: Little, Brown and Company.

——— (1982b). Patterns of expectant fatherhood: A study of the fathers of a group of premature infants. In S. H. Cath, A. R. Gurwitt, and J. M. Ross (Eds.), *Father and child: Developmental and clinical perspectives* (pp. 301-314). Boston: Little, Brown and Company.

Holtzen, D. W. and Agresti, A. A. (1990). Parental responses to gay and lesbian children: Differences in homophobia, self-esteem, and sex-role stereotyping. *Journal of Social and Clinical Psychology, 9* (3), 390-399.

Hooker, E. (1969). Parental relations and male homosexuality in patient and non-patient samples. *Journal of Consulting and Clinical Psychology, 33* (2), 140-142.

Hope, T., Schamus, J., and Lee, A. (Producers) and Lee, A. (Director) (1993). *The wedding banquet* [Film]. (Available from Fox Video, Inc., PO Box 900, Beverly Hills, California, 90213.)

Isay, R. (1987). Fathers and their homosexually inclined sons in childhood. *The Psychoanalytic Study of the Child, 42,* 275-294.

——— (1990). *Being homosexual: Gay men and their development.* New York: Avon Books.

——— (1997). *Becoming gay: The journey to self-acceptance.* New York: Henry Holt and Company.

Jacobs, J. (Ed.). (1967). Jack and the beanstalk. In *English fairy tales* (pp. 59-67). New York: Dover Publications, Inc.

Jacobson, E. (1950). Development of the wish for a child in boys. *The Psychoanalytic Study of the Child, 5,* 139-152.

——— (1964). *The self and the object world.* New York: International Universities Press, Inc.

Jarvis, W. (1962). Some effects of pregnancy and childbirth on men. *Journal of the American Psychoanalytic Association, 10,* 689-700.

Jessner, L., Weigert, E., and Foy, J. L. (1970). The development of parental attitudes during pregnancy. In E. J. Anthony and T. Benedek (Eds.), *Parenthood: Its psychology and psychopathology* (pp. 209-244). Boston: Little, Brown and Company.

Judd, C. M., Smith, E. R., and Kidder, L. H. (1991). *Research methods in social relations* (Sixth edition). Orlando, Florida: Harcourt Brace Jovanovich.

Jung, C. G. (1933). *Modern man in search of a soul.* W. S. Dell and C. F. Baynes (Trans.). New York: Harcourt, Brace, and World, Inc.

———— (1956). *Two essays on analytical psychology.* R. F. C. Hull (Trans.). New York: Meridian Books.

———— (1964). *Man and his symbols.* Garden City, New York: Doubleday and Company, Inc.

Kermode, F. (1981). Secrets and narrative sequence. In W. J. T. Mitchell (Ed.), *On narrative* (pp. 79-97). Chicago: University of Chicago Press.

Kestenberg, J. S. (1970). The effect on parents of the child's transition into and out of latency. In E. J. Anthony and T. Benedek (Eds.), *Parenthood: Its psychology and psychopathology* (pp. 289-306). Boston: Little, Brown and Company.

Klein, M. (1975). The Oedipus complex in the light of early anxieties. In R. E. Money-Kyrle (Ed.), *Love, guilt and reparation and other works 1921-1945* (pp. 370-419). New York: Delacourte Press/Seymour Lawrence.

Kohut, H. (1966). Forms and transformations of narcissism. *Journal of the American Psychoanalytic Association, 14,* 243-272.

———— (1977). *The restoration of the self.* New York: International Universities Press, Inc.

Kübler-Ross, E. (1969). *On death and dying.* New York: Macmillan.

Lacoursiere, R. (1972). The mental health of the prospective father: A new indication for therapeutic abortion? *Bulletin of the Menninger Clinic, 36* (6), 645-650.

Layland, W. R. (1981). In search of a loving father. *International Journal of Psychoanalysis, 62,* 215-223.

Leavitt, D. (1987). *The lost language of cranes.* New York: Bantam Books.

Levinson, D. J., Darrow, C. N., Klein, E. B., Levinson, M. H., and McKee, B. (1978). *The seasons of a man's life.* New York: Alfred A. Knopf.

Lewes, K. (1989). *The psychoanalytic theory of male homosexuality.* New York: New American Library.

Lindemann, E. (1965). Symptomatology and management of acute grief. In H. J. Parad (Ed.), *Crisis intervention: Selected readings* (pp. 7-21). New York: Family Service Association of America.

Loewald, H. W. (1980). Ego and reality. In *Papers on psychoanalysis* (pp. 3-20). New Haven, Connecticut: Yale University Press.

Lowenthal, M. F., Thurnher, M., and Chiriboga, D. (1975). *Four stages of life: A comparative study of women and men facing transitions.* San Francisco: Jossey-Bass Publishers.

Mahler, M. S., Pine, F., and Bergman, A. (1975). *The psychological birth of the human infant: Symbiosis and individuation.* New York: Basic Books, Inc.

Manninen, V. (1992). The ultimate masculine striving: Reflexions on the psychology of two polar explorers. *Scandinavian Psychoanalytic Review, 15,* 1-26.

_____ (1993). For the sake of eternity: On the narcissism of fatherhood and the father-son relationship. *Scandinavian Psychoanalytic Review, 16,* 35-46.

Marshall, C. and Rossman, G. B. (1995). *Designing qualitative research* (Second edition). Thousand Oaks, California: Sage Publications.

McDougall, B. (Ed.). (1998). *My child is gay: How parents react when they hear the news.* Sydney, Australia: Allen and Unwin.

McElroy, H. (Producer), and Dowling, K., and Burton, G. (Directors) (1994). *The Sum of Us* [Film]. (Available from Evergreen Entertainment, 6100 Wilshire Blvd., Suite 1111, Los Angeles, California, 90048.)

Milic, J. H. and Crowne, D. P. (1986). Recalled parent-child relations and need for approval of homosexual and heterosexual men. *Archives of Sexual Behavior, 15* (3), 239-246.

Miller, A. (1949). *Death of a salesman.* New York: The Viking Press.

Mirvis, P. H. and Louis, M. R. (1985). Self-full research: Working through the self as instrument in organizational research. In D. N. Berg and K. K. Smith (Eds.), *Exploring clinical methods for social research* (pp. 229-246). Beverly Hills, California: Sage Publications.

Mishler, E. G. (1986). The analysis of interview-narratives. In T. R. Sarbin (Ed.), *Narrative psychology: The storied nature of human conduct* (pp. 233-255). New York: Praeger Special Studies.

Muller, A. (1987). *Parents matter: Parents' relationships with lesbian daughters and gay sons.* Tallahassee, Florida: Naiad Press.

Myers, M. F. (1982). Counseling the parents of young homosexual male patients. *Journal of Homosexuality, 7* (2/3), 131-143.

Neubauer, P. B. (1986). Reciprocal effects of fathering on parent and child. In G. I. Fogel, F. M. Lane, and R. S. Liebert (Eds.), *The psychology of men: New psychoanalytic perspectives* (pp. 213-228). New York: Basic Books, Inc.

Neuberg, S. L., Smith, D. M., Hoffman, J. C., and Russell, F. J. (1994). When we observe stigmatized and "normal" individuals interacting: Stigma by association. *Personality and Social Psychology Bulletin, 20* (2), 196-209.

Neugarten, B. L. (1968a). Adult personality: Toward a psychology of the life cycle. In B. L. Neugarten (Ed.), *Middle age and aging: A reader in social psychology* (pp. 137-147). Chicago: The University of Chicago Press.

_____ (1968b). The awareness of middle age. In B. L. Neugarten (Ed.), *Middle age and aging: A reader in social psychology* (pp. 93-98). Chicago: The University of Chicago Press.

Neugarten, B. L. and Gutmann, D. L. (1968). Age-sex roles and personality in middle age: A thematic apperception study. In B. L. Neugarten (Ed.), *Middle age and aging: A reader in social psychology* (pp. 58-71). Chicago: The University of Chicago Press.

Nicolosi, J. (1991). *Reparative therapy of male homosexuality: A new clinical approach.* Northvale, New Jersey: Jason Aronson, Inc.

Nugiel, N. (Producer), and Reeve, C. (Director) (1997). *In the gloaming* [Film]. (Available from HBO Home Video, 1100 Avenue of the Americas, New York, New York, 10036.)

Osofsky, H. (1982). Expectant and new fatherhood as a developmental crisis. *Bulletin of the Menninger Clinic, 46* (3), 209-230.

Owen, W. (1964). The parable of the old man and the young. In C. D. Lewis (Ed.), *The collected poems of Wilfred Owen* (p. 42). New York: New Directions Books.

Owens, R. E. Jr. (1998). *Queer kids: The challenges and promise for lesbian, gay, and bisexual youth.* Binghamton, New York: The Haworth Press.

Padgett, D. K. (1998). Does the glove really fit? Qualitative research and clinical social work practice. *Social Work, 43* (4), 373-381.

Paget, M. A. (1983). Experience and knowledge. *Human Studies, 6,* 67-90.

Parad, H. J. and Caplan, G. (1965). A framework for studying families in crisis. In H. J. Parad (Ed.), *Crisis intervention: Selected readings* (pp. 53-72). New York: Family Service Association of America.

Parke, R. D. and Tinsley, B. R. (1984). Fatherhood: Historical and contemporary perspectives. In K. A. McCluskey and H. W. Reese (Eds.), *Life-span developmental psychology: Historical and generational effects* (pp. 203-248). Orlando, Florida: Academic Press, Inc.

Peck, R. C. (1968). Psychological developments in the second half of life. In B. L. Neugarten (Ed.), *Middle age and aging: A reader in social psychology* (pp. 88-92). Chicago: The University of Chicago Press.

Peshkin, A. (1985). Virtuous subjectivity: In the participant-observer's I's. In D. N. Berg and K. K. Smith (Eds.), *Exploring clinical methods for social research* (pp. 267-281). Beverly Hills, California: Sage Publications.

Peskin, H. and Livson, N. (1981). Uses of the past in adult psychological health. In D. H. Eichorn, J. A. Clausen, N. Haan, M. P. Honzik, and P. H. Mussen (Eds.), *Present and past in middle life* (pp. 153-181). New York: Academic Press.

Polkinghorne, D. E. (1988). *Narrative knowing and the human sciences.* Albany, New York: State University of New York Press.

Pruett, K. D. (1983). Infants of primary nurturing fathers. *The Psychoanalytic Study of the Child, 38,* 257-277.

Rangell, L. (1970). The return of the repressed "Oedipus." In E. J. Anthony and T. Benedek (Eds.), *Parenthood: Its psychology and psychopathology* (pp. 325-334). Boston: Little, Brown and Company.

Rapoport, L. (1965). The state of crisis: Some theoretical considerations. In H. J. Parad (Ed.), *Crisis intervention: Selected readings* (pp. 22-31). New York: Family Service Association of America.

Reid, K. E. (1975). Fatherhood and emotional stress: The couvade syndrome. *Journal of Social Welfare, 2* (1), 3-14.

Reid, W. J. and Smith, A. D. (1989). *Research in social work* (Second edition). New York: Columbia University Press.

Riessman, C. K. (Ed.). (1994). *Qualitative studies in social work research.* Thousand Oaks, California: Sage Publications.

Robinson, B. E., Walters, L. H., and Skeen, P. (1989). Response of parents to learning that their child is homosexual and concern over AIDS: A national study. *Journal of Homosexuality, 18* (1/2), 59-80.

Ross, J. M. (1982a). In search of fathering: A review. In S. H. Cath, A. R. Gurwitt, and J. M. Ross (Eds.), *Father and child: Developmental and clinical perspectives* (pp. 21-32). Boston: Little, Brown, and Company.

———— (1982b). Oedipus revisited: Laius and the "Laius complex." *The Psychoanalytic Study of the Child, 37,* 169-200.

———— (1983). Father to the child: Psychoanalytic reflections. *Psychoanalytic Review, 70* (3), 301-320.

———— (1984). Fathers in development: An overview of recent contributions. In R. S. Cohen, B. J. Cohler, and S. H. Weissman (Eds.), *Parenthood: A psychodynamic perspective* (pp. 373-390). New York: The Guilford Press.

———— (1994). *What men want: Mothers, fathers, and manhood.* Cambridge, Massachusetts: Harvard University Press.

Rossi, A. S. (1968). Transition to parenthood. *Journal of Marriage and the Family, 30,* 26-39.

Santrock, J. W. (1970). Paternal absence, sex typing, and identification. *Developmental Psychology, 2* (2), 264-272.

Sarbin, T. R. (Ed.). (1986). *Narrative psychology: The storied nature of human conduct.* New York: Praeger Special Studies.

Savin-Williams, R. C. (1989). Coming out to parents and self-esteem among gay and lesbian youths. *Journal of Homosexuality, 18* (1/2), 1-35.

———— (1994). Verbal and physical abuse as stressors in the lives of lesbian, gay male, and bisexual youths: Associations with school problems, running away, substance abuse, prostitution, and suicide. *Journal of Consulting and Clinical Psychology, 62* (2), 261-269.

Schwartz, D. D. (1984). Psychoanalytic developmental perspectives on parenthood. In R. S. Cohen, B. J. Cohler, and S. H. Weissman (Eds.), *Parenthood: A psychodynamic perspective* (pp. 356-372). New York: The Guilford Press.

Scott, J. (Producer), and Hicks, S. (Director) (1996). *Shine* [Film]. (Available from New Line Home Video, Inc. Australian Film Finance Corporation. Limited Momentum Films Pty, Limited, The South Australian Film Corporation and Film Victoria.)

Selvadurai, S. (1997). *Funny boy.* New York: William Morrow and Company, Inc.

Sheehy, G. (1998). *Understanding men's passages: Discovering the new map of men's lives.* New York: Random House.

Shor, J. and Sanville, J. (1978). *Illusion in loving: A psychoanalytic approach to the evolution of intimacy and autonomy.* Los Angeles: Double Helix Press.

Shyer, M. F. and Shyer, C. (1997). *Not like other boys. Growing up gay: A mother and son look back.* Los Angeles: Alyson Books.

Siegelman, M. (1974). Parental background of male homosexuals and heterosexuals. *Archives of Sexual Behavior, 3* (1), 3-18.

Silverstein, C. (1977). *A family matter: A parents' guide to homosexuality.* New York: McGraw-Hill Book Company.

———— (1981). *Man to man: Gay couples in America.* New York: William Morrow and Company, Inc.

Snortum, J. R., Marshall, J. E., Gillespie, J. F., McLaughlin, J. P., and Mosberg, L. (1969). Family dynamics and homosexuality. *Psychological Reports*, 24, 763-770.

Socarides, C. W. (1982). Abdicating fathers, homosexual sons: Psychoanalytic observations on the contribution of the father to the development of male homosexuality. In S. H. Cath, A. R. Gurwitt, and J. M. Ross (Eds.), *Father and child: Developmental and clinical perspectives* (pp. 509-521). Boston: Little, Brown and Company.

Spence, D. P. (1986). Narrative smoothing and clinical wisdom. In T. R. Sarbin (Ed.), *Narrative psychology: The storied nature of human conduct* (pp. 211- 232). New York: Praeger Special Studies.

Spradley, J. P. (1979). *The ethnographic interview.* New York: Holt, Rinehart and Winston.

Stoller, R. J. (1976). *Sex and gender, volume II: The transsexual experiment* (First American edition). New York: Jason Aronson.

Strauss, A. L. (1987). *Qualitative analysis for social scientists.* New York: Cambridge University Press.

Taylor, S. J. and Bogdan, R. (1984). *Introduction to qualitative research methods: The search for meanings* (Second edition). New York: John Wiley and Sons.

Thompson, N. L. Jr., Schwartz, D. M., McCandless, B. R., and Edwards, D. A. (1973). Parent-child relationships and sexual identity in male and female homosexuals and heterosexuals. *Journal of Consulting and Clinical Psychology, 41* (1), 120-127.

Tippett, M. (1944). *A child of our time: Oratorio for soli, chorus, and orchestra.* London: Schott and Co. LTD.

Tolstoy, L. (1970). *Anna Karenina.* G. Gibian (Ed.), L. Maude and A. Maude (Trans.). New York: W. W. Norton and Company, Inc.

Vargo, M. E. (1998). *Acts of disclosure: The coming-out process of contemporary gay men.* Binghamton, New York: The Haworth Press.

Viorst, J. (1987). *Necessary losses.* New York: Ballantine Books.

Wainwright, W. H. (1966). Fatherhood as a precipitant of mental illness. *The American Journal of Psychiatry, 123* (1), 40-44.

Weinberg, G. (1973). *Society and the healthy homosexual.* Garden City, New York: Doubleday.

Wells-Lurie, L. L. (1996). Working with parents of gay and lesbian children. In C. J. Alexander (Ed.), *Gay and lesbian mental health: A sourcebook for practitioners* (pp. 159-171). Binghamton, New York: The Haworth Press.

West, D. J. (1959). Parental figures in the genesis of male homosexuality. *International Journal of Social Psychiatry, 5*, 85-97.

Whitam, F. L. and Zent, M. (1984). A cross-cultural assessment of early cross-gender behavior and familial factors in male homosexuality. *Archives of Sexual Behavior, 13* (5), 427-439.

White, H. (1981). The value of narrativity in the representation of reality. In W. J. T. Mitchell (Ed.), *On narrative* (pp. 1-23). Chicago: University of Chicago Press.

Whitman, W. (1955). Sea drift: Out of the cradle endlessly rocking (pp. 209-214). *Leaves of grass.* New York: New American Library.

Winnicott, D. W. (1964). What about father? In *The child, the family, and the outside world* (pp. 113-118). Reading, Massachusetts: Addison-Wesley.

—————— (1965a). Ego distortion in terms of true and false self. In M. M. R. Khan (Ed.), *The maturational processes and the facilitating environment* (pp. 140-152). New York: International Universities Press, Inc.

—————— (1965b). The theory of the parent-infant relationship. In M. M. R. Khan (Ed.), *The maturational processes and the facilitating environment* (pp. 37-55). New York: International Universities Press, Inc.

—————— (1993). Communicating and not communicating. In D. Goldman (Ed.), *In one's bones: The clinical genius of Winnicott* (pp. 25-38). Northvale, New Jersey: Jason Aronson Inc.

Wordsworth, W. (1913). Anecdote for father (pp. 25-27), Ode: Intimations of immortality from recollections of early childhood (pp. 461-466). *Selected poems of William Wordsworth.* London: Oxford University Press.

Wortman, C. B. (1976). Causal attributions and personal control. In J. H. Harvey, W. J. Ickes, and R. F. Kidd (Eds.), *New directions in attribution research, volume 1* (pp. 23-52). Hillside, New Jersey: Lawrence Erlbaum Associates.

Wortman, C. B. and Brehm, J. W. (1975). Responses to uncontrollable outcomes: An integration of reactance theory and the learned helplessness model. In L. Berkowitz (Ed.), *Advances in social psychology* (Vol. 8, pp. 277-336). New York: Academic Press.

Zayas, L. H. (1987). Psychodynamic and developmental aspects of expectant and new fatherhood: Clinical derivatives from the literature. *Clinical Social Work Journal, 15* (1), 8-21.

Zilboorg, G. (1931). Depressive reactions related to parenthood. *The American Journal of Psychiatry, 10* (6), 927-962.

Zube, M. (1982). Changing behavior and outlook of aging men and women: Implications for marriage in the middle and later years. *Family Relations, 31,* 147-156.

Index

A Different Light Bookstore, 50
Aarons, L., 32, 41, 164
Abelin, E. L., 2
Abraham and Isaac Story, 9. *See also*
    "Parable of the Old Man and
    the Young, The" (Owen)
Acceptance, 7, 8, 168, 170, 171, 173.
    See also Disclosure;
    Idealizaton; Identification
    and acknowledgment, 32, 159, 172
    characteristics of, 159-160
    as a construct, 58
    and external factors, 161
    factors that may work against, 161
    Gottlieb's typology of, 160
    and internalization, 166-167
    and levels of understanding, 160
    of "the reality of change," 160
    of self, 169
Acknowledgment, 58
    and acceptance, 32, 159, 172
    characteristics of, 32, 159
Active participant, 56
Adaptation
    and attachment, 171
    autoplastic, 170
    and ego integrity, 170
Adjustment, 32, 102, 157
Adult, from child to, 177-178
Adult development, 7. *See also*
    Parenthood; Polarities
    characteristics/tasks of, 167-171
Agresti, A. A., 41, 170
AIDS, 40, 44, 77. *See also* Fear
    advocate, 95
    and loss, 34
    patients, 125
    worry, 98

AIDS Center of Queens County, 51
AIDS Walk, 50
Amsterdam News, 51
"Analytic Play and Its Relationship
    to the Object" (Green), 1
Anderson, D., 32
"Anecdote for Father"
    (Wordsworth), 15
Anger, and guilt, 32
Anna Karenina (Tolstoy), 13-14
Anima, 28, 166
Anthony, E. J., 15-17, 18
Apperson, L. B., 26
Asian and Pacific Islander Coalition
    on HIV/AIDS (APICHA), 51
Asians and Friends, 51
Attachment
    and adaptation, 171
    and identification, 171
    vs. separateness, 167-169
Auditor, 58-59
Avoidance, 113, 144

Bahm, R. M., 176
Baker, J. M., *xii,* 32, 43-44, 164
Balikov, H., 19
Becker, H. S., 56, 61
Bell, A. P., 27, 30, 41
Ben, Blos's case of, 19
Ben-Ari, A., 41, 159
Benedek, T., 8, 162
Berg, D. N., 64
Bergman, A., 1
Berman, E., 12
Berman, P. S., 36
Bernstein, B. E., 34
Bernstein, R. A., 45, 164

Order Your Own Copy of
This Important Book for Your Personal Library!

OUT OF THE TWILIGHT
Fathers of Gay Men Speak

_____ in hardbound at $39.95 (ISBN: 0-7890-0614-6)

_____ in softbound at $19.95 (ISBN: 1-56023-951-4)

COST OF BOOKS _____

OUTSIDE USA/CANADA/
MEXICO: ADD 20% _____

POSTAGE & HANDLING _____
(US: $3.00 for first book & $1.25
for each additional book)
Outside US: $4.75 for first book
& $1.75 for each additional book)

SUBTOTAL _____

IN CANADA: ADD 7% GST _____

STATE TAX _____
(NY, OH & MN residents, please
add appropriate local sales tax)

FINAL TOTAL _____
(If paying in Canadian funds,
convert using the current
exchange rate. UNESCO
coupons welcome.)

☐ **BILL ME LATER:** ($5 service charge will be added)
(Bill-me option is good on US/Canada/Mexico orders only;
not good to jobbers, wholesalers, or subscription agencies.)

☐ Check here if billing address is different from
shipping address and attach purchase order and
billing address information.

Signature _____

☐ **PAYMENT ENCLOSED: $**_____

☐ **PLEASE CHARGE TO MY CREDIT CARD.**

☐ Visa   ☐ MasterCard   ☐ AmEx   ☐ Discover
☐ Diner's Club

Account # _____

Exp. Date _____

Signature _____

Prices in US dollars and subject to change without notice.

NAME _____

INSTITUTION _____

ADDRESS _____

CITY _____

STATE/ZIP _____

COUNTRY _____ COUNTY (NY residents only) _____

TEL _____ FAX _____

E-MAIL_____
May we use your e-mail address for confirmations and other types of information? ☐ Yes   ☐ No

Order From Your Local Bookstore or Directly From
The Haworth Press, Inc.
10 Alice Street, Binghamton, New York 13904-1580 • USA
TELEPHONE: 1-800-HAWORTH (1-800-429-6784) / Outside US/Canada: (607) 722-5857
FAX: 1-800-895-0582 / Outside US/Canada: (607) 772-6362
E-mail: getinfo@haworthpressinc.com
PLEASE PHOTOCOPY THIS FORM FOR YOUR PERSONAL USE.

BOF96